EXPANSIVE POETRY

EXPANSIVE POETRY

ESSAYS ON THE NEW NARRATIVE
&
THE NEW FORMALISM

EDITED BY FREDERICK FEIRSTEIN

INTRODUCTION BY FREDERICK FEIRSTEIN
WITH FREDERICK TURNER

STORY LINE PRESS
Santa Cruz, California

THANKS TO THE GENEROUS SUPPORT
of the
NICHOLAS ROERICH MUSEUM, NEW YORK

ISBN: 0-934257-28-0 (cloth)
ISBN: 0-934257-27-2 (paper)

Book design by Lysa McDowell
Story Line Press
403 Continental Street
Santa Cruz, California 95060

THE NEW NARRATIVE

THE NEW FORMALISM

INTRODUCTION

⌘

Frederick Feirstein With Frederick Turner

We have just passed through a great change both in poetic fashion and in the underlying cultural and philosophical assumptions of poetry. But if we are not to repeat the mistakes we corrected and the new ones we made in that period, we need to preserve some memory of what happened and why. This book of essays is a record of that part of that struggle; it represents the position which, at first attacked from all sides, was eventually to prevail and establish itself.

That position is often referred to in two parts, the New Narrative and the New Formalism. Wade Newman in an essay about our history called it the Expansive Movement — implying an extension of the acceptable forms and resources of poetry beyond the short free verse autobiographical lyric. Some would associate this movement in poetry with literary postmodernism, and compare it with the new figurative trend in the visual arts, the highlighting of narrativity in fiction, the re-introduction of tonality in music, and the rediscovery of classical elements in architecture. Frederick Turner uses the phrase "natural classicism" to describe its underlying ideas.

It is hard to imagine in 1989 how narrow and doctrinaire was the world of poetry in the seventies when the poets in the movement began to mature. Both narrative and meter were considered at best out of date and at worst the instruments of bourgeois capitalism. Ignoring the strict meter and narrative impulses of blues and country and western lyrics, the high priests of the ruling ideology proclaimed that narrative and meter were elitist European importations and that the true American voice could only be heard in "free verse."

These views went together with a pose of the poet as resenting and rebelling against the poet's cultural past and that of the society at large. Although he or she invariably taught in a university, the poseurs would express profound hostility to the intellectual imagination, especially in the forms of science and technology, and a sentimental preference for nature over culture. The poseurs often would be gleefully pessimistic about the future which would seem to justify their solipsistic confessions about their darkly perceived past.

A socio-economic structure involving a peculiar collusion of interests between the poets themselves, the grant-giving organizations such as the National Endowment for the Arts, the academic creative writing workshops, the small magazines and presses, the poetry circuits, and the larger presses, helped to preserve this conception of the role and nature of poetry. Peculiar because of its contradictions. The poets were mostly supported by that same capitalist state which they despised. The small presses, which loathed the large commercial presses, shared with them the cynical opinion that good writing was automatically unpopular, and popular writing was automatically bad. The academy was both the villain and the theater of the poetic act.

In order to fully understand how this situation developed it might be useful to understand its intention as being one like ours, to overthrow the constraints of an earlier establishment. What we might loosely refer to as the free verse movement began as a revolt against the social conventions of Puritan America that permeated all levels of society, epitomized in the fifties, a time comparable in some of its attitudes to Victorian England.

The fifties, besides being tranquil and prosperous, were also boring and stifling. It was particularly stifling to young people who hadn't gone through the Great Depression and World War II and had no need for security and retreat from action.

The fifties were a gray age, as the novel *The Man In The Gray Flannel Suit* showed. People seemed, especially to the young, forced into playing rigid gender roles with their emotional content cut off and replaced by affectation. The poetry that was considered important then reflected those conventions. It was proper in content, unemotional in tone, and often robotic in form. It seemed no different from fifties cerebral British poetry. An underground culture began to develop both in the society and in poetry to counter this. In society it began to find expression in rock and roll—Chuck Berry, Little Richard, Bill Haley, and perhaps most importantly Elvis Presley. In what was to become popular music, the sexual and aggressive instincts began to find expression. The poets that people started turning to were people like Kenneth Rexroth who became known as Father of the Beats, and William Carlos Williams who expressed emotion clearly in an American, not British idiom.

The early counterculture came into the mainstream slowly at first, then with a rush and a vengeance.

America elected a President whose sexuality and passionate optimism symbolized some of its best aspects. Jack Kennedy's very presence expressed the wish to throw off the stifling boring age of Eisenhower. He made the White House a place of open possibilities that would encourage the search for the new and exciting, stimulate the young to adventure. It was the age of the New Frontier.

Poetry reflected this spirit. It became easier to experiment with form and express emotionally wilder content. It became easier, particularly for men, to declare with pride that they were poets. Robert Frost became a fixture at the White House. The Beats made the cover of *Life Magazine*. Suddenly people began to talk of "life styles", as if there was more than one.

The counterculture became a viable choice for the middle classes.

But there was a shadow side to this exuberance and we first saw it in poetry. In this quest to free themselves, many people began to see artistic form itself not as liberating but as confining. Without appreciating any contradiction, they used the theories of conservative (and even fascistic in Pound's case) modernists to make a political attack on form — the linear narrative, meter and rhyme — as being reactionary. Many of us included in this anthology, having begun writing only in free verse, started to question what using form really had to do with politics. In fact we began to see the insistence on writing only in free verse and only the lyric as terribly confining in itself. Though we had begun by writing personal poems, as we became more experienced with life, we wanted to write about others and to try other forms, the narrative and dramatic forms that would allow for this.

We found the change in diction that the free verse movement brought about particularly helpful in writing narrative and dramatic poems, which have to be colloquial because there are real people speaking in them. But we also found we needed meter and sometimes rhyme to create the contrapuntal tensions in the verse that would match the tension in the action.

Furthermore we felt restricted in writing our lyrics too. We began to realize there was an inherent contradiction in writing a lyric with colloquial diction but abandoning those devices —

meter and rhyme — that would make a lyric sing.

The whole purpose of a lyric poem is to sing: to sing in a natural, not puffed up, way so that one can reach an audience. But by removing the elements of song from poetry, by removing meter and rhyme, the poets were alienating the audience, the very audience that comes to lyric poetry for song. Every kid playing a guitar knew better than that, knew you had to use rhyme and meter to sing.

We said and began to say in print that ordinary speech is important for the prose sense of a poem. As Timothy Steele points out, it was important to deflate inflated diction and to capture the audience that wanted to hear themselves. But we also said that what happened in abandoning form was that the devices that came to replace form began to inflate diction all over again. For instance we said that by substituting artificial breaks in grammar for rhyme at the end of lines (as Wyatt Prunty points out) and such rhythmical prose devices as parallelism for meter, free verse poems began to sound as momentous as a preacher's oratory. In fact at readings one witnessed poets relying on such devices — incanting banalities in sonorous, haranguing voices. In magazine after magazine there were prosy little poems propped up by corny rhetorical devices. We began to feel strongly that the true corrective for this was form, form wedded to the diction we had learned from such mentors as Williams.

But we had great difficulty in finding room for this notion and our work that grew out of it. In Dick Moore's terms what had begun as a loosening up of convention, much as Eliot recommended in "Tradition And The Individual Talent," had hardened into ideology. What had begun as experimentation did away with the freedom to truly experiment. The free verse poem was not only supported by rhetoric from within but from without, from theories such as Field Theory and Open Poetry that depended on rhetorical accusation and little substance. Worse, as the counterculture became bureaucratic it became co-opted by the society at large and wound up subtly expressing those very values it rebelled against. As Dana Gioia and Paul Lake point out, such spokespeople as Diane Wakowski began to declaim that anything but the kind of poem she and others like her were writing were un-American. Furthermore, as the pop culture of what was now society began to intermingle with the academic world, notions of what was fashionable rather than aesthetically sound began to infiltrate poetry. Poets became afraid of writing what was not au courant. After all for most of them their livelihoods as creative writing teachers depended on it. No university would keep them if they didn't publish. And the magazines and presses were taking almost uniformly only short free verse autobiographical imagist lyrics. What was a professor to do?

Some of us quit teaching. In the poetry world itself our "experimenting" with form and the narrative led us to become very uncomfortably isolated, even scorned. We had not discovered each other yet; we wouldn't for a decade do that and become an odd underground.

Some of us were lucky enough to get a bit of encouragement from those in the older generation who were misunderstood by their followers or who resisted the drift of the times and were isolated themselves. We found some room for our narrative work in the *Quarterly Review of Literature*, edited by Theodore Weiss who steadfastly remained writing the long narrative poem at the cost of being critically neglected. Our poems in form were eagerly received by *Counter/Measures*, an important but short-lived magazine edited by X. J. Kennedy. We received personal encouragement by misappropriated older poets such as Rexroth whose greatly informed vision and formalism were totally lost on the Beats.

But for the most part, we were as isolated in the poetry world as we'd been in society at the tail end of Gray Flannel culture. We even began to feel the poetry world itself was just another county in the wasteland of television. What had become popular in poetry were poems that required only a short attention span. The content of such poems often resembled the talkiness and domestic values of a situation comedy or the sensationalism of a soap (as in the case of the Confessional Poets).

Irritated and isolated we managed to persist over years, perhaps because we were all young and tenacious. Feirstein's first book, *Survivors*, half a lyric sequence, was selected as an Outstanding Book of 1975 by The American Library Association. But *Manhattan Carnival*, a narrative in Chaucerian couplets written in 1974, would wait until 1981 to find a small press publisher, and at that only after Feirstein had won a Guggenheim. Frederick Turner's free verse poems were published in Wesleyan University Press' poetry series, but his long narrative in dactylics, *The Return*, languished for five years until the same small press, Countryman, brought it out. Turner's resignation from the editorship of *The Kenyon Review*, which published much of the movement's early work, was largely over differences with the English Department at Kenyon College about the value of the new poetry. Three of the essays in this book have been drawn from an issue of *The Kenyon Review* devoted exclusively to the then nascent movement.

Dick Allen and Dana Gioia, also pioneers in the movement, had similar histories. Allen's third book *Overnight In The Guest*

House Of The Mystic, was turned down by twenty-nine
publishers before it came out in 1984 to wide acclaim and a
nomination for the National Book Award. His way was to work
within the system, teaching his subversive ideas on form and
narrative to a new generation of poets, some of whom are now
nationally known, and to find some spiritual sustenance as did
Turner among the literary outcasts of science fiction. Gioia's
way was to leave the academy altogether, to make his living,
like Wallace Stevens, in business, and to refine his formal poetry
slowly toward publication when the time was ripe. His own first
book, *Daily Horoscope,* was eventually published by a small press,
Graywolf; it too has been recognized since as an important work
of American poetry.

The first time we really felt that a genuine movement was
afoot was in early 1981, when Dick Allen, Frederick Feirstein,
and Frederick Turner met for the first time at the Minetta Tavern
in Greenwich Village. As co-editor of a literary magazine whose
editorials had called for a new poetry, and as the author of an
extremely controversial essay in the *Missouri Review,* "Mighty
Poets in their Misery Dead: a Polemic on the Contemporary
Poetic Scene," Turner had already come across a few other voices
crying in the wilderness, as had Dick Allen. Feirstein was corresponding with Dick Moore, Charles Martin, Christopher
Clausen, and very importantly, Dana Gioia.

Gioia was in touch with younger mostly California poets who
all on their own were working in ways very similar to ours. He
particularly called our attention to the work Mark Jarman and
Robert McDowell were doing not only in their own narrative
poetry and criticism but in their outspoken periodical *The
Reaper.* *The Reaper,* begun in 1980 like the *Kenyon* under Turner
and his co-editor Ronald Sharp, had a strong commitment

to narrative poetry and a stronger distaste for the scribbling going on in the Establishment's workshops.

We began to see ourselves as a distinct movement of many people. We saw each other's work begin to appear consistently in the literary journals. Magazines such as *The Hudson Review* began to publish our narrative work. It printed McDowell's "Quiet Money" in its entirety. The *Ontario Review* published some of our dramatic poetry and Turner's essay on the dramatic monologue *Manhattan Carnival. Poetry*, under the editorship of Joseph Parisi, began to not only publish many of our formal poems but for the first time awarded the Levinson prize to an essay, Frederick Turner's essay on meter, "The Neural Lyre."

As we started to make an impact, we began to worry about the harm we would cause if our work was taken up as a new ideology. We even see some signs of it now. So, as we offer this anthology, we would like to close on a note of caution. Our intention is to expand the possibilities for form and content in poetry. We don't want our work as a movement to be transformed into a new conformism in which superficial elements are reduced to a fashion and a set of formulae to be duly retailed in the creative writing schools. The reason to use narrative and meter and rhyme is not to be fashionable but to open worlds of reality and imagination to the poet which might otherwise be shut off. If ever our work is taken up as dogma, we expect we will remain true to our natures and attack it.

❧ THE NEW NARRATIVE ❧

THE DILEMMA OF THE LONG POEM

୧ஜୄஜ୧

Dana Gioia

American poetry prides itself on its great scope and diversity, but one wonders if an outsider might not come away with
a very different notion. Imagine what an intelligent eighteenth-
century reader would conclude if he surveyed the several
hundred books of poetry published in America this past year.
(For simplicity's sake, let us keep this long-suffering gentleman's
conclusions descriptive rather than evaluative. There is no way
of knowing what if anything he would actually enjoy amid this
poetic avalanche.) His overall reaction, I suspect, would be a
deep disappointment over the predictable sameness, the conspicuous lack of diversity in what he read. Where are the narrative poems, he would ask, the verse romances, ballads, hymns,
verse dramas, didactic tracts, burlesques, satires, the songs
actually meant to be sung, and even the pastoral eclogues? Are
stories no longer told in poetry? Important ideas no longer
discussed at length? The panoply of available genres would seem
reduced to a few hardy perennials which poets worked over and
over again with dreary regularity—the short lyric, the ode, the
familiar verse epistle, perhaps the epigram, and one new-fangled
form called the "sequence" which often seemed to be either
just a group of short lyrics stuck together or an ode in the process
of falling apart. Amid this myriad of shorter work he would
see only a few poems longer than six or seven pages—most of
them massive and complex undertakings running many times

First published in *The Kenyon Review*—New Series, Spring 1983, Vol. V., No. 2.
Copyright © by Kenyon College. Reprinted with permission of author and publisher.

the length of the average thin volume. These, he would ascertain, are the epics of this age, but he would probably not be able to classify them further since they are mostly difficult, allusive works not governed by a narrative or expository structure. They undoubtedly belong to a genre whose rules he doesn't understand.

This hypothetical gentleman would also be perplexed by the paucity of technical means he saw employed. Most of what he read would be in free verse (some of which he would recognize as such from his familiarity with Milton, Smart, and, of course, the Old Testament) balanced by a little irregular pentameter, an occasional sestina, and virtually nothing else. What happened to rhyme, he would ask, and all the meters ancient and modern plus all the familiar stanza forms of English? These new poets, he might conclude, are a very monotonous bunch indeed who can only manage the shorter forms and even those only within the slenderest range of technical means. Poems longer than half a dozen pages seem to be beyond their powers altogether. Yes, American poetry would seem to be a very limited enterprise. It not only lacks great poets of the stature of Shakespeare, Spenser, Milton, Dryden, and Pope, it also lacks estimable lesser writers of scope and versatility, like Dyer, Thomson, Collins, Cowper, Young, Shenstone, or Gay.

Such judgements would infuriate our poets and critics alike, but are they so inaccurate? American poetry may be bold and expansive in its moods and subject matter, but it remains timorous and short-winded in its range. Despite its enormous volume, the poetry published each year tends to be conceived almost exclusively in shorter forms. It does not take a university professor to notice this bias. Any reader familiar with at least one other period of literature in English would have to ask why the tremendous talent of contemporary poets has been so narrowly focused.

The orthodox academic reply is that the intensity and concentration of modern poetry has made the long poem impossible. An extended work in verse would perforce break up into shorter fragments. This explanation sounds plausible at first, and indeed it may even have some limited applicability to certain early modern schools such as Imagism, but careful observation proves it untrue in any general sense. Contemporary poetry is not particularly intense or concentrated on either an absolute or relative basis. Certainly concentration and intensity are characteristics of good short poetry in any age, but the twentieth century has little special claim on them. Compare half a dozen widely anthologized contemporary poems with a lyric by George Herbert or a sonnet by Milton and one will usually find the modern work relaxed and casual in comparison. Why then could a poet like Milton, an unquestioned master of the short, concentrated poem, also manage brilliant longer poems whereas our contemporaries cannot? The answer is complex and encompasses several acknowledged factors, such as the increasing identification of all poetry with the lyric mode, the subsequent rejection of narrative and didacticism as available poetic forms, and the neglect of precisely those metrical resources in English which have traditionally provided long poems with an underlying structure. There is another factor, however, which I have never heard discussed but which has had a crucial impact on our literature.

The major problem facing the long poem today is that contemporary theory allows the poet almost no middle ground between the concentration of the short lyric and the vast breadth of the epic (the modern epic, that is, in its distinctive form as the historical culture poem). Of course, our theoreticians have not banned all other kinds of poetry, but the critical emphases on lyric and epic have been so strong over the past seventy years that to poets and teachers alike they have become the distinctive forms of both the modern and so-called post-modern period. The long poem has nearly died as a result. It has become an all-or-nothing proposition, an obsessive, lifelong undertaking. The poet must confront his entire culture and prepare some vast synthesis of its history and values. There may be one or two poets in any age who are capable of bringing off so ambitious an enterprise, but how many geniuses have botched their careers trying it? To take the most conspicuous example in our century, consider Ezra Pound, who stopped writing other poetry at the height of his powers to concentrate on his never completed *Cantos*. Ultimately the *Cantos* may well be the most interesting poem in American literature, but it is surely not a success (if the word *success* has any meaning left in describing a form which has relinquished the conventional standards of literary performance and intends only to recreate an author's private sensibility without any concessions to his audience). Or consider Conrad Aiken, whose entire career was spent in trying repeatedly in vain to write the definitive long poem of his age.

Indeed the long modern poem is virtually doomed to failure by its own ground rules. Any extended work needs a strong overall form to guide both the poet in creating it and the reader in understanding it. By rejecting the traditional epic structures of narrative (as in Vergil) and didactic exposition (as in Lucretius), the modern author has been thrown almost entirely on his own resources. He must not only try to synthesize the complexity of his culture into one long poem, he must also create the form of his discourse as he goes along. It is as if a physicist were asked to make a major new discovery in quantum mechanics but prevented from using any of the established methodologies in arriving at it. Even genius cannot accomplish such a task. Could Milton have succeeded so brilliantly with *Paradise Lost* without the examples of Homer, Vergil, Dante, Tasso, and Spenser behind him? Given that the structure of the modern epic has become an elaborate nonce form, it is not surprising that one finds no incontestable masterpieces among the major long poems of this century but only a group of more or less interesting failures, none widely read in its entirety by the literary public, though all jealously guarded by some particular faction (with no group quite so rabidly partisan as those professors who have staked their academic careers on researching and explicating a particular poem): Williams's *Paterson*, Jones's *The Anathemata*, Olson's *Maximus Poems*, Zukofsky's *A*, Berryman's *Dream Songs*, Dorn's *Gunslinger*, and so forth.

Given the immensity of the commitment and the high odds of failure involved in writing the modern epic, it is hardly surprising that most poets have chosen to concentrate single-mindedly on shorter forms, especially the lyric (both in its simple and conglomerate form, the sequence). Here at least the talented poet can make a lasting place for himself. It is instructive to consider how many contemporary poets have achieved important reputations almost solely on short poems: Elizabeth Bishop, Randall Jarrell, Weldon Kees, James Wright, Sylvia Plath, Robert Graves, Richard Wilbur, Howard Nemerov, Adrienne Rich, Howard Moss, Louis Simpson, J. V. Cunningham, Philip Larkin, Charles Tomlinson, W. S. Merwin, William Stafford. The list could go on and on. Most of these writers have done extended imaginative work, but significantly they avoided poetry as the medium for it. Poets like Graves or Nemerov turned to the novel while others, like Bishop or Kees, chose the short story. Some, like Wilbur and Merwin, concentrated on verse translation or, like Rich, on polemical prose. Even drama, as in Moss's case, or autobiographical prose, as in Simpson's, served as the natural conduit for their most expansive work. The diverse extended work of these poets has only one thing in common—the avoidance of verse as its medium.

American literature needs a more modest aesthetic of the long poem, a less chauvinistic theory which does not vainly seek the great at the expense of the good and genuine. It needs to free poets from the burden of writing the definitive long poem and allow them to work in more manageable albeit limited genres like satire, comedy, unheroic autobiography, discursive writing, pure narrative—wherever, in short, their imagination takes them. It also needs to foster poems of "middle length," extended pieces not long enough to fill up an entire volume. Such poems have played an important role in English from Chaucer's *Canterbury Tales* to Browning's major dramatic monologues, but today they are shunned by editors, publishers, and critics alike. (A sad situation which parallels the almost total extinction of the novella by the novel and short story in contemporary fiction.) Poems of middle length allow a writer to explore a particular theme without overextending it, and they do not require the Herculean effort necessary to complete an epic. Some poets work best in longer forms—Byron, Crabbe, Pope, and Dryden are a few historical examples—but even such talents may not necessarily be suited for the straight epic. Poets need a broad and various array of possible forms, an array which unfortunately does not seem available at present.

THE OTHER LONG POEM

Frederick Feirstein

Over the past two decades the only kind of long poem taken seriously by poetry's readership was the sequence: a series of lyrics thematically rather than dramatically organized and depending for its impact on the intensity of the individual moment and the accumulative effect of its images. At the same time the narrative and dramatic poem, with developed plot and character, was disregarded, much in the same way that Aristotelian drama was shoved aside for Theater of the Absurd with its loosely circular structure and its concentration on atmospheric intensity. This limiting of the form of the long poem was one of the many effects of modernism hardening into dogma.

The great modernists — Yeats, Pound, Stevens, for example — understanding the advantages of using plot, achieved some dramatic movement in their sequences by alluding to plot elements in old myths or texts or to some larger political action offstage. But their most recent followers (though they looked to myth for its primitiveness and politics for its fashionableness) discarded plot — and character as well — finding them to be "irrelevant" to the times. They backed up their practice with certain critical assumptions that the educated but intimidated lay reader learned to take for gospel. For instance, the supporter of Creeley or Ashbery would tell you that the times are chaotic and human life existential; therefore, in a poem there can't be

First published in *The Kenyon Review* — New Series, Spring 1983, Vol. V., No. 2.

any kind of logical structure or characters with coherent histories. Consider this statement by Reg Saner in a recent issue of the *Ohio Review*:

> Still, if poetry is to reflect where we are, it isn't likely to abandon the main feature of 20th century art, fragmentation. We may call it discontinuity or montage. We may refer to "aleatory" sequence or to "suppression of narrative links," but we remain tied to their devices through our sense that life is awash with random events. We admit "chance" is a word describing aspects of our ignorance, but we also admit chance into our designs, knowing that any set of objects tends to become a system.

And a neosurrealist such as James Tate would tell you that there are no rules for the unconscious and, since a poem comes from the unconscious, it must be randomly arranged as well. It was almost futile to challenge these assumptions, to point out to such poets and their readers that contemporary physics and molecular biology were revealing a deep and beautiful orderliness in the universe. Or to point out what every serious student of the unconscious (from Freud to Pinchas Noy to Ephron and Carrington) has discovered: that the unconscious operates by mechanisms of selectivity that are far from random and produces an order that seems illogical only when misunderstood.

Besides these attacks on structure, a contempt for meter developed which also contributed to the abandonment of "the other long poem." It's relatively easy to create dramatic moments in free verse, and a number of poets have managed to knit them together into first-rate sequences. But anyone who's tried it knows that it's virtually impossible to develop a book-length narrative without meter — and call it poetry not prose fiction. The conflict of opposites between the metrical line and the prose rhythm of natural speech sustains and poetically mirrors the tension in the dramatic structure itself. It establishes *in sound* a series of expectations out of which suspense, surprise, reversal, and so on, can come. In effect it does poetically what the content does dramatically. On the other hand, free verse forces the poet to rely on rhetorical devices that tend to create melodrama or to focus the reader on the poet's " voice" instead of on the action—and so distances him perhaps altogether from involvement in the intended drama.

But most of the poets, particularly the younger ones, ill-educated in workshops, simply could not master meter and therefore had no hope of succeeding with narrative. Few admitted this failing unless pressed, and only the rare exception dared do so in print. The *Ohio Review,* sensing that the free verse academy was losing its grip, published an issue (the same one in which the Saner piece appeared) devoted to challenging the notion of an unnamed poet that "free verse is dead." However, one of the essayists, Bim Ramke, had the honesty to say this:

> When I hear talk of exotic, subtle, intellectual use of forms I want to be part of it, but when I try to *do* it, I fail. Of course I fear that my failure may simply result from my laziness, lack of talent, lack of a trained ear. Stephen Spender suggests that if one has not been raised from childhood "speaking sonnet" then the sonnets one writes will have the same order of awkwardness as the foreign language one learns too late. My sonnets are awkward.
>
> Not only my sonnets. I once wrote a two-hundred or so line poem in smooth ballad stanzas with all the proper rhymes. It sat around a while sounding silly, so I got rid of the rhymes and roughed up the meter and sold it. It paid one month's rent so I felt less guilty. If I can't write

sonnets and I can't write ballads, what can I write? And
can I call whatever it is "poetry"?

But unlike Ramke most workshop poets did not even try to
learn meter. In part they were dissuaded by their mentors who —
usually parroting William Carlos Williams — contended that
poetry must be speech, American speech. This was an odd
prescription for the lyric, which traditionally was sung. It was
also a comically chauvinistic pronouncement by a group of poets
who insisted there was a connection between free verse and
political freedom. For instance, Diane Wakoski responding (in
the winter 1981–82 *Missouri Review*) to Frederick Turner's essay
"'Mighty Poets in Their Misery Dead': A Polemic on the Contemporary Poetic Scene," said this:

> Critics (and even some poets) obscure matters by long-
> ing for a neo-British poetry, a new England literature.
> ...But the recognition of Dickinson and Whitman
> depended on readers seeing and appreciating the use of
> an American, rather than English, language. And the
> genius of the writers, themselves, had to be reckoned with
> in American terms — the self-involvment, the unabashed
> lack of concern for the classics, for other literature, and
> for the epic. The complete acceptance of self as impor-
> tant seems to be an American trait, whereas the Euro-
> pean sensibility... requires the writer to justify his impor-
> tance. ...Critics have still not accepted that those savages
> [Dickinson and Whitman] are the Americans, that our
> language is a rougher, wilder, plainer, different one, and
> that our myths do not go back to ancient Greece and
> Rome, but come out of our involvement with this
> immense land here, across the ocean from Europe. ...I
> feel personally in touch with that tradition of Emily and
> Walt. They are ancestors I cherish and love, and it is ex-
> citing for me to see the turn of a nose here, an ankle there,
> the way a mouth moves when certain vowels are spoken.

> I could list at least a hundred poets writing today who
> are exciting, new and old at the same time, who give me
> almost the same excitement that I have writing my own
> poems, when I read and talk about them and their new
> American language

Another reason for the neglect of "the other long poem" had to do with the popularity of confessional poetry. Strong and varied characterization is a crucial element in the narrative or dramatic poem — whether it be fictional or autobiographical. But the confessional poets and their followers had no real interest in any character but the Self, a severely damaged and unappetizing one at that. Whatever little drama inhered in their poems came from their sensationalism, from the poet's making a spectacle of him or her Self. Spectacle is rather low on the list of Aristotle's criteria for effective drama. After a while the total work of such poets as Plath and Sexton seems an endless monologue spoken by a character with little insight, who never grows, who is bathetic rather than tragic. The confessional poets themselves found they had nowhere to go except to become more and more bizarre, more and more melodramatic. The initial attraction to their work is understandable when seen against the background of the deadening fifties. What's more, the very wretchedness of their lives titillated that odd American reader whose fascination with the artist is mixed up with envy and suppressed hatred. But ultimately their work bored as soap operas bore. Even their suicides became a formula.

These reasons for the neglect of the narrative and dramatic poem came from within the poetry world. But they were supported by factors outside that world as well. The popularity of television in the past couple of decades had a strong influence on the form and content of all the arts. The TV generation was conditioned to find emotion difficult to sustain without a commercial break. Naturally, when it came to poetry, they would gravitate toward the lyric sequence because it hit peaks of emotion for short periods and toward confessional poetry because, like television, it was sensational. Also, I might add, there was a distinct parallel between the values of commercial television and the mistaking of Williams's "No ideas but in things" to mean no ideas, and Pound's "Make it new" to mean make it novel.

The rhetoric of 1960s politics also undermined the legitimacy of structure. Everything was being liberated and made new. Anything structured — worse, "linear" — was "over thirty," irrelevant. The narrative, the dramatic, was variously "bourgeois," "elitist," and "nineteenth century." Even now poets such as our friend Bim Ramke sloganeer like this:

> Is it possible that the return, if there is one, to received forms is because the elite wants its badge shined? I noticed a number of comments during the inauguration of Ronald Reagan about "class being restored to the White House." "Class," of course is to be translated "money." Whatever my fellow Georgian Carter lacked which Reagan has could not reasonably be called class, unless the word is understood in an older sense, the sense of demarcations within society. And just maybe the call for sonnets, villanelles, etc. among contemporary poets is a way of setting up class lines too.

Many of the poetry editors at major publishing houses were intimidated by this kind of reasoning. They were often recent graduates of the same schools that produced the poets or weren't sophisticated enough to sort out aesthetics from politics from fashion. Besides, they had books to sell, and what they believed sold poetry was sensationalism of content and its equivalent, "experimentation" with form. They didn't notice that sensationalism was becoming a mannerism and experimentation a convention. To defend their choices they often would talk of *new* form as they would of *relevant* content. As for the small press movement, most of its editors earnestly believed the ideology of the past twenty years and wrote according to it themselves. If the large press editors were fashionably ignorant of the long poem, the small press editors were dogmatically ignorant.

And yet there was a group of poets and critics *rebelling* — to use that dangerous word — against this new *in*formal academy. Some of the most impressive: Dick Allen, Christopher Clausen, Charles Martin, Judith Moffet, Richard Moore, and Frederick Turner. Courageously, and in almost total obscurity, they persisted in writing their narratives and dramas. When they discovered each other, they would exchange their unpublished manuscripts much as the formally censored Russian writers do. Then they began to find their way to a few daring magazines and presses. Now (while continuing to write lyrics and lyric sequences as well as narrative and dramatic poems) they have begun to publish dissident essays designed to expand the capacity of poetry and poetry criticism. Eventually they will bring plot and character back to poetry and perhaps recapture some of the audience that has been lost.

FROM TRISTRAM'S RHAPSODY:
TRISTRAM'S ATTACK ON MODERN POETRY

ᴄ⅊ᴏᴄ⅊ᴏ

Richard Moore

Society, said Paul Valéry, is held together by fictions. We tend to think that the police hold society together, with the threat of pistols, truncheons, and prison making everyone behave. But without the pious fictions in which almost everyone—even now—believes, no mere brute force would be adequate to keep us organized. O surely when the ruling power has machine guns, cannon, helicopters, and tear gas! No, even they aren't enough. As always the gifts of progress are dubious. The more technologically advanced a society becomes, the more interdependent it is and the more vulnerable to guerrilla attack. One may say that apathy holds a tyranny together; but apathy too is a belief, a presumption, a fiction. Change that, and the helicopters begin to fly crazily because of those crazed human beings at the controls. A few well-placed sticks of dynamite, and the city

---

AUTHOR'S NOTE: In this book the disgruntled suburbanite, Tristram Brodie, recounts his life in comic detail and presents his odd and desperate meditations on a variety of subjects. This particular excerpt concerns modern poetry. I find Tristram deeply embarrassing. He is well enough educated evidently, but there is something crabbed and querulous about him. His opinions attract me—I admit that—but I find him crude, reckless, and intemperate. Couldn't he have toned down his remarks on Pound, Eliot, and others just a little? I am, after all, a modern poet myself and have to be careful of what I say.

First published in *The Georgia Review*, Winter 1981. Copyright © by University of Georgia. Reprinted with permission of the author and publisher.

comes to a standstill. Behold Vietnam. We came home because our army was disintegrating.

In this essay, therefore, let me say a few things about these conventions, these clichés and stereotypes, these fictions which seem to make human society possible. Let me first use them as a theme in making some remarks about poetry; and let me begin with a poem by Thomas Hardy:

THE DARK-EYED GENTLEMAN

I

I pitched my day's leazings in Crimmercrock Lane,
To tie up my garter and jog on again,
When a dear dark-eyed gentleman passed there and said,
In a way that made all o' me colour rose-red,
    'What do I see —
    O pretty knee!"
And he came and he tied up my garter for me.

II

'Twixt sunset and moonrise it was, I can mind:
Ah, 'tis easy to lose what we nevermore find! —
Of the dear stranger's home, of his name, I knew nought,
But I soon knew his nature and all that it brought.
    Then bitterly
    Sobbed I that he
Should ever have tied up my garter for me!

III

Yet now I've beside me a fine lissom lad,
And my slip's nigh forgot, and my days are not sad;
My own dearest joy is he, comrade, and friend,
He it is who safe-guards me, on him I depend;
    No sorrow brings he,
    And thankful I be
That his daddy once tied up my garter for me!

Is this a poem at all? Or is it merely a bit of buffoonery, a

sally of light verse, tripping along in its bouncy anapestic measure
(the measure, uncommon in English, of limericks and "'Twas
the Night Before Christmas") — simple, superficial and unworthy
of the notice of the critic? We might say, perhaps, that it is clever
and full of surprises, with its refrain line innocently comic in
the first stanza, bitter in the second, and triumphantly ridiculous
in the third.

In truth it is a marvelous poem: complex, deeply comic, and
sad; and it is a perfect example of how poems, as all art, use
conventions, clichés, and stereotypes in order to attain their
significance and impact. Hardy's point of view was Victorian,
though he lived until 1928; and in Victorian times there was
the cliché about women who allowed themselves to be seduced:
they would get pregnant from the briefest encounter (this was
partly only a literary convention) and they would suffer terribly for their transgression. The wages of sin are, if not death,
at least a lifetime of regret. Although the first stanza might leave
us with some misgivings about whether the subject was being
reverently handled, at the end of the second we are sure that
the poem is going to be a ringing endorsement of the cliché.
Maybe we have even begun, with some embarrassment, to expect
a moralizing third stanza. But with the third stanza the lid comes
off. The shameful pregnancy has become, in the course of time,
a full-grown son who gives his erring mother nothing but joy.
Hardy has blown the mindless cliché into a thousand pieces.

Or has he? Take another look at that third stanza. Run it
through again with your ear open to false notes in the woman's
tone of triumph. Check her reasons for feeling good; to anyone
without the courage and gaiety of this "simple" harvest girl they
would be reasons for feeling terrible: "my slip's *nigh* forgot"
— that is, even after all these years the nasty little village she

must live in still remembers her mishap; "not sad" — she doesn't say she's happy, does she? Her son is her "comrade, and friend, / He it is who safe-guards me, on him I depend." It is impossible to hear these words more than once and not reflect that her son is filling the social role conventionally played by a husband. The girl has remained unmarried. She will never have a husband because no one will have her. Her silence about the years it took the son to grow up, during which, presumably, nobody safe-guarded her, becomes deafening. And finally that wonderful "No sorrow brings he" with its emphasis on "he" both triumphant and ironic: her son is the only one who has *not* brought her sorrow.

Is her irony conscious? The poem is beautifully balanced on this point. Of course she is aware — how could she not be? But she chooses to forget; she chooses to put a good face on things, to accept her circumstances and in so doing to rise above them. After so many years of sorrow, it is still "the *dear* dark-eyed gentleman" and "the *dear* stranger" — the "dear" with a metrical emphasis each time. In spite of everything, she remains true to her first and only experience of him. Looked at in this way, the woman's simple, comic testimony takes on a quality of greatness, of heroism.

But note that, in this magical process, the cliché is affirmed after all. Her sexual transgression *has* made her suffer and, underneath her bravado, continues to do so. The fiction has worked simply by being believed. As Valéry puts it, "Toute societé est un édifice d'enchantements." A rather vile little "edifice of enchantments" in this case — but enchantments nevertheless: for it is by them, measuring herself against them, that the speaker of this wonderful poem achieves her humanity.

Hardy loathed Victorian sexual mores, and it is easy to look at the poem as an attack on them. It shows us a case where the conventional wisdom is untrue: an illicit pregnancy brings joy. But Hardy is not satisfied with this, since it only shows the convention to be ridiculous and, by implication, harmless. He wants us to feel that it is monstrous as well; and so the implications of misery creep in, the suggestions of bigotry in the background. But they are only allowed to creep in so far; they are not permitted to break the woman's spirit and transform the poem into message-laden melodrama, because at this point Hardy's interest in his character and her tone takes over: he forgets himself and his opinions and becomes an artist. His character has her greatness (and we our joy in the poem), but since she has it only in her response to the convention, the convention is affirmed by the process in a way that Hardy, the polemicist, could not possibly have intended.

Many curious paths of thought lead out from this illustration. Leaving convention for the moment, let us first observe that we have a concrete, documented instance of the selflessness of the artist implied by Keats's theory of negative capability. The poet forgets his personal convictions and is taken over instead by the life of his subject. Next, the poem raises the very interesting question of the relationship of art to propaganda and persuasion. Hardy had to choose between making a persuasive argument and creating an exciting character, and there is no sign of hesitation on his part. He is at one with the other poets of the world in this. Even Euripides in his play which shows us the Trojan women, Hecuba and others, lamenting the fall of their city and being led off into slavery — even in this closest approximation in antiquity to an antiwar tract, Euripides, the artist, can't resist including statements like these: "Even in Hector's death, Mother, there is something besides sorrow. He did not die till he had made himself a heroic name; and it was the coming of the Greeks that made that possible. If they had stayed at home, we would never have known how great Hector was." As the play progresses and the stature of Hecuba slowly increases to heroic proportions, we begin to sense that a similar logic applies to her: suffering makes her greatness possible and generates the exaltation of tragedy. When the Greeks kill Hector's infant son, she scorns them for being afraid of a baby; and her last words—"forward into slavery!"—have an almost triumphant ring. At points like these, the antiwar tract is forgotten, and that is why the play is moving as a work of art.

Critics of poetry have been fond of presenting exciting new definitions and images of the poet: the poet as forerunner, the poet as ephebe, the poet as the keeper of the keys to dreamland, the poet as the unacknowledged legislator of mankind. I would like to propose an addition to this impressive list: the poet as unsuccessful used-car salesman.

He is, of course, eloquent with his customers, amusing them, putting them at their ease, filling them with awe for the wonders of mechanics, impressing them, as did Jimmy Carter, with the childlike genuineness of his manner. There is only one fatal flaw in his otherwise brilliant performance. Just when the customer has been persuaded, has taken out his checkbook, and is ready to sign his name and drive off in the glossy beauty, our salesman develops an uncontrollable giggle and can't resist saying, "And won't you be surprised, a month or two from now, when the transmission falls out." The impulse to say this is none other than the child's aimless impulse of delight as he plays in his sandbox; for as Aristotle said, the essence of art is imitation and the origin of imitation is in the play of children. Poets may think sometimes that they have the urge of the politician, the urge to lead and persuade; but insofar as they remain poets, their controlling urge is to tell the truth and be exact about experience, reckless of the cost.

"Nonsense, Tristram," I hear someone reply. "Your salesman is an exhibitionist. His uncontrollable urge is not to tell the truth, but to show off. He wants to say something extraordinary and be patted on the head for it. He wants attention, which he knows he will get with a surprising statement. But — and here you come to the futility and waste of the whole operation — he makes his statement surprising by making it self-destructive. That's his sure formula for success. No one could have expected him to undo his whole sale and go home to bread and water and starving children. So he achieves his poor momentary thrill of making others think him wild, feckless, and free at an insane cost to himself. Is this what you think constitutes the essential urge to poetry?"

I submit that answering this objection amounts to answering the simple question: *Will* the transmission fall out of the car in a month or two? If it will, then the poet has uttered a truth in a dramatic manner and we have to respect whatever motives led him to his utterance, and further: we cannot possibly think of him as an exhibitionist because the thrill of finding and expressing a truth is incomparably greater than the titillation of attracting an audience.

Thomas Hardy has another poem, "The Convergence of the Twain," about the ocean liner *Titanic*, which was said to be "iceberg-proof" and which sank by collision with an iceberg on her maiden voyage in 1911. The poem has a shocking quality like our salesman's statement: while man was building his ship, God was building an iceberg, "a sinister mate for her":

> And as the smart ship grew
> In stature, grace, and hue,
> In shadowy silent distance grew the Iceberg too.

The two are like future lovers growing up apart and as yet unknown to each other, and Hardy calls their first and final meeting a "consummation." The question one has to ask about this, it seems to me, is whether the poet is merely making a tasteless joke about the catastrophe, which ended the lives of more than a thousand people, or whether the poem presents a true perception. Every time we shock, we create implications, and the implication here is that man's technological achievements are inevitably undone as part of a pattern he has failed to understand. The bigger, stronger ship only serves to find the bigger, stronger iceberg. Is this true? Suffice it to say in answer that the idea seems a good deal less strange today than it must have seemed in 1911. The poem has deepened in validity and gained in power since it was written. One cannot sense this and not also feel in contact with a true perception. The poem resides at a point where the truth of poetry enters upon the truth of prophecy.

As Robert Frost said, "We are back in poetry as merely one more art of having something to say." If the car is sound and the salesman has only made his comment for effect, then there is no artistic selflessness, and his case is indeed pitiable and absurd: it was not his subject, but only another ego motive, that led him to forget his obvious self-interest. As Pope describes him:

> His wit, all see-saw, between *that* and *this*,
> Now high, now low, now muster up, now miss,
> And he himself one vile Antithesis.

This self-destructive, exhibitionist tendency is very real and can actually lead to suicides, of which there have been a number among modern poets. I shall have something to say about these, but meanwhile let me return to the subject of convention.

For the sake of clarity, let me define some terms as I shall be using them.

1) A custom or convention is a pattern of behavior or a belief held in a society without the support of reasoned argument and developed over a long period of time.

2) A cliché is a derogatory term for a convention of language.

3) A stereotype is a conventional belief about people, as that little boys are made of rats and snails.

4) An ideology is a rationally argued system of beliefs proposed by a person or persons.

It should be plain from these definitions that a system of conventions is something radically different from an ideology, though they both involve belief and both guide human behavior. The difference is that the one develops unquestioned in the course of generations, the product of a process beyond human reason—of chance, the collective unconscious, or whatever else one chooses to postulate—while the other, the ideology, originates in more-or-less acceptably reasoned argument and is adopted or rejected on the spot as a conscious decision. This contrast suggests another definition, a nifty little horror in which the twentieth century has specialized:

5) A true-believer is a person who accepts an ideology without question, as though it were a system of conventions.

Why are these nasty things—these conventions and ideologies—necessary? Why can't we all just be sweetly reasonable, order and think out our own lives for ourselves? Isn't that, after all, the American ideal? Valéry proposed one answer: since we must fit into a society, control is necessary and force alone is not enough to effect it. Another, perhaps more fundamental answer is to be found in a basic property of human experience: the scope of sensation must be arbitrarily narrowed in order to become negotiable. Because the simplist sensation can have endless interpretations, arbitrary choices have to be made before anything can become intelligible. The situation is like the problem of the hundred variables. In algebra, if you have a problem with two unknowns—two variables—then you need two independent equations—mathematical statements—about the variables in order to fix a unique situation. For three variables, you need three equations, and so on to any number of variables and equations. The human, that is, the social situation, is like a problem with a hundred variables and only five equations supplied by the exigencies of the environment. The only possible way to proceed is to assign values arbitrarily, that is, to *pretend* that ninety-five of the variables are fixed values. These are Valéry's fictions. No society can work without making assumptions.

It's summer now, and yesterday I went for a swim in the local pool. Afterwards I wanted a patch of grass to sit on while I put on my shoes for the walk home. I looked the dried grass over with careful thought before finally selecting the lushest, shadiest patch available. After my swim today I went directly to the same patch without any thought or conscious observation. A custom had been formed.

Note that this argument also shows that a completely rational ideology is impossible. The human intelligence cannot construct a social system—even in conception—without leaving the vast preponderance of it to arbitrary choice and chance, which will, in turn, have incalculable consequences. Thus, when the conventionalist stubbornly clings to old and tried usages, his very irrationality has a firm basis in reason. It is reasonable to prefer something which works badly to something which may not work at all.

Is there any special reason, then, why "The Dark-Eyed Gentleman"—along with most other good poetry—tends to support social conventions, even when at first it seems to be attacking them? Art for the artist is a rapt, selfless contemplation and working out of some aspect of experience. The process is aimless in that it is open to all possibilities, but the conditions under which it is carried out—the loss of self, the essential passivity of the artist—predispose it toward harmony with one's surroundings, that is, mainly, with one's society, one's tribe. And since a society is primarily a structure of conventions, art necessarily leads toward a reconciliation between the individual and convention. Therein lies much of its enormous social value.

But what of that especially modern and perhaps universal phenomenon, the artist who rebels against the status quo? Does he finally seek to overthrow convention and legislate a new order? I would suggest that such a course would remove him from the artistic process altogether and that, insofar as he remains true to that process, the effect of his art will be, not to overthrow convention, but to *loosen* it: to qualify it with ironies and thereby render it less rigid and more accommodating to human individuality. In this respect too the social value of art is incalculable.

Thus, in the Hardy poem the final effect is of reconciliation with the conventional wisdom about errant women, not as an absolute statement, but as a principle whose fulfillment is likely to be ironic and paradoxical. Instead of remaining a stern requirement, the stereotype becomes, more tolerantly, a measure of deviation, a scheme of reference useful precisely because it never exactly fits the variety of actual life.

It is Shakespeare's deep insight into the complex and subtle relationships between stereotypes and actual human possibilities that most accounts, I think, for the enormous power and variety of his characterizations. *King Lear*, for example, can be viewed as an elaborate and harrowing investigation of the stereotype of the wise old man. Like Hardy's poem, the play moves from blatant contradiction of the stereotype to final ironic affirmation. In the beginning the old king is not wise at all, but almost unbelievably foolish. The ensuing scenes show us the remorseless consequences of this foolishness and conclude with the old king's death; but at the same time there is a counterdevelopment of great power and complexity. The protean changes of Lear's character, always surprising, yet with an eerie logic of their own, have an underlying direction, and at the end, the old man has achieved a wisdom through his suffering that could have been obtained in no other way. The stereotype has been affirmed—terrifyingly.

Years before this, there was for Shakespeare the essential and perhaps decisive case of Falstaff, the delightfully corrupt outcast from the upper classes who flaunts every convention and riddles every stereotype with his supremely rational mockery. There is, for example, the famous speech on honor, the conventional virtue of a soldier:

> Honor pricks me on. Yea, but how if honor prick me off when I come on? How then? Can honor set a leg? No. Or an arm? No. Or take away the grief of a wound? No. Honor hath no skill in surgery then? No. What is honor? A word. What is that word honor? Air—a trim reckoning. Who hath it? He that died a Wednesday. Doth he

feel it? No. Doth he hear it? No. 'Tis insensible then? Yea,
to the dead. But will it not live with the living? No. Why?
Detraction will not suffer it. Therefore I'll none of it.

He is all charm and wit in the first of the two plays on Henry
IV, where we see him almost entirely in public among his friends;
but in the second play, where he reveals more of his private
thoughts and plots, we grow increasingly aware of the seamy
corrupt side of his character; and finally at the end he must
be banished from the new king's presence. Yet when he is driven
off, much of our sympathy and emotion goes with him. He is
something fundamental, a force that every healthy society both
desperately needs and must ultimately reject: he represents the awareness that society is essentially a fiction and
he has the power to distort, loosen, and modify that fiction
through wit and mockery. The young king must banish Falstaff
because the ultimate tendency of the old man's games is the
dissolution of society itself; and yet the king will be a better
king for having known Falstaff and for continuing to know that
Falstaff exists.

But perhaps the greatest triumphs in Shakespeare's gallery
of characterizations are his portraits of women. There was a very
strong and definite female stereotype in Shakespeare's day. In
the vast hierarchy of creation women were a notch lower than
men. They were more lovely perhaps, but they were less rational
and had no wills of their own. An unmarried man and woman
could not be left alone together for even the briefest time: for
the man, because of his nature, would inevitably try to seduce
the woman, and the woman, because of hers—her lack of
will—would inevitably yield. Although women derived a certain de facto power through being the objects of desire, this
power was not in the ordained order of things and therefore,

especially for religious reformers, the work of the Devil. The only godly way for a woman to behave was to be meek and yielding in all things. A contemporary of Shakespeare's, Thomas Heywood, wrote a play which embodies the stereotypes perfectly and which, as a result, is today unreadable. Milton in his presentation of Eve in *Paradise Lost* has to adhere pretty strictly to the conventional image, for she, being the mother of mankind, has to be typical of all women. The currency of the stereotype in the minds of the poem's readers is what makes such a universal image possible. Milton's genius is evident in the fact that Eve is very much alive as a person as well. He seems to have been aided in obtaining this personal touch by his own very ambiguous feelings about women, at once open and tender in his sensuality and prone to anger and distrust. His Eve has a little of the witch about her.

Shakespeare seems to have had no illusion that the stereotype had much to do with the actual women of his time, and as a dramatist, he was relatively free to play imaginative variations on it. Yet always the presence of the stereotype is felt, giving form to the individual character, who surprises us in her departures from it and then surprises us again in her unexpected returns.

Cleopatra stands above them all—violent, sensual, yet completely feminine in every line. She is about to kill a messenger for bringing her bad news when her serving woman protests, "The man is innocent." Cleopatra replies magnificently, "Some innocents 'scape not the thunderbolt." I would stigmatize myself as a male chauvinist, I suppose, if I dared say that this line is perfectly logical, but that it is a woman's logic; but how else can I appreciate its quality? That her feminine logic controls Antony completely, in spite of his better knowledge, is felt as tragic in terms of the stereotype; and yet she is so much more interesting as a person that he seems like a silly little boy tagging after her. How is this violent inversion of the conventional state of affairs to be resolved? For it must be resolved. Shakespeare has made use of the convention in the minds of his audience in order to make his play deeply exciting. He must calm this excitement somehow; he must give the convention its due. His audience (including himself) requires it for its peace of mind — for that sensation of harmony which is the end of art. But in another sense, his society requires it. His society has given him the stereotype through which he obtains his effects and he, in justice, must give it back unharmed. The solution is brilliant. Cleopatra becomes Antony's meek, humble, and devoted follower *after he is dead*. True, she hesitates a little until she is sure that Caesar means to dishonor her; but then she follows him:

> Methinks I hear
> Antony call: I see him rouse himself
> To praise my noble act. I hear him mock
> The luck of Ceasar, which the gods give men
> To excuse their after wrath. Husband, I come:
> Now to that name my courage prove my title!

In the centuries since Shakespeare, conventions have slowly but surely — and with some strong countermovements — fallen on evil days. The conventions of literature itself have undergone similar transformations. One may take the changes in verse forms as an illustration. There was a certain artificiality in the adoption of the iambic line in Elizabethan times, but once it had become universal, it underwent a marvelous development in sinuousness and accommodation to the natural rhythms of speech. Finally in the late seventeenth and in the eighteenth centuries, it achieved great organization and polish at the cost of a narrowing of effect and a restriction of variety. An attempt to break out of this mold with the Romantic Movement around the turn of the nineteenth century only led in the following decades to a greater stiffening. Ballad measures were rediscovered and a great variety of stanza forms introduced, inspired by deepening studies of the past; but the iambic line itself was beginning to lose its life and naturalness. At last in our own century the free verse movement has proposed its abolition, and the modern poet must choose between trying to breathe life into old measures that have lost their naturalness and writing in a way that his readers (if there are any) will hardly recognize as verse at all.

A notorious little poem by Ezra Pound illustrates the situation. I quote it entire:

IN A STATION OF THE METRO

The apparition of these faces in the crowd;
Petals on a wet, black bough.

This poem is a good example of Pound's free verse at its best and of the way it achieves its effects. The first line is in perfectly regular iambic with six feet and is, in fact, rather lame and monotonous with its weak accents on *of* and *in*. The second line breaks this rhythm completely — or so it seems at first: one would have to scan it as — ◡ ◡ ◡ — — — (where " — " means a stressed and " ◡ " an unstressed syllable), and this makes no metric sense at all. The point of the poem is the sudden appearance of the image in the second line, like an explosion — the faces are like petals — and this explosion in the image is paralleled by an explosion in the rhythm. Well and good; but this still leaves something to be desired. Explosions — especially metric explosions — are too easy. We want some final sense of form, of inevitability. And as we contemplate the poem (if indeed we find the thing worth contemplating), we sense a further formal presence that is hovering there somehow. How, then?

Suppose that for the second line the poet had written, "Like petals on a wet, black bough" — since he means *like*, after all? A little mouthing of this quickly convinces us that the change would weaken the effect. But there is something else: the new line scans. For the addition of *like* gives a slight accent on *on*, so that we have ⌣ — ⌣ — ⌣ — — —, in iambic pattern with an ordinary substitution of a spondee (— —) in the last foot. What his little experiment shows us is that the second line, as Pound wrote it, is, in fact, very close to the regular rhythm of verse in English. One may say that it *alludes* to iambic verse. The presence of the word *like*, which would have made the line regular, is grammatically *understood* by the reader. Having said all this, we next realize that the whole poem also alludes to being a couplet: *crowd* and *bough* do not rhyme, but their vowel sounds echo.

Am I at last reduced, then, to admiration by these discoveries? Or are they merely inventions on my part — over-clever fabrications that might have been gotten up with any random collection of fourteen words for a text? No, contemplation of these fourteen words produced a sense of melody and rightness, so my observations go toward explaining an actual experience and are, therefore, not mere inventions, but pertinent discoveries. Nevertheless I am indignant. I admire this poem, but I also feel that it has imposed itself on me in a way that is arrogant and unjust. I want to say that it has put me through too much for too little. Poetry can do so much, give so much, and this thing only gives one little impersonal impression. But maybe that objection is ill-founded. It is never the destination that matters, but only the game of going, the ingenuity of arrival — as in a mathematics problem. And yet, taking that into consideration, I still feel indignant and imposed upon. I can't like the man who did that poem. He has used what I have brought to it and given me nothing in return. He has used my sense of the iambic line in English, but instead of strengthening, making it firmer in me in return, he has weakened it in me and made me less apt to appreciate it elsewhere. He has preyed upon me, exploited me — and also exploited the tradition he inherited. His poem depends on the metric conventions in English as surely as any other English poem and yet at the same time it overthrows the convention in scorn. That is arrogance.

Am I being too fussy about niceties? I invite those who think a tradition of poetry is important to consider the situation after two generations of free verse. The accentual-syllabic system of prosody in which almost all of the great poetry in English has been written has become a dead language. It is now possible to become a Ph.D. in our literature and not have the foggiest notion of the few simple rules that Milton used in composing his lines; and poets busy collecting government grants to go on mystifying one another need not trouble to learn them either. Milton, after all, is irrelevant. They only need and read modern poetry, and that has such rules. But where will even the good free verse, like Pound's poem, be when all the rules have been forgotten?

The requirements for the language of a poem embody a general principle which we see in all the arts: the unity of opposites or the resolution of contradictions. The artist does the apparently impossible, and the result, seemingly magical, produces the delight that we recognize. The language of a poem must be both familiar and unfamiliar; it must be ordinary living speech, but at the same time it must be different from ordinary speech, stylized, raised above it—or maybe sunk below it—sublime or comic. Formal pattern—rhyme, meter, or whatever other rule of regularity the poet can devise and his listeners appreciate—can play a role in creating this magical effect. Milton in *Paradise Lost* loosened the formal pattern by discarding the rhymes which were customary in the narrative verse of his time and said that this gave him greater freedom. A century later, the critic Samuel Johnson observed that, on the contrary, Milton's freedom constrained him to make his language unfamiliar in other ways; and indeed the language of the poem is so heavily influenced by the vocabulary and grammar of Latin that it has seemed artificial to some and unnecessarily difficult to others.

The tradition of modern poetry stemming from Whitman's and Pound's free verse, in discarding formal pattern altogether, has produced a far more intense version of this situation. Poetry has been transformed from a game of counting syllables and finding rhymes to a game of twisting syntax. There has been so much of this kind of poetry now that it has produced as a byproduct the expectation in those few who still read poetry that the syntax of poems be dislocated and that each new poet present us with a distortion uniquely his own—a "voice" of his own, as the current critical jargon expresses it. Yet language—like a society with its conventions—can function only by preserving accepted conventions of syntax. They are so much more efficient when one has something to say. But if a poet is going to permit himself the luxury and freedom of using ordinary speech and if his poem is going to seem any more heightened and memorable than peculiarly printed prose, then he has only one recourse: the formal patterns provided by his tradition and still—with increasing dimness—recognized by his readers.

My use of the idea of convention as a key to unlock some of the secrets of poetry has turned into an attack on contemporary poetry and society. I am in danger of seeming like a crank of some kind, a simple-minded hermit among his gadgets, a Barry Goldwater of poetry. It can't be helped. Have out with it, then! We are all worshipers of spontaneity, are we not?

Let me go on, then, with the decay in the conventions of language. "It is a great matter to observe propriety in these several modes of expression," says Aristotle, "But the greatest thing by far is to have a command of metaphor. This alone cannot be imparted by another; it is the mark of genius,—for to make good metaphors implies an eye for resemblances." These words carried me directly into my first months as a college teacher years ago—a freshman English class in the Boston University "School of Education." Translated into plain English, that phrase in quotes means "gridiron fodder." All the males in my class were destined for the BU football team. Great hulks towering above their Lilliputian teacher, they were not stupid (you need intelligence and cunning to play football), but their size and physical gifts were permitting them to get through the American educational system without acquiring any verbal skills whatsoever. Emil Bombast, who could have pulled the pillars of Gaza down on the screaming Philistines, returned from the post-war occupation of Japan with a nagging urge to say something about Mount Fujiyama. He could say that in the sunrise it was pink, and that, alas, was all he could say. How do you use up 300 words reasserting the pinkness of Mount Fujiyama? It was agonizing... And then there was John Belfour. Out of the depths of his wondrous consciousness, he could spin long intricate sentences, each so convoluted, so inveterately convolved and twisted in its own mad lapses of grammar and incomprehensible connections, that it reduced me to helpless laughter. I should have known that there was something extraordinary about a mind that could construct those splendid cathedrals of error that seemed to mock the arty subjects he felt himself obligated to write about.

Then one day he handed in a theme that described a bee colony he had begun some years before. In the late autumn, he explained with unusual clarity, you order a small package of hibernating bees through the mail and, when it arrives, you put it in the box that you have prepared in your yard. All through the winter there is no sign of the bees, and you wonder whether they are still alive; and you don't know whether they are or not until the snow falls and you notice that it melts more quickly off the box than off other things. When I read that detail, something happened in my body — a shiver in the gut, a wateriness about the eyes. When the spring came, the bees began to fly, taking off from the box like planes from an aircraft carrier. They were going out into the battle of existence. And like the carrier planes, many failed to return and many returned with damaged bodies and torn wings. Aristotle was right. John Belfour had genius. I weep now, writing about him and wondering about his fate.

And what has become of metaphor — that testimony of man's triumphant eye for resemblances — in the playpen of the modern lyric? In answer, let me quote some of the swinging prose of Robert Kelly, one of our many defenders of all that is new and modern in poetic practice. After showing some proper scorn for traditional poetry, Mr. Kelly continues: "For the past

hundred years (as, again, with preliminary flickers of anticipation all through man's verbal history) there has been a better
possibility: to sustain life by the creation of new forms, genuine
new verbal structures arising out of our condition to sing to
us of all times. The work of Whitman and Rimbaud in the nineteenth century—with awful slowness—has at last alerted us
to the possibility of a poem that means something. . . . I mean
a poem that means something because it is no longer *about*
something but *is* something." This is a fair sample—more than
usually intelligible, perhaps—of the sort of prose one gets from
the apologists—Pound, Williams, Olson—when they set out
to tell us about the exciting "new forms" of avant-garde poetry.
Aside from occasional phrases of sentimental bombast, like "to
sing to us of all times," there is the problem of what precisely
is meant by all those *meanings, meanings* of *meanings,* and
somethings. I quoted this passage because it will tell us what has
happened to metaphor in modern poetry.

Let us start first with the idea that a modern poem, unlike
an old-fashioned poem, is not "*about* something but *is*
something." Mr. Kelly is here echoing a better known but equally
silly statement by Archibald MacLeish: "A poem should not
mean/But be." Insofar as this assertion means anything, it means
the denial of the Aristotelian concept of imitation: the work
of art need no longer imitate, reflect, or portray anything in
the rest of experience, but is henceforth to be considered as
an object entirely in its own right, possessing only a harmony
and a coherence with itself and *unrelated* to anything else. The
trouble with this view, as one might remark in connection with
the parallel movement in mathematics, is simply that it makes
the game too easy to play and, therefore, uninteresting to watch.
In terms of poetry it is an attempt to get rid of relation and

resemblance: the hard part, the part that Aristotle says takes genius.

Next we are ready to consider what Kelly means by the "better possibility" for poetry that we have had "for the past hundred years"—with only a few dim "flickers of anticipation" to light all the other benighted centuries of "man's verbal history." He means, I presume, symbolism and surrealism, movements in French poetry that have had wide influence. Let me give what I hope is not a too outrageously simplified definition of the first of these terms. Symbolism is where you name an object in your poem in such a way that it suggests qualities, feelings, etc., which are not named and are, indeed, nameless. Wordsworth, for example, in a poem about Yew trees describes them in such a way as to suggest ancient time, deep mystery, death, long forgotten battles, shadowy pagan rites—one knows not what. One isn't supposed to know. The aim is an aura, a feeling. The meaning is there somehow, but it can be stated in no other terms. As the illustration suggests—because it was drawn from an earlier period—almost all poetry and a great deal of prose uses symbolism in some degree; but symbolism, the movement, attempts to make this mood-engendering property of words the central feature of the poem and to found a technique on it.

This brings us back to metaphor. The word means, literally, a "bearing across" and originally it named that rhetorical device by which we speak of something with terms properly applied to something else, as when I speak of "the playpen of the modern lyric." A metaphor always implies a comparison and is often suggestive. Thus, my phrase implies that modern poets resemble puling infants in some way and invites us to picture them throwing tantrums and sucking their thumbs. The word has, however, long been used to signify comparisons of any kind.

One therefore, speaks of "the two terms of a metaphor," meaning the items compared—the terms of Mr. Belfour's metaphor being, for example, "bees" and "carrier planes." The paradoxical nature of art, the seemingly irreconcilable aims which give difficulty to the artist and, when overcome, a sense of magic to the audience also appear in our estimation of a good metaphor: we want to be surprised and excited by how unlike the things are which are compared; but we also expect the comparison to be just, that is, we wish to be able to see that the things compared really do resemble each other. A good metaphor is a genuine discovery.

With all this in mind, we can take a fresh look at symbolism. For the symbolist poet, a symbol is a metaphor with one term left vague. Ultimately the origins of the technique lie in medieval allegory, but it will be sufficient for our purpose to consider one development of this European allegorical tendency in the lyric poetry of the Renaissance: the customary metaphor. Poets in Renaissance times were not expected to be original—at least not in their choice of subjects and comparisons. In fact, they were expected *not* to be original in this way. Comparisons tend to be used and reused and so to become customary. This makes it possible for a first-rate poet like Wyatt or Shakespeare to use certain images—the hunter and the deer, standing for the lover and the beloved, was a favorite of Wyatt's—in a way that relies upon their being charged with conventional meaning and gives the poem great intensity as a result. The symbolist poet tries to do the same thing without the benefit of such a system of conventional meanings, which, indeed, no longer exists in his society. In the absence of convention, he has to suggest such meanings in the texture of his poem. Some of the results are exquisite, but always and inevitably there is a certain doubt

whether the suggested term of the metaphor is indeed present—
whether, in fact, it is a metaphor at all, let alone whether it
is a good metaphor. "Say it with images!" has been the cry of
"advanced" poetry for generations now, but there is always the
question in the mind of the reader—especially the general
reader—whether the images are saying anything at all: whether
the poet is not, in fact, using the technique and its fashionable
acceptance to cover up his inability to make metaphors in the
traditional way: by discovering interesting and recognizable
resemblances. It is possible, for example, for some to believe that
Ezra Pound's *Cantos* are endlessly allusive; but it is equally possible for others to find them almost totally capricious and
incoherent.

One would have thought—considering only the art of poetry
and paying no attention to the crisis Western Civilization was
reaching—that so limited and questionable a technique of
poetry would have been quickly laid aside in favor of an
approach more accessible to ordinary common sense; but symbolism not only thrived; it developed into surrealism.

Let us look at a hint of surrealism in the first three lines of
a familiar nonsurrealist poem:

> Let us go then, you and I,
> When the evening is spread out against the sky
> Like a patient etherized upon a table.

The usual way of explaining this comparison, of the evening
to a patient, is to say that it expresses the state of mind of J.
Alfred Prufrock, the speaker, named in the poem's title. He feels
numbed and passive, and so that's how he sees the evening,
like a patient under ether, unnaturally put to sleep, ready to
be cut open—as Prufrock is himself to be cut open and examined

in the course of the poem. (That last bit of suggestiveness about the cutting open would make the image symbolic as well as psychological. Is that meaning really part of the poem? There is no telling. That's the way symbolist poems are.) But such a gloss does not do justice to the actual effect of this opening. There is something wild and kinky about it. That third line about the "patient etherized upon a table" with its tone of flat, clinical prose comes as a shocker after the vaguely romantic and "poetic"-sounding "evening . . . spread out against the sky." Our first requirement for a good metaphor — that the things compared be surprisingly unlike — is met brilliantly. But what about the other — that there be an actual resemblance between the terms? I have had these lines in my consciousness for more than thirty years, and I am still unable to visualize that evening "spread out against" the sky — certainly not in the sense of someone lying on a table. "Evening" and "sky" simply do not go together in this way. They are only *put* together to *set us up* for that whammy in the next line. This poet is not about to forget himself in order to discover the truth of his experience but, with his ego securely intact, he is going to manipulate his experience to get an effect. Like the used-car salesman who remains true to his trade, this man is motivated by the designs he has on us; and I, for one, feel perfectly free to reject his pitch by saying simply: it's a bad metaphor because there is no real resemblance; the resemblance is only asserted. With this as a lead, I can then go on to say that I reject the whole phony, hoked-up character of J. Alfred Prufrock as well. He is not a deeply perceived person, not really a person at all, a man who is growing old, but only a bundle of the self-centered fears of a young man who is terrified at the prospect of growing old. Such fears are banal and tiresome, and there is a failure of imagination in the perfunctory attempt to mask them. I would not deny the brilliance of the poem; in its flawed art, it frighteningly reflects the predicament of our civilized notion of the self.

The hint of surrealism in those opening lines is in the arbitrariness of the metaphor. In answer to my objection, the surrealist would answer that the "image" has psychological validity and is therefore justified. Henceforth, as Mr. Kelley says, the poem is to be an object in its own right with no need to reflect anything else — especially anything else in merely physical reality, which the scientists have neatly sewn up into their own domain. (The modernist poets, for all their hatred of science, are remarkably docile to its precepts. Charles Olson thinks that the introduction of the typewriter, with its ability to space more accurately, has revolutionized modern verse.) No longer is the poet to make intelligible statements and discover fresh resemblances in the realm of common experience: the sole aim of the modern poem henceforth is to be self-expression. The words of the poem are to reflect the self — and only the self — of the poet, and the less they have to do with their ordinary prose meanings, the more torn from their usual contexts, the better. As Mr. Kelley puts it: "The prime material of the poem is words. Let there be no doubt about that. In general, the new poetry is the product of those poets who believe in the word . . . the wood of our world that grows from the roots of our consciousness. Modern linguistics hypothesizes a tyranny which language, as a system, exerts over its unconscious users. The radical poetry of the American language would liberate us from that tyranny."

The great modern theme of liberation is upon us here again, that runs its course from Milton to this, the liberation from the very language we speak, from our very humanity. Metaphor is now gone altogether, both terms of it, the second now following the first that had already vanished into the mists of symbolism; for metaphor is a part of the tyranny of logic and language, one more odious convention. Poems now will be praised only for their "breath-taking and exciting imagery," their "fireworks of words," without any hint of how easy it is to put on such displays: it only requires a certain shamelessness. The aim is self-expression. The Self! What can be left after all this peeling off of our cultural layers but something more naked than any primitive ever was — the pure savage at last; the pure savage that only a thousand years of city life can produce — a man as artificial as his meaningless poems?

Do I grow too hot? Why should we, who dwell in America with its wonders of science, its unemployment, its atomic armadas, its towers reaching to the sky, its corporations — why should we worry about what a few mad poets are doing? Perhaps if we were concerned, they wouldn't be doing it. There have, indeed, been societies that have interested themselves in such matters. The Greeks were intensely aware of the social implications of art. Aristophanes' comments on certain types of music of which he disapproved remind us uncomfortably of the Russian government's censure of Shostakovich. We think art should be "free." To the disgruntled little band of artists among us, this is an article of faith; to the rest of us, it is a polite way of saying that art is too insignificant to worry about. The best way is to devote a minuscule fraction of the national budget to making grants to a few of the artists and to getting applications from them all. If they are busy filling out forms, they will be less likely to be making bombs.

But in fact, developments in the arts today are highly significant in that they express and represent a far more general movement in the societies of Western Europe and America. Let us call it Modernism and define it as the attempt to overthrow a system of customs and conventions felt to have become rigid and stultifying and to create in its place a completely liberated society based on the individual self. Modernism in this sense may easily be seen to underlie and give ideological support to a number of more specific movements of varying merit that have made social life in the West since the Second World War so exciting: the peace movement, the New Left, Black liberation, women's liberation, gay liberation, and of course, Mr. Kelley's liberation from language. To an amazing degree, being a poet — or any other kind of serious artist — in our present society has meant to be in sympathy with one or another of these movements — and most likely with all of them: to be, in a word, a Modernist. This gives us perhaps the most significant peculiarity of contemporary poetry: it is free in form and stereotyped in attitude. One senses the ghost of Samuel Johnson saying that this is but one more instance of paying for the freedoms we take with new, more odious forms of bondage. Indeed, it should be apparent that this movement, as I have defined it, cannot ultimately have much of a future: for is not the individual self, which it opposes to the hated world of convention, also entirely a matter of convention? Pope in his marvelous Augustan prescience provides us with Modernism's proper label: it is "one vile Antithesis."

Modernism begins in America (for the French were deeply affected by Poe and Whitman), and rightly so. It was in America that convention became intolerably rigid and produced the break. The settlement of an alien continent with its palpable and impalpable threats on every side necessarily involved a rigid assertion of a Western Civilization that had, at the same time, been shorn and simplified in the ocean crossing. Moral codes and the stereotypes governing the relations of the sexes, for example, tended to become subject to a brutal sentimentality and to lose all their nuance and flexibility. A few simple beliefs could be brought on the voyage, apparently, but all the qualifications, subtleties, and paradoxes established by art and the aristocratic tradition had to be left behind. William Carlos Williams in his book *In the American Grain* laments the spiritual inflexibility of the English-speaking settlers, which prevented them from responding more creatively to their new surroundings, and compares them unfavorably to the French trappers and missionaries to the north. Whereas the French sympathized and mixed freely with the Indians and responded to the new continent with love and openness, says Williams, the English felt mainly hate and fear. This is very interesting, even profound, but in the end, I think, sentimental; for Williams only regrets the fact that almost the whole continent has since become English-speaking and makes no attempt to explain why. The explanation is obvious: the French he admires were single adventurers; the English came with their families. For this reason it was clear from the beginning which nationality would develop a powerful, settled life and become dominant. But this difference also explains the difference that Williams notes. A man afraid for his wife, his children, and his cultivated land can hardly be expected to show much interest or sympathy with Indians. Loneliness, after all, is not his problem. The omission is symptomatic of the refusal of Williams, and of others with his prejudices, to consider any of the virtues of conventional American life.

Another revealing instance of this prejudice came my way a couple of years ago when I ordered a paperback collection of short stories for my class of freshman English. Along with the stories that I knew, came one I had never heard of, originally published in *The New Yorker* in 1948, and a very famous item, as my freshmen told me with a sigh at the prospect of reading it again. They had all had it assigned to them in high school. The story was "The Lottery" by Shirley Jackson. Apparently those in high-school administrations who have a finger on the pulse of modern culture consider it good material with which to blow the minds of the young. "This is a story," the editor assures us, "that reaches down to expose some deep and terrifying flaw in human nature. The reader will leave it profoundly moved and intensely disturbed." I hope that my discussion of it will convince the reader that the story is profoundly untrue and, in essence, vulgar and disgusting.

We are presented with a rather insipidly drawn rural town with a middle-western flavor. Everybody is getting ready for the big annual event in the town, the Lottery. Boys are gathering stones for it, as in so many years past; the old customary lottery box for the tickets is brought out. Everywhere there is the stultification and mindless adherence to customs justified by nothing more than long habit. Everything is thoroughly familiar, tedious, and ordinary, except for one thing: the reward for the winner of the lottery is to be stoned to death by his fellow townsmen.

The story is topical. The post-war revelations of the Nazi Holocaust, the mass murder of more than twelve million Jews, Gypsies, Poles, and Russians, was fresh in the minds of its original readers, and the story implies an explanation of how such things can happen. Clearly man's tendency to adhere without question to ancient customs and conventions is to blame. Custom makes robots of us, and under its behests we can be induced to carry out any horror. And where do such customs come from? Presumably from some deep core of savage cruelty that lurks in all of us — the flaw mentioned by the editor. One thinks of the Aztecs and their gory sacrifices, forgetting that we learned almost nothing about their society before we destroyed it in the name of Christianity.

Is there any truth in these implications? The story is based firmly and without any sort of qualification on a familiar American stereotype: the scorn of the urban intellectual of the East Coast for small-town farmers, the hicks of the hinterland. A barbarous act of unprecedented proportions occurred in the advanced civilization of the twentieth century. How comforting it is to blame it on the Elmer Snerds — and what a perfect story for *The New Yorker*! It is for this reason that I consider the story to be vulgar and disgusting. But an element of truth could still redeem it. Did the Nazi genocide result from a blind adherence to immemorial custom? The idea is ridiculous. The Holocaust was carefully thought out and meticulously organized. It's leaders thought they were solving "the Jewish problem" and can only be described as bold, innovative and, in their own terms, thoroughly rational. The horrors did not follow from ancient custom, but from fresh ideology. This is, or ought to be, the real horror for us, who have been committed to the reorganization of society on what we call rational principles. But instead we allow ourselves to be duped and soothed by shallow myths like this.

The prejudices and assumptions of Modernism can be deadly as well as ridiculous. Let me briefly consider, as a final example, the so-called confessional movement in poetry. It represents in many ways a sharp and important break with the tendencies toward chaos and incoherence that I have already described. The confessional poet is committed to writing about his own experience in a language close to prose, intelligible, and often intensified by traditional meters and rhetorical devices; and profound and beautiful work has been done by Snodgrass and others. But Modernism has deeply influenced the work of these writers as well. There is also the curious fact that suicide, as I mentioned earlier, has become almost a fashion among them. Sylvia Plath, John Berryman, Anne Sexton: these writers have staged a little holocaust of their own. Explaining this phenomenon has become one of the more macabre occupations of modern critics; and with due humility, I should like to tender my own theory on the subject.

I would suggest that the confessional poet who is influenced by Modernism is caught in the toils of a cruel syllogism which runs as follows: 1) The poet must find the materials for his poetry in the circumstances of his life. 2) The circumstances of his life are banal, suburban, and conventional, and therefore, by the tenets of Modernism, intolerable to the self. 3) Therefore, his poetry must be agonized and desperate. The essential feature is that Modernism induces the poet to adopt an ideologically stereotyped attitude towards his materials. He cannot, for example, regard the banality of his existence as essentially comic, because that would be to denigrate the pristine purity of the self in its heroic struggle against convention. His problem as a poet then becomes: to demonstrate in his poems the agony and desperation of his life in the twentieth century. But in poetic demonstrations, as in other kinds, the actual circumstances presented must justify the conclusion to the reasonably impartial observer — that is, to a reader who is not necessarily a Modernist. This is impossible to do; for the poets under consideration have all had lives in which, on the surface, there has been very little to complain about. True, they have tended to have overweening egos and been consumed by overwhelming ambition to be great poets. But such sources of discomfort can-not be included as substantiating detail in the poem; our reasonable reader would find such details laughable. Such childish crazes are the poet's problem, not his.

The modernist confessional poet, then, is in the dilemma of trying to demonstrate in the detail and mythical implications of his life an agony and desperation which is justified neither in those details nor in the beliefs of the society as a whole. That is to say, he is a sentimentalist. The resulting poems, no matter how brilliantly worked out, will inevitably be open to a simple devastating criticism: "What on earth is this person complain-ing about?" No matter how many sympathetic followers the poet may gather about him who will share his assumptions and protect him from this question and no matter what personal disasters he may cultivate in order to put the attitude of his poems on a firmer basis, as long as he lives, that question re-mains, sitting there like Mount Everest—or like an ugly little monkey perched on his bookcase. Finally the poet must prove—outside his poems, since there is no way for the poems to prove it—that there *is* something to complain about, something that renders life supremely desperate. He can do this only by committing suicide. He kills himself to validate his own poems.

In *Erlkönig*, the great ballad-poem of Goethe and song of Schubert, a child carried by his father on horseback through the night sees, hears, and finally feels the terrifying King of the Goblins, cajoling him, then snatching at him. Everything the child experiences as part of the goblin world, the father also experiences as part of the rationally explained world of civilized adults. The king's train is a streak of mist, his whispered pro-mises the wind in dry leaves, his daughters the old willows shin-ing in the moonlight. The two realms of experience are parallel but totally disparate — until the child screams. The scream the father can hear. The irony up to this point is that we adults experiencing the poem see as the father sees and take the child's experiences to be "vivid imagination." The father spurs his horse in terror, but when he arrives in the warmth and light of civilization, the child is dead. This last turn of events, which ends the poem, alters the state of affairs completely. There is now no longer any way to reconcile the child's view with that of the adult: so it becomes independent, valid in its own terms, unanswerable. Death has validated it. Before his death, we could say to the child, "You are only seeing things," and thus express and believe in our social truth: our faith that the child will grow into our view. But with his death our mouths are stopped, and he escapes, firm in his world, untouched by ours.

The poem presents us with two irreconcilable interpretations, two truths, and no way to prefer one to the other. The child's death has defeated society, the only possible arbiter. And when I mentioned Valéry's idea of society as "an edifice of enchantments," this poem was waiting nearby. Valéry posits a reality underlying such enchantments, such conventions: "Il y a une réalité antérieure aux fictions et aux mythes"; and says that poetry can regain contact with it: "La poésie permet à l'esprit de reprendre contact avec une réalité antérieure aux monstres méchaniques que cet esprit engendra et qui sont nos hypothèses et nos connaissances." In Goethe's poem, it is the child's death that plunges us, helpless and without thought, into this "réalité antérieure."

The poem does this, not by being, but by meaning. It is something other than what it represents. In this sense, the *child's* vision of Erlkönig is *not* a poem: it does not mean; it simply is; and this is why the child's death can validate it. The complaint has been made that Sylvia Plath, after her death, has become a cult, to the detriment of a proper appreciation of her poems *as poems*. But this is exactly the proper thing to have happened. By her act of suicide in order to validate her poems, she took them out of the realm of poetry altogether and placed them in the realm of absolute belief, that is, in the realm of religion. I could quote one of her poems and say, "This is brilliant, but unconvincing." I could as well have stood before The Cross and said, "This display is exciting, but excessive."

Is there any way at all, then, for poetry to go in these modern times of chaos and impasse? The Modernists remain a small minority in society as a whole. Do other people write poems? One doesn't often hear of them, but they exist; and going back only a few years, one comes upon large presences that don't fit this modern ambience and seem like irrelevant leftovers from the forgotton past. The movement that has Rimbaud as it's patron saint does not include Thomas Hardy or Robert Frost. That brilliant schoolboy, who gave up poetry altogether at the age of nineteen in order to take up gunrunning, condemned all of French literature before him, and especially the plays of Racine, its greatest dramatist, as being mere "versified prose." Goethe's *Erlkönig*, being in very simple unadorned and undis-located German in the style of eighteenth-century rationalism, would undoubtedly come under the ban as well. I suspect that this lowly versified prose is, in fact, the only viable possibility for a basic style in poetry in this—or in any other—age. And I submit that the only poet in the twentieth century to see this fact with absolutely unwavering clarity was Robert Frost. In his pronouncements about the relation of the fluid rhythms of natural speech to the fixed patterns of meter, he shows himself to have been completely aware of what he was doing; and it seems to me that his popular narrative poems in blank verse, so often looked down on by critics as, at best, mere peculiarities, are the most thoroughly original work by any poet in the modern age: for no other poems oppose so clearly and authoritatively as these the direction that European poetry has taken since the work of Blake and Hölderlin.

Indeed, there was an immediate forerunner in the copious but strangely flawed work of E. A. Robinson. In spite of its gaucheries, there is a kind of homemade, do-it-yourself epic style in Robinson that repays study; but it is in Frost's pastoral mode that the new approach, resembling nothing since the work of Goethe, becomes entirely convincing. One might speculate on the reasons why both of these poets should be Americans associated with New England—the only section of America that had experienced significant decline and decay—and note that, like other great innovators in literature, they seem to have been far more deeply influenced by ancient Greek poetry than by any of their contemporaries. I shall content myself with looking at one brief passage: the opening of Frost's "The Death of the Hired Man," which I have chosen deliberately because it is very low key and shows how the style can accept flat, prosaic materials on their own terms and heighten them nevertheless.

> Mary sat musing on the lamp-flame at the table
> Waiting for Warren. When she heard his step,
> She ran on tip-toe down the darkened passage
> To meet him at the doorway with the news
> And put him on his guard. "Silas is back."

Considered as prose, this would rate as a good opening for a short story. One has to consider what being in blank verse adds to it. The most striking answer comes in the third line with the tripping staccato rhythm of "She ran on tip-toe down the darkened passage." The fact that this marvelously expressive rhythm strains against, but does not break, the regular metric pattern, of which we are subliminally aware, enormously enhances its effect. The passage has other effects as well. The first line has two weak accents (syllables that would not normally be accented in speech, but which tend to be accented because of the metric pattern) on *on* and *at*. An English iambic pentameter line tends to have one of these (a consequence, perhaps, of the fact that a thousand years ago the "English" poetic line, which did not count syllables then, had only four accents); and when one varies the number of these weak accents, making lines with none or with two, one gets special effects. Here the effect is of wavering and suspense, and it is repeated in the fourth line, "To meet him at the doorway with the news," with its weak accents on "at" and "with." Finally, the last phrase, "Silas is back," presents us with a trochee ($-\smile$) substituted for an iamb ($\smile -$), which sets off the abruptness of the words.

More important, however than all this is the sense of the *proper length* of every phrase and sentence. Any good prose stylist has a sense of this, but when it is done in meter, the effects created are much stronger because the meter clearly and precisely measures the length of every grammatical element. As Milton puts it, the "true musical delight" of poetry consists in "the sense variously drawn out from one Verse into another." But the rhythms of Frost's blank verse are utterly different from Milton's. The metric stereotype accepted by both permits — and enhances — the originality of tone and attitude in each.

Frost's great originality lay in his bold return of poetry to its immemorial and rightful place: the art of storytelling. A French symbolist poet of the last century said once that he could never write a novel because he could never bring himself to write such banal phrases as, "Then he opened the door." I would not be at all surprised to learn that Frost was thinking of this poet when he opened one of his own poems with the line, "I let myself in at the kitchen door." Not only a door, but a *kitchen* door! And the line is quite interesting metrically.

So there is, indeed, a way for poetry to go: the old way that it has always gone. As Frost himself remarked, it comes down to one simple requirement: an artist must have something to say — something new that he discovers. A difference between music and poetry is that in music this something must, it seems, always be about the medium itself, whereas in poetry it need not be. The poet can revivify old forms and conventions with discoveries about experience. Music, like mathematics, appears to be wholly at the mercy of its medium.

I would have the poet leave the revolutions in art and society alone; for they are amply staffed with madmen already. I would have him return to his ancient role: neither to reject the stereotypes of his society nor to accept them but, in the comic vein, to show how ridiculous they are and how necessary and, in the tragic, to portray their grievous and ennobling consequences; in short, to qualify them with a humor and sadness that glances into the mystery beneath and thereby makes a life of gaiety and dignity possible.

There are the conventions of society, and there is art, and neither can function properly without the other.

EXPLORATIONS OF AMERICA

cʒoɕʒ

Christopher Clausen

I

With a few important exceptions, nationalism as a strongly
held attitude is conspicuously absent from modern poetry in
English. An overtly nationalistic poem like Drayton's "Ballad
of Agincourt" has hardly any parallels in the twentieth century. For a variety of reasons, skepticism about the value and
an awareness of the dangers of national self-assertiveness have
entered the language and attitudes available to modern poets.
The cosmopolitanism of the most influential modernists and
the disillusionments of the first World War are two obvious
sources of this skepticism, but perhaps there are older and deeper
ones as well: for example, the fact that English poetry became
a trans-national enterprise precisely at the time, in the nineteenth century, when modern nationalism was taking shape.
An American, Australian, or Canadian who has been educated
on British poetic models finds it difficult to use them in the
service of national self-assertion without some obvious ironies
arising in his mind.

For whatever combination of reasons, highly regarded poetry
that is explicitly nationalistic (as opposed to merely patriotic
in a general way) has in the twentieth century been restricted
on the whole to small or embattled nations in conditions of
crisis: Yeats's poems about Irish independence, for example, or

First published in *Verse*, III 1985. Copyright © by Christopher Clausen. Reprinted
with permission of the author and publisher.

Hugh MacDiarmid's about Scotland, or the more nationalistic passages of Eliot's *Four Quartets*. "Highly regarded," of course, raises the possibility that skepticism about nationalism is an attitude of critics rather than of poets, and no doubt one could find in the twentieth century a great deal of nationalistic verse that in previous centuries would have been labelled "popular" as opposed to serious or literary poetry. Nonetheless, it is a fact that the major poets of the twentieth century, even Kipling, are far less comfortable asserting nationalistic attitudes in verse than their predecessors from the Renaissance through the eighteenth century. If James Thomson were alive today, he might very well write a series of poems thematically similar to "The Seasons"; it is much less likely that he would write a modern equivalent of "Rule, Britannia."

None of this means that nationality and the exploration of its constituents has not been a major theme in the literature of our time. It has, perhaps all the more so as the differences between one place and another seem to lessen. I am speaking here not of the regionalism that is such a common feature in modern British and American literature, but of national self-definition. Self-definition is an entirely different activity from self-assertion, and an inevitable one in nations that have been created in recent times by settlers whose descendants are often at a loss to know what makes them a nation besides their ancestors' common, willed act of immigration. It is hardly too much to say that this need to create a national identity in the act of understanding it has obsessed the literature of America and the Commonwealth countries since their beginnings. Much American writing from the seventeenth century onwards has embodied a heroic attempt at national definition, which reached its nineteenth-century peak in the poetry of Whitman. The history of this literary theme—of an Eden settled by Europeans, who overcame the original inhabitants and declared their independent identity by an act of self-creative will—has in turn been traced exhaustively by scholars and critics, and there is neither space nor need to summarize it here.

Since Whitman's time until recently, the literary definition of America has been carried on more conspicuously and effectively by novelists than by poets. The works of Mark Twain, Henry James, F. Scott Fitzgerald, Ernest Hemingway, and William Faulkner are obvious examples, and occasional attempts at this sort of thing in the poems of Robert Frost (e.g., "The Gift Outright") and others do not weigh heavily against them. Because the adequate exploration of national identity involves history, characters, and complex attitudes, novelists are at an obvious advantage in a time when the dominant poetic form is the short or "lyric" poem. In *The Place of Poetry* (University Press of Kentucky, 1981) I described the decline of the book-length narrative or meditative poem and gave some reasons for the dominance of the short poem since the middle of the nineteenth century. Since book-length poems that tell a story or expound ideas in detail are precisely the kind best suited to the task we are discussing, we should not be surprised that prose fiction largely appropriated it, along with so many other tasks and themes, once the scale of *Leaves of Grass* had come to seem ungainly or merely impracticable by Whitman's successors.

"Are stories no longer told in poetry?" Dana Gioia asked in the *Kenyon Review* for spring 1983. "Important ideas no longer discussed at length? The panoply of available genres would seem reduced to a few hardy perennials which poets worked over and over again with dreary regularity—the short lyric, the ode, the familiar verse epistle, perhaps the epigram, and one new-fangled form called the 'sequence' which often seemed to be either just a group of short lyrics stuck together or an ode in the process of falling apart." Gioia discussed some of the advantages of longer forms and then put his finger on an important reason for their decline in the wake of modernism: "The main problem facing the long poem today is that contemporary theory allows the poet almost no middle ground between the concentration of the lyric and the vast breadth of the epic (the modern epic, that is, in its distinctive form as the historical cultural poem). . . . American literature needs a more modest aesthetic of the long poem, a less chauvinistic theory which does not vainly seek the great at the expense of the good and genuine. It needs to free poets from the burden of writing the definitive long poem and allow them to work in more manageable albeit limited genres like satire, comedy, unheroic autobiography, discursive writing, pure narrative — be it fictional or historic . . . "

Drawing attention to the eclipse of a literary form is often a step towards reviving it, and as Frederick Feirstein pointed out in the same issue of the *Kenyon Review*, most of the genres that Gioia called for are again being practiced in a variety of ways. The lyric poem could accommodate some themes and ambitions supremely well and offered many poets a welcome discipline after the verbosity of the most celebrated Victorians. But the very successes of its practitioners, from Hopkins and Yeats through Frost and Eliot to the present, exhausted many of its possibilities in the act of exploiting them. Sooner or later, new poets would wish to escape from the shadow of their immediate predecessors — just as the modernists had once done with theirs — by trying themes and forms that had fewer recent associations. One result has been a widespread but mostly unheralded revival of the book-length poem in America during the last decade or so. Another, closely related, has been a return to the theme of national identity in an era which, like Whitman's, makes that identity a matter of obsessive concern. The end of the twentieth century is in most respects a more troubling time than Whitman's, and the identity to be explored is not the same as it was in the first century of the republic. Nonetheless, Whitman, Cooper, Emerson, and their contemporaries would recognize important continuities, if only because searching for the essence of America is such a characteristically American thing to do.

From many poems that might be chosen to illustrate these assertions, I have selected three: Robert Pinsky's *An Explanation of America*, Frederick Feirstein's *Manhattan Carnival*, and Robert Penn Warren's *Chief Joseph of the Nez Perce*. They are a diverse group in their forms, in their settings, in their authors' outlooks on life in general and America in particular; yet they all embody a deep desire to get to the heart of American identity, which in varying ways all three writers (like most Americans since Jamestown) feel to be unique. None of these poems is an epic; all are ambitious "public" poems. My concern in examining them is not so much to evaluate them as to see how three contemporary poets have experimented with long forms — blank-verse meditation, fictional narrative in heroic couplets, and historical narrative in free verse — while exploring a theme of overriding significance. Looked at together, they incarnate three ways of writing a book-length poem today and also three approaches to what might be called, in medieval romance fashion, the Matter of America.

II

In *The Situation of Poetry* (1976), Robert Pinsky celebrated the

bicentennial of American independence by calling for a return
to the "prose virtues" in poetry. Poetry, he declared, should be
as well written, and sometimes as discursive, as good prose.
"Colorless and reactionary as such a position may seem," he
added, mindful of the recent history of American verse, "it is
worth taking up." Then he went on to explain what he had
in mind by "prose virtues" and to assert that late-twentieth-
century poets might find them to be necessities: "If the plural
is analyzed, the virtues turn out to be a drab, unglamorous group,
including perhaps Clarity, Flexibility, Efficiency, Cohesive-
ness . . . a puritanical assortment of shrews. They do not as a
rule appear in blurbs. And yet when they are courted by those
who understand them — William Carlos Williams and Elizabeth
Bishop would be examples — the Prose Virtues are transformed
from a supporting chorus to the performers of virtuoso marvels.
They can become not merely the poem's minimum requirement,
but the poetic essence." Pinsky's *An Explanation of America*
(1979), subtitled in Yeatsian fashion "A Poem to my Daughter,"
puts most of those virtues to use in an extended meditation
whose discursive purpose is proclaimed by its title.

To explain America poetically, it is necessary first to delineate
the person for whom the explanation is intended. The rhetoric
of explanation must be *ad hominem*, in the correct sense of that
commonly abused phrase. The daughter for whom the explanation is nominally devised seems hardly the sort of child thought
to be typically American: she is imaginative, solitary, infantile
in many ways but with the dreams of an adult — "not / A type
(the solitary flights at night; / The dreams mature, the spirit
infantile)/ Which America has always known to prize." She is,
in short, an outsider, not a joiner, not likely to be at home with
American gregariousness, a potential object of persecution, a

disconcertingly intelligent child whose eyes behind their owlish glasses betray "The gaze of liberty and independence / Uneasy in groups and making groups uneasy." Already a note of alienation has been struck between the person to whom the explanation is directed (the explainer himself is not yet an issue) and the thing to be explained. We are a long way from Whitman's uncontradictory sense of America as a unified mass of individualists.

The possibility that America in the fullness of its development has become a less benign creation than Whitman hoped inheres in the daughter's childish forms of alienation. Dreams and reality have parted, leaving behind the wake of ambiguities that require the poet's explanation. Thus the first question is what, after the variety and empty vastness of the American continent, to show.

> What do I want for you to see? I want—
> Beyond the states and corporations, each
> Hiding and showing after their kind the forms
> Of their atrocities, beyond their power
> For evil—the greater evil in ourselves,
> And greater images more vast than *Time*.
> I want for you to see the thing I see
> And more, Colonial Diners, Disney, films
> Of concentration camps, the napalmed child
> Trotting through famous newsfilm in her diaper
> And tattered flaps of skin, *Deep Throat*, the rest.

In its content, its emphases, its development, its juxtaposition of the horrific and the banal, this catalogue of American realities is far different from anything in "Song of Myself." Evil and banality infect not only institutions but American selves. Television and Vietnam have both happened. If the New World was ever Eden, the Fall was a long time ago. Democracy, however desirable, has solved few problems (as the daughter puts it, "Voting *is not* fair").

> I want our country like a common dream
> To be between us in what we want to see—
> Not that I want for you to have to see
> Atrocity itself, or that its image
> Is harmless. I mean the way we need to see
> With shared, imperfect memory: the quiet
> Of tourists shuffling with their different awes
> Through well-kept Rushmore, Chiswick House, or
>   Belsen . . .

Not discoverers or pioneers, not Columbus or Lewis and Clark, but tourists.

What follows is predictably fragmentary, impressions of a land and history described in the last line of the poem as "So large, and strangely broken, and unforseen." It is not on the whole an attractive portrait.

> The plural-headed Empire, manifold
> Beyond my outrage or my admiration,
> Is like a prison which I leave to you
> (And like a shelter)—where the people vote,
> And where the threats of riot and oppression
> Inspire the inmates as they whittle, scribble,
> Jockey for places in the choir, or smile
> Passing out books on weekdays.

An empire is characterized, in Pinsky's terms, by variety, mobility, and above all power. Americans move around so much that regional differences, indeed all sense of place, become themselves "a kind of motion." An image of unmotivated suicide in the endless prairies of the Middle West suggests the aimlessness of so much American mobility, which is perhaps little more at bottom than a love of death. In a nation whose inhabitants have to create it imaginatively out of such a vast emptiness, a lasting individual or corporate identity is hard to come by. No wonder that the official symbol of the United States, the eagle who represents flight and power, is a "wild bird with its hardware in its claws."

What Whitman would have made of America a century after his death is anybody's guess, but he would almost certainly have resisted the notion that classical European parallels could offer useful insights. For him and his followers, America was unique in the world's history, subject to few of the limitations that affected other empires. Pinsky, however, follows many twentieth-century historians and political commentators in seeing close parallels between America and Rome, frugal republics that begat decadent empires. The centre of his poem is a free translation from a letter in which Horace reflected on private versus public life in an imperial society. *Public* and *private* meant different things in an empire from what they meant in a small republic, Roman or American. For Pinsky's Horace, a detached retirement is the only way to lead a life that is both free and dignified. A public life in which those virtues can be maintained has become, if not absolutely impossible, at least very difficult. What can traditional civic virtues mean in such a civilization? At bottom, the willingness to commit suicide rather than submit to tyranny is the only solid basis for liberty — a liberty which only detached individuals can possess, not one that undergirds the whole social structure. The republic is gone forever; only in the isolated, detached self of the Stoic does anything of its spirit survive.

Republics liberate, empire imprisons. Thomas Jefferson on his mountaintop at Monticello represented an altogether different classicism from Horace at his Sabine farm. A third civic

possibility is Brutus. Pinsky finds it hard to decide what kind
of fortune to wish for a daughter who must live in an age of
Caesarism. Whatever one's talents, to be a Jefferson is now
impossible.

> Since aspirations need not (some say, should not)
> Be likely, should I wish for you to be
> A hero, like Brutus—who at the finish-line
> Declared himself to be a happy man?
> Or is the right wish health, the just proportion
> Of sun, the acorns and cold pure water, a nest
> Out in the country and a place in Rome...

The question is never resolved.

Despite the optimism of its title, "Its Everlasting Possibility,"
the last section of the poem remains equally uncertain. With
the instincts of a classicist, Pinsky sees the denial of limit as
a "pride, or failing" common to all the races, classes, and regions
of America. That denial may well be what transformed America
from a republic to an empire. Vietnam ought finally to have
taught America a lesson about limits.

> On television, I used to see, each week,
> Americans descending in machines
> With wasted bravery and blood; to spread
> Pain and vast fires amid a foreign place...
> I think it made our country older, forever.

Older, but not wiser. The lesson was not learned. A curious
amalgam of "Nostalgia and Progress" continues to dominate
the collective mind. No doubt every recent observer of America
has been struck by the bizarre coexistence of an unlimited faith
in technology with an assertion of what are imagined to be old-
fashioned family and religious values. As Pinsky puts it,

> The country, boasting that it cannot see
> The past, waits dreaming ever of the past,
> Or all the plural pasts: the way a fetus
> Dreams vaguely of heaven . . .

Even the ageless mountains need protection, in the form of environmental laws, from the irresponsibility of technological somnambulism.

In the epilogue, the ambiguous tale of America is tacitly compared with Shakespeare's *Winter's Tale*. Hope may be reborn, despite appearances; the size and mobility of the country once again militate against a definitive conclusion. What can a classicist make of so unclassical a spectacle?

> Where nothing will stand still
> Nothing can end—but recoils into the past,
> Or is improvised into the dream or nightmare
> Romance of new beginnings.

A skeptical half-hope for the national future, by a mind that does not even know what it would be best to hope for, is the paradoxically patriotic conclusion to this uncertain explanation.

III

If it is to be less ambiguous, the romance of new beginnings may have to be a private rather than a national renewal. The year after Pinsky's poem was published, Ronald Reagan was elected president on the slogan "Together, a new beginning." It seems unlikely that Pinsky's hopes for his country or his daughter were advanced by such an appropriation, but there can be no doubt that the concept of new beginnings, on the level of advertising if not of poetry, had developed a mass appeal. The public consequences of that appeal are well known. For poets and thinkers, the most important effect was probably to intensify the division between public and privte life that Richard Sennett described a decade ago in *The Fall of Public Man*. We shall be looking presently at one contemporary poet's jaundiced view of public life during the period when America was transforming itself into an imperial power. Before that, however, I want to examine a more private romance of new beginnings in Frederick Feirstein's *Manhattan Carnival* (1981), a poem whose exploration of American identity rarely becomes as explicit as Pinsky's and yet is perhaps, for that very reason, all the more searching and symptomatic.

If Pinsky's points of reference are on the whole classical, Feirstein's most immediately obvious ones are eighteenth-century and neoclassical. The poem is written in heroic couplets like a satire of Pope's, but its content and idiom are 1970's New York Jewish. To confuse matters further, the subtitle is "A Dramatic Monologue." The poem's antecedents, like America's, are too various to fit clearly in a single line of development. We might best think of it as a novel in verse that begins when Mark Stern, a New York playwright whose wife has left him, wakes up one morning and decides to rediscover himself.

> I shout into the mirror football cheers:
> "You've lived on this stone island thirty years
> And loved it for its faults; you are depressed.
> Get out, discover it again, get dressed.

If the city where he finds himself (in more senses than one) is not quite Whitman's "my own Manhattan," the search itself in its enthusiasm and inclusiveness is an expedition on which Whitman would have found himself entirely at home.

> My eye is like a child's; the smog is pot.
> Shining cratefuls of plum, peach, apricot
> Are flung out of the fruit man's tiny store.
> Behind the supermarket glass next door:
> Landslides of grapefruit, orange, tangerine,
> Persimmon, boysenberry, nectarine.
> The florist tilts his giant crayon box
> Of yellow roses, daffodils, and phlox.
> A Disney sun breaks through . . .

and on and on, a Whitman catalogue in which (*pace* Pinsky)
Disney is as real and acceptable as daffodils, rock-and-roll as
Mozart: contemporary America in the eye of the beholder.

There are no villains in *Manhattan Carnival* — how could such
a frenetically inclusive work have villains? — but not all people
and things arouse Mark Stern's sympathy equally. Landlords,
bankers, sexual hypocrites, developers who destroy the urban
landscape ("Helpless I watch as wreckers mug and rape / The
Greek Revival houses . . .") are bad, but not inhuman. Children,
and above all childlike adults, are good, but not unflawed. Reviving the child in himself is one of Stern's goals; the child and
the city are somehow bound together, and neither can be properly enjoyed without the other. In the simple plot of the poem,
Stern's aim is to become childlike again partly for its own sake,
partly so that his estranged wife Marlene will return to him.
Somehow, their lives have gone wrong; instead of being filled
with wonder and enthusiasm, both of them were merely infantile.

> We lived inside a mirrored garbage can.
> Each day I grew more passive, you more wild.
> The child is only father of the child.

The solution, Stern feels, is to have a child of their own.

It must be obvious by now that Manhattan is more than a

setting for this domestic drama. The exploration of self is also an exploration of the city-state; healing the self requires a new relation to the environment. That relation is always emotional and tactile, never political as in earlier city-states. The mirrored garbage can has to become a carnival, not a *polis*. In that sense, we are still wandering in Pinsky's empire. On the other hand, variety and mobility are less threatening here than in Pinsky's poem. New York is filled with all kinds of people and things, many of them transient.

> A tourist wearing giveaway white gloves,
> A straw hat with a pin of turtle doves,
> Asks for the flavors in a Southern drawl.
> The ices-man snaps, "Just one left, that's all."
> "A typical New Yorker," she replies.
> Stunned by those words, tears welling in his eyes,
> He lifts her hand and kisses it. "For you
> —For free! dear lady, take my special brew."
> She sucks a cup of all his remnants mixed.
> A rainbow "Typical New York" has fixed.
> She walks away perplexed: is this one mad?
> He beams, "Two years an immigrant, not bad!"

Two kinds of Americans on the move encounter each other, are baffled, but make the best of it, more or less. It may not be an ideal way to create a nation, but there is no atrocity in it.

On the whole, the city is a good place, and people who reject it are rejecting themselves. To be sure, it has its frauds, financial and artistic. As in Pinsky, though to a much lesser extent, the American refusal to recognize limits leads, if not to catastrophe, at least to bad taste.

> The New World's paved with dog-shit, not with gold
> And tasteless in its art. These galleries

> Are filled with junk the touring Japanese
> Cart home with moccasins, tin Empire States,
> Key chains with footballs, paper license plates.

Nonetheless, the one point at which Stern momentarily repudiates the city is a moment of self-hatred.

> I hate this Spring, rebirth, no birth, this city.
> I hate my monomania, self-pity.
> I hate that Hasid, hate his button shop.
> I hate that jeweler, hate that traffic cop.
> I hate the Gotham Bookmart, Berger's Deli.

Only the most dehumanized monuments to greed, such as Sixth Avenue (officially the Avenue of the Americas) and the Hilton Hotel, deserve this reaction.

Manhattan, like life itself, is an opportunity for affirmation in this affirmative poem. Whatever our individual and collective histories may have done to us, however flawed or impaired we may be, carnival is still possible. The relatively optimistic conclusion of the poem is effective because so much stands in its way:

> In other words Corinna what I'm saying:
> We're crazy, wounded, but we are a-maying.

The poem ends with the Sterns apparently in the act of begetting a child to whom America may someday have to be explained anew; but one suspects that the explanation will be less skeptical and ironic than Pinsky's. *Manhattan Carnival*, unlike *An Explanation of America*, is rooted in a place whose identity is reasonably secure. Perhaps that limit to possibility allows the poet to be less threatened by the scale and transiency of life in contemporary America.

New York City, as most Americans will concede or proclaim,

is not a typically American place; but then what is? The ancestors of most living Americans entered the New World through
its harbor. The identity that Mark Stern discovers and the city
in which it has meaning are as centrally American as any of
the other selves that rot or flourish in what F. Scott Fitzgerald
defined forever as the dark fields of the republic.

IV

An Explanation of America and *Manhattan Carnival* might,
in different senses, be described as poems of the Age of Carter,
that humane season in which American introspection seemed
to revive. Publicly and politically if not poetically, it soon became
evident that the reach of the new idealism exceeded its grasp.
Robert Penn Warren's *Chief Joseph of the Nez Perce* (1983)[1] is
a poem for the harsher Age of Reagan, by which I mean not
so much a harsher poem as one whose portrayal of American
expansiveness and potentiality is bitterly ironic rather than even
guardedly optimistic. The "atrocities" that Pinsky mentioned
abstractly come to full historical life in this meditative narra-
tion about a nation of Indians, the Nez Perce of the Pacific
Northwest, obliterated by a brutal notion of progress.

Warren would undoubtedly disagree with Pinsky that ignorance of limit is common to "all this country's regions, / Races,
and classes." He would except the South. Because the South
lost its war of independence, was devastated and conquered,
its inhabitants ever since have been more aware than other
Americans that the strength and boldness of a people's aspirations do not guarantee their success. Warren has made a career

---

[1]A shorter version was published by the *Georgia Review* in 1982. I
make use here of the later text.

of writing about the durable (though perhaps not unqualified) effects of defeat on the Southern mind; his most famous novel, *All the King's Men*, is a tragedy of political corruption and hubris in Louisiana. In writing about the Nez Perce, he ascribes to them a Southern sense of the limits of self-assertion, a reverence for the earth and for their ancestors, in sharp contrast to the victorious Union veterans, insatiable conquerors of land and people, who defeat them. An advantage of writing about the traditional lives of Indians or other primitive peoples is that one can project upon them almost any set of attitudes one wishes. Their literary usefulness as a reflector of contemporary needs is unrivalled because so little is known about them. Warren has clearly mastered the few records that survive about the lives of the Nez Perce before their conquest; the mind of his Chief Joseph is an imaginative construct, however, that inevitably embodies historical realities less than the needs and anxieties of the 1980's as Warren senses them.

Thus the Indians at the beginning of the poem live in an Eden of nakedness, harmony with the natural world, truthfulness, and "unbridled glory."

> It is their land, and the bones of their fathers
> Yet love them, and in that darkness, lynxlike,
> See how their sons still thrive without fear,
> Not lying, not speaking with forked tongue.
> Men know, in night-darkness, what wisdom thrives
>   with the fathers.

In this paradise there are no serpents until the white men come, first in the form of French trappers, then Lewis and Clark, finally the United States army and "the makers of treaties." Joseph's father signs the treaty of 1855 that guarantees the homeland of his people. For a time all is well. In 1873 President

Grant again guarantees the land of Joseph's band; but the promise is not kept, and a few years later all the Nez Perce are ordered
to a reservation. They fail to understand the white man's concept of truth and reality as determined by marks on paper that
can be changed at will by other marks. Not only their concept
of truth is different; so is their idea of national identity. By this
time Joseph's father has died and Joseph himself is chief, but
throughout the poem he feels himself guided by his father's voice
and watched by his father's eyes.

> "But then, my heart, it heard
> My father's voice, like a great sky-cry
> From snow-peaks in sunlight, and my voice
> Was saying the Truth that no
> White man can know, how the Great Spirit
> Had made the earth but had drawn no lines
> Of separation upon it, and all
> Must remain as He made, for to each man
> Earth is the Mother and Nurse, and to that spot
> Where he was nursed, he must,
> In love cling."

The greatest failing of white men in this poem, the flaw that
motivates their brutality and greed, their perfidy and the cor-
ruptness of their public life, is their failure to love the land. For
them, country and national identity are matters of documents
and possession, not tradition and association—a frequent complaint of Southern writers about their Northern countrymen.
America as a nation began, to be sure, with documents—the
Declaration of Independence and the Constitution; the spontaneity of Joseph's feelings about his land has always been impossible for most white Americans. Ultimately the Indians fight
for their land, the whites for gold and empire. Warren quotes
a battlefield marker with bitter irony:

> Before you . . . lies the historic battle ground of the Nez
> Perce Indian War in which 34 men gave their lives in
> service for their country.

Whatever they gave their lives for, Warren seems to be saying,
it was not "country" in any sense that the natives who were
fighting for their homeland would have understood. The white
men are found "clutching earth as though they had loved her"
only after they have been killed.

The flaw of the white men is also their strength, and as the
story unfolds in its inevitable way we experience no surprise
at the tactics by which they overcome Joseph's people. When
two hostile nations track their way through mountains alien
to both, the one trying to reach safety in Canada, the other
trying to cut off his escape, the winner is likely to be the one
who understands maps and compasses. So it proves in this case,
although the Indians' instincts for the land enable them to hold
off white attacks more than once and almost, in the end, to
make their escape. For a time the white soldiers are more brutal
than effective.

> "Near dawn they struck us, new horse-soldiers. Shot
> Into tepees. Women, children, old died.
> Some mother might stand in the river's cold coil
> And hold up the infant and weep, and cry mercy.
> What heart beneath blue coat has fruited in mercy?
> When the slug plugged her bosom, unfooting her
> To the current's swirl and last darkness, what last
> Did she hear? It was laughter . . ."

But we know, if we know anything at all about how the West
was won, that eventually the soldiers will surround the Indians,
that the Indians will surrender after being promised to be allowed
to return to their homeland, that the promise will be broken,

that many of them will die of white men's diseases on a reservation . . . The "Sky-Chief" smiles on his worshippers for a time, then betrays them in an alien landscape. It is the endlessly depressing story of the Indians of the West.

Although the white men act in the service of impersonal forces, not all of them are wholly depersonalized. General O.O. Howard lost an arm in the Civil War and feels himself driven by God's will and the love of glory. Colonel Miles, even more driven, flings his men across mountain ranges in the hope of capturing Joseph's band before Howard does. Their battle for reputation is with each other rather than with the Indians, who represent (to them) little more than a reproof and an opportunity. Both men are nearly demented with ambition. In the end, however, both draw back from their worst excesses. Arriving before the surrender, Howard sacrifices his longing:

> Stood there, commander, enduring the only
> Outlet of rage and hatred Miles
> Could give vent to: ironical courtesy, cold,
> Gray as snot. But Howard,
> Whose sweat had soaked sheets in wrestling with God,
> Laid his remaining hand on the steel-stiff shoulder
> That quivered beneath it. Howard, almost
> As soft as a whisper, promises him the surrender.
>
> And hearing his own words, he knew a pure
> And never-before-known bliss swell his heart.

Likewise Miles, his own ambition appeased, offers mercy to the Indians, and later even advocacy:

> And was it integrity, or some
> Sad division of self, torn in ambition
> And ambition's price, that at last made Miles
> The only staunch friend of Joseph for all

> The years? In his rising success, did something make
>   Miles
> Wonder what was the price of a star?

As at Appomattox, the conquerors are capable of mercy, chari-
ty, and ultimately some degree of self-knowledge. But the price
of serving impersonal forces is irrelevance once one decides to
stop serving them. Joseph wishes throughout to be a man in
the eyes of his father. The eyes in whose gaze Howard and Miles
perform — public opinion as expressed by newspapers — are not
so easily placated. The Indians find that once he has befriended
them, Miles carries no weight.

> How could they know that Miles, whom they trusted,
> Was only a brigadier behind whom
> Moved forces, faceless, timeless, dim,
> And in such dimness, merciless?

Ambition, greed, and lust for empire are forces too powerful
for mere Indians to stand in their way. Nor is any personal ideal
of manhood a match for them. Heroes like Grant, Sherman,
Howard and Miles become figures of straw in the wind when
they try to mitigate the destructiveness of their own victories.
Brooding on his long-dead father and the destiny that has over-
taken his own life, Joseph has the last word about men and
nations:

> "But what is a man? An autumn-tossed aspen,
> Pony-fart in the wind, the melting of snow-slush?
> Yes, that is all. Unless — unless —
> We can learn to live the Great Spirit's meaning
> As the old and wise grope for it . . ."

Glib and inadequate as this prescription may sound, Warren
seems to be saying, it represents a wisdom beyond the grasp,

let alone the practice, of the driven civilization that puts an end to the Nez Perce way of life and simultaneously to its own public virtues.

Except in those rare cases where it arises from attachment to a place, American identity is a matter of documents and pledges and rituals. In this conclusion Warren, Pinsky, and Feirstein would probably all agree. The Indians might have educated us in less destructive attitudes and ways of living, of being a people, if we had listened before we dispossessed them. Like Southerners, Warren's Nez Perce represent the rooted victims of an abstract, implacable American destiny. They even get beaten by the same men. (Of course, white Southerners are less amenable to this kind of idealization: they helped displace the Indians, they kept slaves, and they left more records of themselves.) When it comes to the making or maintaining of a national self, W. H. Auden put it most memorably:

> History to the defeated
> May say Alas but cannot help or pardon.

Poets, likewise, can do no more than explore and try to explain.

THE FOREST FOR THE TREES:
PRELIMINARY THOUGHTS
ON EVALUATING THE LONG POEM

꧁꧂

Dick Allen

It is at once disturbing and revealing to find that contemporary attitudes toward the long poem still basically derive from Edgar Allen Poe's "The Poetic Principle," published over 150 years ago. Poe wrote, we recall, "I hold that a long poem does not exist." By maintaining poetry is only poetry when it "excites, by elevating the soul," he helped set in motion a way of composing and judging poetry which is greatly beneficial to short lyric poetry but downgrades the two other major types, the narrative and the dramatic. As a result, the short lyric has come to seem synonymous with "poetry" itself. Today's critics — whether practical or theoretical — seldom are comfortable in judging the qualities or lack of them in a poem which is "long."

Poe felt that the poem's "elevating excitement" — a quality at the heart of his aesthetic — "cannot be sustained throughout a composition of any great length. After the lapse of half an hour, at the very utmost, it flags — fails — a revulsion ensues — and then the poem is, in effect, and in fact, no longer such." A long poem such as *Paradise Lost*, he maintained, should be regarded as poetical "only when, losing sight of that vital requisite in all works of art, unity, we view it merely as a series of minor poems."

First published in *The Kenyon Review* — New Series, Spring 1983, Vol. V., No. 2.

However, what Poe and the long line of critics following him
(I include most of those usually discussed under the general label
of "New Critics") disregarded was that, in judging the poem
which extends beyond the length of the usual lyric, in judging
poetry which is not written under the influence of Poe's criteria,
we approach and must deal with considerations applied to judging prose fiction. The long poem is not a "pure" form, nor is
it aimed to produce what Poe called "the rhythmical creation
of beauty." Like the drama, the long poem is a "mixed" form
and our criticism of it cannot be based solely upon its "poetical"
qualities or lack of them. Most important, with the aid of critical
insights and ways of evaluation taken from prose fiction, the
critic can and should treat the long poem as a whole, rather
than as a collection of parts.

If we grant the right of existence to the long poem, one thing
becomes clear: the long poem must engage our attention and
contain enough devices — usually those we associate with fiction
— to hold it. The longer the poem, the more we must be interested in the story and, since involvement with character is the
primary way of creating suspense and continual interest, with
the characters in the poem. Unless we are to consider the long
poem as a series of shorter poems, we must have some kind
of plot or, as in John Ashbery's best longer poems, at the very
least a sequence of actions and observations so acute that our
interest is sustained, our sensibilities kept involved.

Most of the noble failures of the long poem in our century —
and there have been many, Pound's *Cantos*, William's *Paterson*,
among others — result from the poet's trying to write the long
poem as if it were an extended imagistic lyric: with a minimum
of explicit narrative and dramatic elements. Long poems which
are pitched at high intensity, containing all the elements we have

come to value in the lyric, particularly the "academic" lyric — ambiguity, layered meanings, a multitude of sophisticated rhythmic effects, concentration on the central image, primary attention to "how" a poem means — fail just as Poe said they would, and can only be treated adequately as a collection of parts. Those written more or less in "open" or "naked" form after a few pages come to seem merely rhythmical prose, interesting mainly to those interested in the poet and his or her sensibility, or as a way of shedding light on the poet's shorter works. None have achieved major importance in and of themselves.

We should, then, rightly anticipate that the longer the poem is the more we can *expect* and *welcome* sections which are not of high intensity, which exist to round out the characters, further the plot, add suspense, provide an interesting setting, enhance the mood. Just as one would not wish to remove all those elements from Shakespeare's plays — the sections seldom discussed in a classroom but utterly necessary if the play is to hold the attention of an audience not composed solely of critics and scholars — neither should we ask that the long poem be lacking in them. Critics have for too long been unchallenged when they dismiss long poems by quoting from their lesser parts — offering these, unfairly, as characteristic of the poem as a whole. Indeed, sections of lesser intensity prepare us to appreciate and be moved by sections of greater intensity — as the practiced orator's jokes and asides give us an opportunity to digest his points of major concern and relax our attention so we are ready to consider deeply what major points might follow.

Conversely, we cannot give up all the gains achieved by the century's concentration on complex language. We must expect from the long poem a form — whether this be blank verse, rhyming couplets, or even fabulously "organic" structure — which is capable of intensifying the theme, of giving a major place to the role of language in the poem's overall pattern. The contemporary long poem cannot be regarded as successful if it simply tells a story in poetic form. The commercial short story and novel have justifiably replaced such works and we would not really wish back into vogue long poems which imitate those by Browning and Tennyson. Complex use of language, and form, however, must always be viewed as secondary to the drama of the poem as a whole. If the language, the imagery, the form of the poem obviously overwhelm the poem's plot, the poem ultimately is not successful.

A short lyric poem is a concentrated work of art which can be explicated valuably by the sensitive reader and is especially valuable in the college classroom or creative writing class. The long poem cannot be handled so easily, nor can its types of ambiguity be dredged up so neatly for consideration. The longer the poem is the more we have a right to expect that its concerns break the bonds of literary and musical considerations. It is right to ask that the long poem justify its length. The critic can be expected to ask of the long poem a purpose beyond the poet's defense of his own position to himself. Is the poem more than reporting and more than history? Does the poem present or imply a belief it seems necessary for us to understand? Does it tell a story we have not heard told this way, with this emphasis? If it does not use traditional closed form — a form particularly suited to providing unity and technical interest to the long poem's lesser parts — what is the loss or gain? We could even be forgiven for asking that the contemporary poem in some way at least acknowledge the presence of the technological-industrial society and its impact on us; in some way explicitly or implicitly illuminate and be involved with the changes of the twentieth century; contain some understanding of such matters as television, space flight, nuclear age politics, modern astronomy, and modern physics. As Lee T. Lemon reminded us in *The Partial Critics*, "form is filled only by content."

Additionally, in evaluating the long poem the critic will fail if he dismisses, out of hand, a poem's didactic elements. Here again, he must set aside criteria for judging the lyric poem, in which didactic elements are so often scorned. Obvious didactic intention should not be cause for downgrading the poem; indeed, a lack of obvious conscious intention is a main factor in making so much of twentieth-century poetry seem irrelevant to even well-educated readers. Further, slavishly applying to the long nonlyric poem the "intentional," "affective," and "biographical" fallacies so limits our criticism that we are apt to miss completely how a poem's success or failure may depend on its persuading as well as entertaining readers.

We can expect to read the long poem differently than we do the lyric poem. For a poem of three to twenty pages, our reading should be akin to the reading of a complex short story; for a longer poem, we can expect to engage in a reading experience not dissimilar to that of reading a novella or novel, an experience which we may extend for several days, treating each new section of the poem as we would another new chapter in a novel. When we finish, we can expect to be able to turn back to particularly important and rewarding sections and episodes. But the sense of the whole should overwhelm the parts, put weaker parts into proper perspective. Again, the experience of having a work grow more unified, more important to us, is seen in fiction. We may be reminded of the way Cooper's *The Prairie*, for instance, becomes stronger and more important in retrospect (despite our having to read through many of its silly and grossly written chapters). We may also remember that when we think back on our own reading experiences with such extensive poems as *The Iliad*, *The Odyssey*, *The Divine Comedy*, individual *Canterbury Tales*, *Paradise Lost*, *Don Juan*, we remember episodes, ideas, feelings, the great interwoven themes and concerns and stories of these poems more often than the exact ways in which the poems were written, the precise lines which were used, the manner in which language and imagery were handled. To a lesser degree, the same applies to "The Rime of the Ancient Mariner," "Sunday Morning," even "Directive," "Howl," Lowell's "Skunk Hour," and Dickey's "Falling."

The achievement of imagistic poetry and the new critical methods which have so long supported it do not have to be disparaged by one interested in the long poem, so long as we realize they basically concern the lyric. The twentieth century has given us an abundance of major and minor lyric masterpieces, a golden age of lyric poetry. Yet just as the century began with the critical work of Coleridge and Poe influencing French poets' views, and these in turn influencing Pound and Eliot and a host of influential poet-critics whose sensibility persists to this day — so we have entered a time in which critical structures and methods have become so codified, so turned into classroom slogans, that we would do well to remember their limitations.

All poetry is not, to cite Robert Frost's popular observation, "a momentary stay against confusion." That "a poem should not mean / but be" is simplistic. And the famous Imagist criteria for judging poetry, necessary in its own time, has become too limiting. Too much criticism of contemporary poetry still concentrates upon the more than fifty-year-old questions of proper use of imagery. What was once revolutionary has become a method which takes few risks, excludes those who have not been classroom trained in explication methodology, and contains no new insights. What it actually does is squelch any type of poetry which is not primarily image-centered. Criticism of the lyric, centered around questions of form and image, can let us know the good from the bad, sometimes even the better from the good, but it sees trees, not forest.

And "no ideas but in things" — our key phrase for understanding modern poetry — has led too many poets and critics mistakenly to think that ideas in and of themselves have no place in poetry. Until the prevailing critical attitudes change — and they are essentially the same for judging beat, academic, new surrealistic, and confessional lyric poetry — we shall continue to have more of the same and we shall continue to discourage the understanding and furtherance of poetry which does not accept the limiting and temporal thing-oriented views of reality so strongly expressed by William Carlos Williams and Wallace Stevens.

When a critical climate has become as stale as ours has, when it actively discourages the nonlyrical longer poem (and even discourages or ignores nonlyric elements in the extended lyric), it is time to move outside prevailing frames of reference and ask of poetry — as did those in much earlier centuries — that it once more obviously entertain and instruct. Sir Philip Sidney, in "The Defence of Poesy," felt the poet was defined by his "imaginative and judging power." The poet, he wrote, is "the right popular philosopher" and "of all sciences . . . is our poet the monarch" who "with a tale forsooth he cometh unto you: with a tale which holdeth children from play, and old men from the chimney corner." Poetry, for Sidney as for the ancients, was inventing and prophesying. It tells "not what is or is not, but what should or should not be."

If these concepts of poetry and poets sound strange and wrong to the modern ear, they indicate what minor conceptions of poetry float on our century's final decades. It is time we ask that poets rejoin literature's major rivers and that critics judge the full journey and its accomplishments rather than concentrate on minute inspection of the often imperfect large vessels built for long passages. The small and beautiful boat of the lyric was never meant to reach and chart the larger seas.

ROBINSON, FROST, AND JEFFERS AND THE NEW NARRATIVE POETRY

࿇

Mark Jarman

There is a twofold difference between those Americans writing narrative poetry today, especially among the younger generation who make up what is being called increasingly the neo-narrative movement, and their forerunners, Edwin Arlington Robinson, Robert Frost, and Robinson Jeffers. First, whereas Robinson might have looked to George Crabbe for his example, and Robert Frost might have looked to William Wordsworth and over his shoulder at Robinson, and Robinson Jeffers might well have had in mind the anonymous border ballads and the poems and novels of Thomas Hardy, today's young American narrative poet must look to Robinson, Frost, and Jeffers. If he or she looks beyond them, to their own English masters, these modern American figures intervene. The second difference is that modernism itself intervenes between Robinson, Frost, and Jeffers and the contemporary view of them. Unlike Eliot or Pound, neither Robinson, Frost, nor Jeffers was part of a transatlantic axis or took part in describing the modernist aesthetic. Only Frost proposed a poetics, his modest but sheerly original method of sentence-sounds. Robinson and Jeffers worked by example and neither would be included among what is now called the high modernists. Their narrative approaches, like Frost's, were linear and not spatial, coherent and not fragmented.

Their intentions, too, in telling their stories might have been recognized by Crabbe, Wordsworth, or Hardy as moral, formally reflecting humanity's proper relationship to the world. It is doubtful that these older English poets would have recognized much in Eliot's and Pound's deliberately skewed and fragmented approaches to the narrative mode.

Although I am convinced that Crabbe, Wordsworth, and Hardy would have looked kindly on Robinson, Frost, and Jeffers, would Robinson, Frost, and Jeffers approve of what is going on in the narrative movement today? I am not sure. In fact, I have some serious doubts about whether they would. However, despite the doubts that I can imagine they would have, I think their skepticism might be applied to real virtues in the neo-narrative movement and only a few shortcomings.

The successes of these three masters of American narrative poetry are notable for their difference in length. Robinson is best short, Frost at a medium stretch, and Jeffers, who reserved his narrative skill for his longer poems, is best when extending himself.

Although Robinson could and did write long narrative poems, his greatest stories are told in poems that are often shorter than "The Ballad of Sir Patrick Spens." Sometimes they are sonnets, like the one about the butcher Reuben Bright or the mysteriously happy Cliff Klingenhagen. There are the brief poems in quatrains about Richard Cory and Minniver Cheevy; there are the lyrical tetrameters about the miller and his wife who kill themselves; there is the old anthology piece, "Mr. Flood's Party," which is still a great poem, despite our familiarity and the undergraduate contempt it may have bred. Robinson's forays into the longer poem, like his Tennysonian retellings of the Camelot stories, are about as interesting, now, as Tennyson's own. An argument for the resurgence of narrative verse cannot be based on *Lancelot* as it could not be on *Idylls of the King*. There is a friendly, ambling, yet profound movement to the medium-length "Isaac and Archibald," but for narrative compression that pivots on a fully created character, sometimes complete with tragic flaw, Robinson is the master — Dickens in fourteen lines.

One looks around today for anyone who chooses to work in his mode, to set out the entire story, naming the names resonantly, in a small space. When a contemporary narrative poet works that small, and that formally, the story is usually an autobiographical portion of the life or it is a series of events involving a persona. T.R. Hummer's marvelous "Carrier," a sonnet sequence from his first book *The Angelic Orders*, is an example of the latter. Hummer displays Robinson's compassion for his characters, for their tragic as well as their comic fates. Here is "Looking in His Rearview Mirror, the Rural Carrier Thinks He Catches a Glimpse of the Angel of Death Hanging over George Gillespie's Mailbox."

> A clear day, not even a crow in the air
> Over George Gillespie's as I put the mail
> In his box. The usual stuff, except for the one bill,
> The one he's been waiting for, from the funeral parlor.
> He's asked about it twice. the first time was the day
> After his wife was buried. He came to the road
> When he saw my car. Asked if I had it. Said he owed
> Somebody something. Said he was ready to pay.
>
> The second time was some days later. He just stood there,
> And when I shook my head he walked off, nodding.
> I haven't seen him since, though every morning
> When I come by, his curtains tremble. He knows I'm here.

He knows my moves, how I hang out my window to slip
Something in his box. He knows how to add things up.

When a contemporary poet interested in telling a story invents
a character as rich as Hummer's mail carrier, he is more likely
to give him an entire series of poems than to compress everything
into one sonnet. Certain characters of Robinson's make more
than one appearance in his poems (one thinks of Flammonde),
but he would have made the one story work—as Hummer
makes the story of George Gillespie work, albeit as an episode
in the mail carrier's life. Robinson's legacy to the neo-narrative
is the episodic power of the short form, which has now been
extended to the sequence through the contemporary interest
in personae. Our current extension of character through
sequence may have been seen by Robinson as an attenuation,
either in search of a moral center or in flight from one. The
intervention of modernism may be seen in not wanting to round
off the life—to send Richard Cory home to the pistol or Minniver Cheevy and Eben Flood to the bottle. The dilemma for
the neo-narrative poet, then, is whether or not to commit
himself to a character's fate. Unless he does commit himself,
he may find he has created characters more like Edgar Lee
Masters' small town stereotypes than like Robinson's sharp-edged
yet three dimensional human beings.

In fact, it may be Masters who appeals to us, though I say
so with great reluctance. What intervenes between us and Robinson is modern relativism, the reticence to judge, unless the
character is part of a historical sequence (consider the numerous
historical poems of late, for example, about Nazis) and history
has already judged. Perhaps the most successful Robinsonian
character created in a narrative poem in recent years is Robert

McDowell's bootlegger in "Quiet Money," the title poem of his first book. Named "Joe," as in "average Joe," this character flies the Atlantic before Lindbergh; his job is to bring liquor in from Norway. Joe is forced to endure his obscurity while Lindbergh enjoys celebrity then suffers the tragedy of his child's kidnap and murder. Joe must come to terms with his own absence from history, which he decides is preferable to Lindbergh's place in history, and thus enjoys the rounded fate of a Robinsonian character. "Quiet Money," however, is a poem of over 200 lines and hard to imagine as a sonnet.

Robert Frost's approach to narrative, his poems of medium length in his early books, *North of Boston, Mountain Interval,* and *New Hampshire,* may be better suited to contemporary workers in the form. Many of Frost's narratives are based on the classical eclogue, a conversation between rustics, as in "Home Burial" and "Death of a Hired Man"; in others, a single voice dominates, although a narrator usually introduces the speech-maker and lets him or her go on, as in "The Black Cottage;" another example is the conversation between the mother and son in "The Witch of Coös" for the benefit of their overnight guest. The dramatic monologue takes an interesting form in Frost that can be seen in today's monologue poems. Unlike Browning's dramatic monologues, in which we can imagine the stage, the other characters, Frost's dramatic monologues tend more to be voiced ruminations about the speaker's life or inner life with no audience in mind, except the reader, as in "Wild Grapes" and "The Pauper Witch of Grafton." Only "A Servant to Servants" has Browning's sense of the full stage being acknowledged, the play being stopped for the speech, but there the poor woman uses her audience as an excuse to talk to herself. Frost does not make a point with names, either, the way

Robinson does, unless the name is the point as in the Starks who gather in "Generations of Men" and chat about the streak of madness in the family or the little girl in "Maple" who must contend with people who do not believe that "Maple" is a proper name for a child. If a name is unusual, like Toffile Lajway in "The Witch of Coös," it is only as an odd fact, to be verified on the mailbox. Frost is interested in what his people *say* and not so much in what happens to them, what their fates are or are to be. What they say and how they say it in blank verse are the pleasures of Frost's narrative poetry, more than the stories he is telling. As the critic Vereen Bell has pointed out, one does not necessarily go to Frost for his plots. This is not to say that plot does not exist in Frost's narrative poems, but it is more as a portion of a life, an episode with the rest of the life left to speculation, sometimes certain, more often not.

Frost's narrator is rarely central, but usually is along for the walk or the ride, as in "A Fountain, A Bottle, a Donkey's Ears, and Some Books," or he is the scene-setter, as in "The Witch of Coös" or, again, the person who goes along with the minister in "The Black Cottage" or who serves as an ear for the cranky mother-in-law in "The Housekeeper." This is an appealing role for the contemporary narrative poet who cannot, as Frost rarely could, completely dispense with himself or herself in a narrative poem. To serve as witness, bringing his own character or situation to bear while letting the subject shine forth, shine brighter than the poet in word or deed, was Frost's goal in his narratives, one he abandoned, as he abandoned narrative, as his fame increased and he realized that it was his pithy lyrics people wanted. Two poets who are working particularly well in the narrative tradition that Frost adapted from Wordsworth and made his own are Andrew Hudgins and Garrett Hongo.

Since Hudgins works primarily in the blank verse line, it would be good to look first at him. "Sotto Voce," from his first book *Saints and Strangers*, adapts its title from music and gives the phrase dramatic meaning. Hudgins presents himself as our narrator, but in more of a comic light than Frost ever would have presented *himself*. Like Frost, Hudgins wants to turn a phrase into a dramatic moment, to make the emotion of the poem come from the way he tells the story. Here are the poem's opening lines.

> I'm standing in the university
> library, staring at the German books
> and I don't parle eine word of Allemand.
> Actually I'm listening to a girl named Beth
> call her boyfriend in El Paso.
> He's leaving her for work in Mexico
> and other reasons. She doesn't understand,
> repeats out loud the things he says, as if
> the sound of her own voice will help make sense
> of what is happening. And even now
> her voice is airy, cool, and beautiful;
> only her humor perks into uncertainty
> as she tries to turn around his serious
> long distance voice.

Although I am not arguing that Hudgins *sounds* like Frost (there are still actual Frost imitators around), it is hard not to see the Frostian touch in how the girl repeats what her boyfriend says out loud, "as if / the sound of her own voice will help make sense / of what is happening." The simple language and the sense of that phrase fall out along the blank verse arrangement as Frost would have had it. Also, we are given a multiplicity of view points: the speaker's, the girl's, the imagined party on the other end of the line, and the poet's. We're not supposed to be overhearing the girl's conversation, but how can we help it? One thinks of Frost's late and brilliant short poem, "Loud Talk," in which the speaker and his companions overhear an argument coming from a house at night as they pass by. Frost reports the substance of the fight between a married couple and some of its actual phrasing, because the phrasing contains the truth of the matter.

Hudgins watches Beth "pull pink tissues from her purse."

> With practiced hands she shreds them into strips
> then floats them to the phone booth's tiny floor,
> the phone held lovingly between her ear and shoulder.
> As if it were already painless, she's
> reminding him of the evening they made love
> (her alto — half in music — lingers on
> the simple words) in her parents' queen-size bed.

Clearly, it is the way she is talking, the "alto" of her "sotto voce," as much as what she is talking about that moves the poet. She tells her boyfriend that she had to change the sheets and make up an excuse for her mother, saying she'd fallen asleep there herself and, for the first time since she was a child, wet the bed.

> She talks until he starts, I think, to laugh,
> and she laughs back in harmony with him,
> the laughs oddly resonant though his
> is still in Texas and I can't really hear it.

Almost everything is imagined here. One can recall Frost warning, "Let's be accurate, but not too accurate." When the girl glances up and catches the poet watching, he quickly sticks his head in a copy of *The Tin Drum*, "Which by fifty-fifty chance is right / side up." The poem ends with a parting word and a final dramatic scene.

> *Regret*
> is the only word that I can make out clearly,
> and even then I can't decide if it's hers
> or if she's repeating what he said.
> But with a smile she hangs the phone up and
> clicks down the hall to the elevator, leaving
> the bottom of the booth fluffed with pink tissue.
> Over the whole of German literature
> I see her smiling, framed in the closing doors;
> her afterimage holds the same sure pose,
> floating on air, in the empty shaft, and fading.

Earlier in the poem Hudgins admits, having regarded her with a stranger's intimacy, that he can understand why the boyfriend "had to run to El Paso / to leave her." The poet has fallen in love with her a little himself, as I think we do as readers, and the final depiction of her smiling and in a sure pose, floating on air, is an imagined triumph. But the poem ends, as it began, in a kind of *medias res* for the speaker; though the episode is over, the portion of the subject's life has taken shape in the speaker's own. This provisional quality, which characterizes much of Frost's narrative poetry, is attractive in a way that Robinson's fuller, tragic version may not be.

Yet Hudgins' comic self-portrait is in conflict, somewhat, with the character of the girl. It asks for our sympathy, too. Usually Frost's narrator has little or no character, and may seem much less vivid, much less alive than the character he allows us to meet. Garrett Hongo puts himself in a perfect situation to observe in this way in "Metered Onramp," from his second book, *The River of Heaven*. All that he observes in the poem, though he claims it "pursues (him) through sleep / and waking day-dream," originates from his car window as he waits to get on the freeway in L. A. on the "Alondra onramp." There, he would

see, in "a swale of new fieldgrass. . . / sloping under the
powerlines,"

> the bums and ragpickers,
> the shopping bag people
> with their makeshift rakes
> and scavenged handtrowels,
> sifting through the loose dirt and refuse piles
> for whatever treasure they could find. . .

If this seems to be a typical urban desolation, consider again
its roots in Frost, who could give us equally defeated places and
people in New England, or Wordsworth who could show the
moors dotted with dismal little ponds where leeches bred. From
such unpromising material, these poets work with a faith that
meaning is inherent. Hongo discovers his leech-gatherer, his
mudtime tramp.

> Her name was Sally, I think,
> and she reeked of wine and excrement
> but always had money, wadded up
> like pads of Kleenex mixed with carrot tops
> and cabbage leaves stuffed in the deep pockets
> of her long Joseph's coat.

Hongo's prosody is not the traditional one of counted feet, the
one Frost would have recognized, but rather of repetition,
parallelism, increment, and the laying down of interesting
sentences over lines. The poem ends with a long cadenza of
such free verse techniques as he remembers one day seeing Sally
launch herself from the crest of the hill, as if for the delight
of those waiting their turn to enter the freeway.

> She seemed to stop more than a couple of times,
> blocked by a tie or a trough in the dirt,
> splashing in the puddles,

> but kept going, shoving herself downhill
> flinging her body shoulders first
> and scuffling over the crusts of mud
> and small piles of broken fencing.
> All the while she flailed her arms,
> billowing her open coat that,
> now drenched in fresh doses of mud,
> slapped and whispered sexually
> against her spindly thighs.
> *Hallelujah*, she was saying,
> *A-le-leu*, over and over
> as we marvelled, crouching in our cars.

Certainly Frost might have cited more than one opportunity to make Hongo's poem metrical. In Hudgins, he would have taken exception to the count in some lines. But the example present in both poems is of the Frost who trusted the narrative and the mystery of the story to which he might not be able to draw a conclusion. The marvellous life that goes on as we shrink from it was a theme Frost expressed himself (Think of the professor sliding down his pillow at the end of "One Hundred Collars"); it is also the life that draws us out of ourselves, out of our hiding places, like Hudgins behind his ridiculous book or Hongo in his car.

It is much more difficult to discuss Jeffers' relationship to the neo-narrative movement in American poetry because his example is at once the most daunting and least appealing. His characters act out dramas unmitigated by Robinson's compassion or Frost's moral relativism, but determined by Jeffers' merciless vision of humanity as an aberration of nature. Jeffers' determinism derives from Hardy's "Immanent Will," from his own Calvinist background (his father was an ordained Presbyterian minister), his belief in contemporary science, and his Spenglerian vision of western civilization's decline. He preferred to see man as a biological phenomenon rather than as little less than the angels. His philosophy is the moral foundation of his poetry, especially his narrative poetry. He set about in his long narratives to make humanity enact social and biological forces that he saw working to bring about the end of civilization. It is a much simpler matter to find the influence of Robinson or Frost at work today than of this austere soulmate of Thomas Hardy. Would Jeffers be more appealing if, like Hardy, he had written novels instead? For if one considers Jeffers' narrative poems beside Hardy's bleakest books, *Jude the Obscure*, *The Mayor of Casterbridge*, *Tess of the D'Urbervilles*, *The Return of the Native*, one finds the same fools damned by much the same fate. In Jeffers' case, the isolation on a coast too grand for their aspirations twists his characters to madness: man doesn't measure up to nature, to the creation. Whether we like it or not, this profound moral vision is the motivating force of Jeffers' narrative poems.

Though it is impossible to find anyone working on Jeffers' terms, some do see the long poem as a way of exploring a unified deterministic vision. Chase Twichell's "My Ruby of Lasting Sadness," from her second book *The Odds*, is held together by a scientific understanding of fate. Part narrative, part meditation, the poem relates a love affair the poet had when very young and her reunion, later in life, with the man who broke her heart. He has "laid claim / to the demimonde" and apparently is a drug dealer in Southeast Asia. She has "retired / to the regions of the north," a poet living in New England. Though the two have "divided the world" between them, a deep connection remains, one that seems to have determined who they are, and which is symbolized by a ruby in a golden lotus that he gives her as a gift. To explain their connection, Twichell appropriates

one of the most speculative theories of recent physics, Bell's
Theorem:

>   that at a fundamental level,
>   disparate parts of the universe
>   may make an intimate connection,
>   and furthermore
>   that things once joined remain
>   even over vast distances
>   and through the shifts of time
>   attached by an unknown force
>   its speed exceeding that of light,
>   a force which Bell called
>   "that-which-is."

Like Jeffers, Twichell has found her own definition for God.
Instead of "I am that I am," which is close to Jeffers' belief that
the creation itself is God, it is "that-which-is." Thus, Twichell
echoes Jeffers, but in a reductive way that resonates with a pathos
I believe he would have recognized.

>   The physics of connection
>   is all that matters.
>   The heart matters, and the mind.
>   Sensation matters, as long as it lasts.
>   The world does not think of us at all.
>   It is animated dust, and that is all,
>   a flower of atoms pulsing in space,
>   a flower of ash, a flower of soot.

There are some poets working on Jeffers' scale, that of the book-
length poem. Recent attempts include Frederick Turner's *The
New World* and Frederick Pollack's *The Adventure*. But these
poems are more properly considered epics and make use of the
hero as a central figure. Both require us to imagine a science-
fiction world where man is remade. Their visions are political,

especially in Pollack's long poem, and veer away from Jeffers' moral absolutism for very good reasons. Jeffer's book-length and other long narrative poems hew closer to the drama and, I believe, the dramatic form of novels like Hardy's. If we think of them as naturalistic, then we can see why they must occur in their local confines; Jeffers' northern California coast is his Wessex. Thus his locality (I hesitate to say regionalism) is also essential to his vision. For Jeffers' work to be of more use to the neo-narrative movement, the terms of his great story-telling verse may have to be changed. But since those terms — the enormous beauty of creation, particularly around Carmel, California, and the insignificant ugliness of humanity — inhere in his stories, it is hard to say what a neo-narrative poem in Jeffers' style would look like without them.

My aim here has been to sketch briefly the relation of each of the American masters of narrative poetry to the current scene. It should be clear that I believe Frost is the one we find most engaging to younger poets, whether or not they recognize the influence, because of the fluidity of his medium-length narratives, especially their moral relativism when compared to Robinson's narratives or Jeffers'. Frost's own moral vision is perfectly clear in his body of work, and we might infer from it that the characters he has created express his belief in self-reliance. Still, I would argue that because of the nature of narrative as Frost uses it, there is an essential mystery of character and motivation and, in the end, meaning, that appeals to many working in the narrative verse form today. E. A. Robinson requires a fuller, more rounded story, with a manifest plot and a strong sense of closure. He feels love for his characters as human beings and pity for their fates, emotions we do not see as clearly in Frost. Finally, as I have tried to suggest, the challenge of Jeffers remains to be met. Only now that we have passed his centennial year is he being reconsidered, critically reevaluated, in a way neither Frost nor Robinson has had to be. This is all to the good. But if Jeffers is going to have the powerful effect that I, for one, believe he can have, he will have to be recognized for what he is — the most troublesome and imposing of the three figures.

THE NEW NARRATIVE POETRY

❧❀❧

Robert McDowell

The return of form and the rise of narrative have been the most compelling developments in American poetry in the nineteen-eighties. In some quarters an argument for including the Language Poets might be made, but in fact that aggressively experimental work has not yet exerted significant influence outside a small coterie. Though the critic Marjorie Perloff has argued eloquently for it, though poets like Jorie Graham have attempted to draw on its lessons in their work, Language Poetry cannot overcome the undeniable liabilities of its effects. Its practitioners believe in language as a set of symbols set apart from a human context. Such linguistic exercises cannot speak directly to others, and therefore most people find the writing emotionally and intellectually barren and do not care. This sterility is not found in the new formalism and the new narrative. It is the intention of all poets working in form and in narrative to speak to a large audience, to say what is true about our collective experience by accurately illuminating the particular details of that experience.

Historically, the current flowering of narrative marks the boldest and most unexpected innovation in our poetry since the work of the great Modernist poets in the early decades of this century. This is not to argue, however, that narrative, or form, are new developments.

Our formal tradition stretches back to the beginning of

First published in *Crosscurrents*, A Quarterly, Vol. 8, No. 2, 1988. Copyright © by Robert McDowell. Reprinted with permission of the author and publisher.

American poetry. Even though in the middle decades of this century free verse supplanted form as the dominant mode of expression, some poets continued to write in traditional forms (Richard Wilbur is the most obvious example, but there were many others). But in the sense that the current young poets writing in form are making demands while seen as outsiders by both the free verse camp and the followers of Wilbur, and are backing up their demands by producing some of the best poems of this decade, the label New Formalists is appropriate. Their argument, it seems to me, is a call for more expansively down to earth subjects in poetry and, most importantly, recognition of the poetic line as distinct from the prose sentence.

The new narrative poets, many who also work in traditional forms and some who do not, share a fundamental sympathy with this argument. Hence the frequent critical alignment of the two schools. Though the best new American formalist poetry clearly springs from a rich tradition the new narrative poetry does not feel at home with the longstanding native tradition of verse storytelling that reached its pinnacle in the nineteenth century with Longfellow, Whittier, and a host of imitators. These poets were capable of writing good narrative verse, but more often they wrote badly, rendering their subjects as popular entertainments or moral instruction and violating the integrity of the line (and frequently the forms they worked in). By the time the Modernist innovators had done their work, and despite the fact that Ezra Pound, T.S. Eliot, and William Carlos Williams left behind a few narrative poems of note, narrative no longer had a respected place among mainstream poets. Still, some poets stepped outside the mainstream to write strong narratives.

The most important contributors, of course, were Edwin

Arlington Robinson, Robert Frost, and Robinson Jeffers. Yet
all three of these poets were isolationists in their influence on
narrative art. Robinson, one of the most popular American poets
ever, lived long enough to see his reputation with the critics,
though not with readers, wane. Sadly, a general critical indifference towards his work persists to this day. Frost, that shrewd
sculptor of a career, did much of his most significant work in
the narrative, and in poetry, relatively early in his canon. Jeffers enjoyed a brief celebrity, then critical banishment for his
unrelentingly harsh and bitter interpretation of the world.

Though the narrative work of all three poets contributed
greatly to their ultimate reputations, none spawned a narrative
movement or argued consistently for the virtues of narrative.
In their time it was not necessary, for narrative had not yet been
ostracized from the field. This occurred as successive movements—Academic, Beat, Confessional, Projective, Deep Image,
Surrealism—stressed the importance of the poet's interior
landscape rather than the poet's place in the larger community.
The rejection of narrative gradually became so complete that
occasional attempts by poets to work it were greeted with hostility by critics, editors, and other poets. A representative example
of a poet-critic's reaction is James Dickey's attack on the linear
structure of George Keithley's *The Donner Party*, an impressive
book-length poem appearing in 1972. Poets writing narrative
could not reasonably expect to find magazine outlets for their
work, for most magazine editors would not consider publishing
a poem whose length exceeded one or two pages. Meanwhile,
in creative writing classrooms and at writing conferences poets
with strong opinions, but without the fortitude, organization,
and ambition to state them in print, informally lobbied against
the intrusion of a form they considered best left to prose fiction.

But this sutuation had changed considerably by the middle of the eighties. Though most critics, editors, and poets still violently oppose the concept of verse narrative, a significant number now support it. Poet-critics such as Mark Jarman, Dana Gioia, Dick Allen, Frederick Turner, Bruce Bawer, Frederick Feirstein, Robert McPhillips, Frederick Pollack and others have convincingly argued for the essential place of narrative in poetry. Magazines once closed to longer poems now accommodate them. Some have recently devoted special issues to narrative, such as the Spring 1983 issue of *The Kenyon Review* (edited by Frederick Turner), the Autumn 1985 narrative symposium issue of the *New England Review/Breadloaf Quarterly* (edited by Mark Jarman), and the January 1989 issue of *Crosscurrents* (edited by Dick Allen).

Writers abroad such as Herbert Lomas in England and John Millett, the editor of *Poetry Australia,* have recently credited the new narrative with rejuvenating American poetry. Some older American writers have also assisted this rebirth. Frederick Morgan, in addition to writing many memorable verse narratives, as editor of *The Hudson Review* has also provided a sympathetic forum for the poetry and criticism of the New Narrative and New Formalist movements. Donald Hall has both written important shorter narrative poems and turned a wise critical eye on the new narrative work of others.

But Louis Simpson, a pivotal figure in the emergence of narrative, has more consistently led by example than any other poet of his generation. After winning the Pulitzer Prize in 1963 with his fourth volume, *At the End of the Open Road,* Simpson two years later had this to say in *Harper's:* "Most poetry is mere fantasy; most prose is merely reporting the surface of things. We are still waiting for the poetry of feeling, words as common as a loaf of bread, which yet give off vibrations." In successive volumes Simpson has himself created that poetry of feeling he called for, and he has done so by developing a unique narrative style. At the same time he has fought in his criticism for the recognition of narrative as an essential element in poetry that will communicate openly with others. I refer readers here to Simpson's two collections of essays in the Michigan *Poets on Poetry* Series, *The Character of the Poet* and *A Company of Poets*, and *Definite Connections: Selected Prose* from Paragon House. Also important, not only for its focus on Simpson's work but for its portrayal of the literary climate that opposed narrative and is now breaking down, is *Depths Beyond Happiness*, edited by Hank Lazer and appearing in Michigan's *Under Discussion* Series.

The current argument for or against narrative poetry is really about whether poetry should be inclusive or exclusive. The new narrative poets—we may allow this label by recognizing that their individual efforts in poetry and criticism over the last decade are now perceived as a united front—insist that poetry must include public as well as private experience. The poet's personal psychological drama must be presented in the context of a community that exists outside the poet and also includes him. Whether narrative poems are written in traditional forms or free verse they must observe the integrity of the poetic line rather than embrace the prose sentence. Flatly reporting the news is not enough.

In 1985 in the eleventh issue of *The Reaper*, a magazine founded in 1980 and devoted to the resurgence of narrative, Mark Jarman and I presented a checklist of the ten elements that a new narrative poem needs in order to be successful:

1. *A beginning, a middle, and an end*

   Just as it is hard to get the whole story, it is hard to allow a story to tell itself. Poets become enamored of a segment, an anecdote, and are content with nothing more. When this occurs, like the detached tail of a lizard, the story just wriggles and dies.

2. *Observation*

   The poet whose senses are attuned to all of the elements of the story can create the impression of participation. In a good narrative poem the narrator is a witness.

3. *Compression of time*

   Whether a narrative poem is 4,600 or 46 lines long, the poet must handle the passage of time in far less space than prose would require. This restriction demands the poet's restraints in choice of language. A rhythm is necessary, too, one that arises out of the story. No matter how a poet captures it, in meter or typography, rhythm is movement, movement is time, and time must be compressed.

4. *Containment*

   No character and no action may violate the essence of that character or act. A character must be consistent; an act must logically follow acts preceding it. Even illogical acts must be logically constructed.

4. *Illumination of private gestures*

   A character's gestures define that character. They also bind that character to other characters. A poet who makes a character's private gestures accessible is engaged in the act of definition, not by proclamation but by presentation.

5. *Understatement*

   This device sustains and contributes to the development of drama. Without drama there is no tension; without tension the story sags.

7. *Humor*

Humor is an exploitation of intimacy. The most frequent form of this, in poetry anyway, is irony. But humor in a narrative poem might display more tenderness than irony allows. Humor may also change the pace subtly, allowing the reader to reflect on what has been read and prepare for what is to come.

8. *Location*

Memorable literature is the history of authors who have successfully presented their intimate involvement with an identifiable region.

9. *Memorable Characters*

Any character is potentially memorable. One might tell us something about ourselves we did not know (or own up to) before we met him or her. But our fascination with character is also a desire to connect with someone who is not ourselves, not even like us, as far as we can tell. Obviously, we have always read stories in order to find out what happens to others and to see how they act and why.

10. *A compelling subject*

The way any story is told will determine whether or not it is compelling to readers who know how to read narrative in poems. Subjects resist authors lacking the experience, knowledge, and staying power to tell them. This alone explains the inability of many poets to write narrative. It also explains their reluctance to try, their fear of form, and their fearful denigration of it.

Most of these elements can be found in any of the successful narrative poems of a number of younger writers. The poet Ai in three books, *Cruelty*, *Killing Floor*, and *Sin*, has consistently produced tough and distinctive dramatic monologues and haunting third person narratives in which she has mastered compression, containment, memorable characters, and the

illumination of private gestures. Rita Dove's Pulitzer Prize winning *Thomas and Beulah* is a sequence of short narrative poems
that tells the story of her maternal grandparents' move from
the south to settle in Akron, Ohio. Location, containment and
understatement are the chief virtues of this collection.

The same can be said of Brooks Haxton's novel-in-verse, *Dead
Reckoning*, which tells the story of a war vet's unlikely but
believable love affair amidst drug trafficking in rural America,
and Brenda Marie Osbey's *Ceremony for Minneconjoux*, a
sequence focusing on Black and Creole New Orleans. Frederick
Pollack's epic poem, *The Adventure*, takes place entirely in the
Afterlife where the protagonist gets what he wants simply by
wishing for it. The one hundred eighty-two page poem makes
extensive use of philosophy, psychology, and economics, but
never at the expense of the storyline.

Several of the new narrative poets eschew free verse for traditional forms. Frederick Feirstein's *Manhattan Carnival* is a
dramatic monologue in five hundred and thirty-three rhymed
couplets that tells the love story of a modern couple in New
York City. His *Family History*, in rhymed stanzas, is a poignant,
humorous account of a Jewish family's migration to America
and its struggles through three generatrions to make a new life.
Frederick Turner's epics in meter and rhyme, *The New World*
and *Genesis*, make potent use of history, science fiction, science,
and philosophy in presenting the future world we all may be
creating. Andrew Hudgins (*Saints & Strangers*, *After the Lost
War*) and Mark Jarman (*Far and Away* and *The Black Riviera*)
most often employ a supple blank verse line to write narratives
of middle length (four to twelve pages). Hudgins' gothic narratives create a unique portrait of the current and historical
South; Jarman's poems concentrate on couples, troubled

adolescents, and estranged individuals in the Midwest and the beach communities of Southern California.

In addition to these writers, poets like Dick Allen, Dana Gioia, and Liam Rector work equally well in narrative free verse and traditional forms. Allen, the author of four books and most recently *Flight and Pursuit,* in long and short narratives has evoked the small town American boyhood of the forties. He has also contributed powerfully, and with wit, to the dramatic monologue with his poem "Cliff Painting." In his first book, *Daily Horoscope,* Dana Gioia also extends the Frostian tradition of the monologue with "The Room Upstairs" and builds on this success in monologues of middle length in "The Homecoming" and "Counting the Children." Liam Rector, who would probably not consider himself a narrative poet, has still made important use of the form in the title poem of his 1984 book, *The Sorrow of Architecture,* and in the cinematic "Getting over Cookie", which appeared in *The Paris Review.*

Though all of these poets would argue fine points when it comes to discussing the shape and mission of narrative in poetry, all would agree that the most frequently published poetry of the sixties and seventies had become increasingly self-conscious and remote to the general reader. They would agree that what poetry then lacked most was compelling subjects and poets who could tell the stories of our time.

Some of the frequently heard arguments against these poets — that their poems sound like prose, that they do not "sing" — are the ignorant, defensive complaints of readers who have either forgotten or never learned how to read stories in verse. Comfortable with the short attention span required by the brief *personal* poem, we can imagine these readers turning with dismay from the pages of Homer, Dante, Chaucer, Milton, Byron, and

Browning. If these detractors fully learned how to read, if they learned how to stick with a good story in verse, they might discover what most other readers already know: That the new narrative poems contain many of the finest lyric and meditative passages in our poetry. The difference in these new poems is that the lyric and meditation are always *in service to a story* and not to the poet's fragile ego.

What the opponents of the new narrative are actually arguing for is a poetry of exclusion. Because poets once surrendered narrative to the province of prose, they reason, it is better to leave it there. Further, poetry should not concern itself with subjects but with essences, the fragrant and refined life of the isolated mind. This argument is reactionary, a wish for things to stay the same. It is also wishful thinking.

By contrast, the new narrative poets argue for a poetry of inclusion in which the lyric, the meditation, and the story are seamless partners. No field of human thought, endeavor, or experience are considered outside the range of poetry. Science, philosophy, religion, politics, popular culture, the family, film and the other visual arts, and psychology are all richly to be mined, for they make up the human experience it is the poet's responsibility to chronicle.

This is no easy task. Because writing good narrative is the most ambitious endeavor a poet can attempt, the failures are everywhere present for all to see in books and the pages of our literary magazines. Most often, as in the work of Norman Dubie, Dave Smith, and Alfred Corn, three poets frequently celebrated for their expertise in narrative, the poems fail because the poet does not believe enough in the story he is telling to let it develop as it wants to. Such poets give in to the impulse to intrude, trusting the authority of the author more than the integrity of the story they are trying to tell. Failing to tell it well, they reduce a good story to anecdote and lapse into tedious meditation.

If the new narrative poets collectively believe in anything, they believe in the integrity of the story. Their challenge is to avoid repetition and unintentional self-parody and continue to create the essential stories of our communal experience. They must continue to acknowledge and make use of the virtues of the lyric and meditation and remain sensitive to inevitable aesthetic and cultural currents that will affect not only narrative poetry, but all poetry. So far the new narrative poets have produced work that is profoundly accessible to that much discussed and dreamed of larger audience. It is such progress that may rejuvenate our poetry in the next century.

❧ THE NEW FORMALISM ❧

TOWARD A LIBERAL POETICS

୯ୡ୦ଓ୰

Paul Lake

One of the most remarkable developments in recent American letters has been the emergence of a group of younger poets, now in their thirties and forties, who have rebelled against the poetic orthodoxies of the past two or three decades to revitalize American poetry. Often called the "new formalists" — a misleading title, as I will later argue — they represent a diverse group of men and women who are united only in their shared devotion to widening the formal possibilities of poetry in our time. At a time when the hegemony of free verse seemed firmly established — when to write in a tradition that extends beyond the formal and prosodic possibilities of the verse of William Carlos Williams and his epigones was to court silence or critical disdain — these young poets began their careers and came of age, writing poems that employed a whole array of forbidden poetic strategies. They rhymed their line endings, they used meter skillfully to create interesting and memorable rhythms, they shaped their lines into functionally significant stanzas, they used a wide-ranging, unspecialized diction to say interesting and meaningful things. And what is perhaps most remarkable, given the climate in which they matured, they published their poems and books, and now they have even begun to enjoy some measure of critical regard and national prominence. As with all revolutions in politics or art, though, this one has already met with hostility and resistance.

First published in *The Threepenny Review*, Winter 1988, Vol. 8 No. 4, Copyright © 1988 by Paul Lake. Reprinted with permission of the author and publisher.

What is ironic is that opponents of formalism in poetry still regard themselves as innovators and the new generation of poets as conservatives and reactionaries. Still employing an old shibboleth in the now decades-long debate, partisans of an American poetry limited exclusively to free verse sometimes even describe the new poetry as "academic" in their attempt to discredit it. The irony resides in the fact that the person using the term often makes his or her living teaching creative writing in a university writing program.

What the opponents of the new formalism fail to realize is that if numerical superiority is a criterion, they are now by a vast majority the real academics. For some time now, free verse has reigned virtually unchallenged in our university writing workshops. Formal poetry has been either ignored or viewed with amusement or hostility. One can't help wondering sometimes if this intolerance of formalism might not be engendered by fear. For what if students should question the theoretical foundations of the poetry their instructors write and publish? What if students should demand to learn about poetic forms concerning which their instructors are apparently either ignorant or in which they are unskilled? Their work suddenly regarded as passé, how could many professors of creative writing maintain their prestige in the academic establishment where they make their living?

Perhaps to silence just these sorts of questions, a number of apologists of the status quo have resorted to equating "traditional" poetics with "conservative" politics; formal poetics with Reaganomics. It's a theory that won't stand critical evaluation; it's simply a rather shabby rhetorical device employed to frighten the sheep back into the fold. There are honest and honorable arguments that can be used to justify free verse — which hardly

anyone wants to abolish as a legitimate alternative to formal
verse, anyway. This is not one of them. Diane Wakoski, for
instance, writes in an article entitled "The New Conservatism
in American Poetry: Part II" published in *Caliban* that "there
is a new conservatism in this country, and it is in our poetry
exactly as in our politics." And somewhat more confusedly,
she adds:

> But maybe for every William Carlos Williams, there is
> a T. S. Eliot, who becomes more beloved during his time
> precisely because he is *not* making any changes in the insti-
> tutions of poetry, only appearing to do so, like Reagan
> sincerely convinced he is right and (poetically) too dumb
> or deceived to know he isn't.

When T. S. Eliot, one of the great inventors of modern free
verse, is viewed as a literary reactionary simply because he wrote
poetry in a manner different from that of William Carlos
Williams, it is time to take stock of the literary culture which
makes such bizarre judgements possible and gives them currency. One can only wonder what other strange notions young
poets are imbibing in our nation's institutions of higher learning.

Not all of the opponents of formalism are quite this obviously
misguided, but there is a surprising consistency in the way they
try to define the issues. Many regard any departure from free
verse orthodoxy as quite literally un-American. Wayne Dodd,
editor of the *Ohio Review*, recently asserted in an article in that
journal that the new formalists, or the "neo-classicists," as he
called them, were "the Reaganites of poetry," and later implied
that there was something downright subversive and dangerous
about this new development; indeed, he implies, regarding some
remarks in literary magazines "bemoaning the slackness of
American poetry over the past two decades," there is something

not quite American about it:

> This reactionary zeal worries me. I know it is the
> zeitgeist, the temper of the times, but that is no consola-
> tion. Intolerance and mean-spiritedness are dangerous in
> literature as in politics and religion. I am worried that these
> responses seem to be all a part of the same "cultural" move-
> ment. Are these not, in fact, simply further examples of
> the new outbreak of "know-nothingism" that is attacking
> us like a polio of the spirit? Is this reactionary, revisionist
> response not an instance of what one might call the
> Reaganism of poetics—*Reaganetics*, maybe (the president's
> favorite poet is, of course, Robert Service)?
>
> The question for American Poetry, it seems to me, is,
> "What *is* the voice of America?" . . .

Another rhetorical trick Dodd employs is his not-so-subtle equa-
tion of all formal poetry with the barbaric simplicities of the
verse of Robert Service. Apparently Dodd sees—or wishes his
readers to see—little distinction between the work of poets such
as Anthony Hecht and Richard Wilbur and Thom Gunn on
the one hand and that of Robert Service on the other.

In other parts of his essay, Dodd tries to discredit formal poetry
by claiming that it is a betrayal of modernism, and in turn, he
sees contemporary free verse as modernism's only rightful heir.
This, of course, is to simplify and distort the truth. Modernism
is a much more varied and capacious thing than Dodd describes.

What, in fact, many free verse apologists wish us to believe
is that the tradition of modernism is, much more narrowly,
simply the tradition of William Carlos Williams. Ezra Pound,
the inventor of free verse for our century, used in his own mature
work a prosody much more complex and developed than that
of Williams (whom Pound influenced), a "free" prosody derived
in large part from Greek and Latin metrics—as Jim Powell,

one of the most innovative of the new formalists, showed in his article "The Light of Verse Libre" in *Paideuma* several years ago. T.S. Eliot's long poems "The Waste Land" and *Four Quartets* are both veritable textbooks of prosody, employing along with free verse everything from accentual verse to rhyming quatrains to blank verse — and nearly everything in between. Most of the poetry of Wallace Stevens was in blank verse, that old standby of English poetry, and some of what looks like free verse in his *corpus* is really accentual. Marianne Moore wrote syllabics. What Dodd calls the "dominant movement in poetry in America for several decades" is more ramified and various than he imagines. Where would one place Hart Crane, for instance, in the "dominant movement" of this century?

The very term "the new formalism," which is used most often by its opponents, is misleading. It implies that formalism is new, when in fact it has been with us all along, running beside and influencing, and being influenced in turn by, the stream that passes from Williams to the Objectivists (with a large tributary from Pound) to the Black Mountain poets and the Beats. Later, Dylan Thomas (who was surely also a formalist) exerted his influence across the Atlantic. And the careers of native American poets are no less instructive in this regard. John Berryman's synthesis of formalism and modernism involved the use of stanzas and rhymes. Theodore Roethke and Robert Lowell vacillated back and forth between free and formal verse throughout their lives. And poets such as Wilbur and Nemerov and Hecht, to name only a few, have continued to write formal verse to this day without apology for their un-Americanness.

No, what is unprecedented and new about the new formalism is the fact that the best young poets in America — who grew up in various regions of the country during a period when the

Williams influence predominated — have rejected the limitations imposed by that rather circumscribed and exhausted poetics to explore richer prosodic fields — the greener pastures of formalism. They have seen through the rhetoric of "open form" and the "deep image" and don't accept the myth of "organic form," as it is usually presented, having observed that the poems of those who advocate a poem's "evolution of its own form" nearly always finish by sounding only like William Carlos Williams — never like Eliot, or Frost, or any other modernist master. Apparently, it is not permissible for a poem to evolve a form such as terza rima, or blank verse, or rhymed quatrains. As a result, most poets today reproduce nothing more musical than Williams' speech-like cadences or the abbreviated nervous asides to the reader of Robert Creeley.

The poets of the Williams tradition, citing Charles Olson's seminal essay on "projective verse" for support, have espoused for nearly four decades now a poetry that imitates American *speech*. Williams himself described his poetic line as an expression of his nervous habits of speech. What the new formalists know that the advocates of "projective verse" and "open form" don't is that though the electric guitar might have replaced the lyre, *lyric* poetry was never meant to be strictly a spoken art, but something far more musical, something chanted or sung. Song lyrics, whether of Rock or Country or Pop music, still have meter and rhyme — and millions of listeners. Why then — simply because the accompanying musical instrument has been removed — should a lyrical poetic art want always to remove the song-like rhythms and rhymes of formal verse to imitate mere speech — and nervous speech, at that?

The advocates of "open form" have stacked the rhetoric of modern poetry in their favor for far too long. The opposite of "open," as everyone knows, is "closed," and who wants to write "closed" poetry? It is an adjective as unappealing as the dour "traditional." The new formalists share a disregard for such obvious rhetorical tactics practiced by the custodians of a limited and increasingly overworked tradition. They know that the opposite of "free" verse isn't "unfree" verse; that the opposite of "organic" form isn't "inorganic" or "mechanical" form. The opposition itself is false — merely the product of literary politics. Why otherwise would poetry which depends on the typewriter for its visual prosody and on print technology for its reproduction and dissemination be termed "organic," while poetry which relies on meter and rhyme for its aural prosody and the human memory for its reproduction and dissemination be termed "mechanical?" Poetry is too important and enduring an art to be long vitiated by a terminology so clearly polemical in origin and inaccurate or misleading when applied. Right now, the best young practitioners of the art in America are reaching beyond literary politics to once again broaden poetry's resources.

The new formalists are a diverse group, including poets as various as Timothy Steele, Charles Martin, Vikram Seth, Mary Jo Salter, Jim Powell, Gjertrud Schnackenberg, Alan Shapiro, Dana Gioia, Tom Sleigh, Robert Shaw, and others, and are from various regions in the country, including the South, where poets such as Andrew Hudgins, Wyatt Prunty, and Jack Butler live and write. Some of the young poets using a more formal poetics include among the major influences on their writing the great modernists of the early part of this century — despite their alleged conservatism; the only modernist poet that seems to have had little or no influence on form is Williams, for reasons I've discussed above. Jim Powell has learned from Ezra Pound, Dana Gioia from Wallace Stevens, Brad Leithauser from Marianne

Moore. Others such as Timothy Steele and Charles Martin show no apparent influence of the modernists but are no less modern or exciting for all that—and are certainly no less American, despite the innuendoes of those who would have them establish their free verse credentials as a kind of loyalty oath. We don't need a House Committee on Un-American Poetic Activities in this country; we need good poems. The new formalists, as they seem destined to be called, are writing them.

Here, for instance, is an epigram by Timothy Steele which shows that the charge that the new formalism reflects a movement toward political conservatism is false. Its title is "Social Reform":

> A prince of rational behavior,
> Satan informs us that our Savior
> Remarks we'll always have the poor,
> Which moral saves expenditure.
> We'll have the poor? Okay.
> Yet, looked at whole, the text will say
> Something more lenitive, and truer.
> We'll have the poor: let's make them fewer.

Far from being a paean to Reaganomics, the poem expresses the very spirit of liberalism. Gjertrud Schnackenberg in her poem "The Heavenly Feast" gives voice to a more radical idea, suggesting through the persona of Simone Weil that the only proper action to take in a world of poverty and hunger is "To refuse to eat till none / On earth has less than you."

Charles Martin is another of the new formalists whose work gives the lie to the claim that the new formalism reflects a political leaning to the right, that meter and rhyme somehow represent a withdrawal into the security of older political and poetic traditions. While those who make such claims continue to write poems about their personal lives, evading larger political issues altogether or writing of them with the stridency and simplicity of the propagandist, Charles Martin writes with a refreshing boldness and subtlety on the larger issues of our time. Here is a poem, quoted entire, which no one can accuse of Reaganism. The title and epigraph are essential to the poem, so read them first.

EASTER SUNDAY, 1985

To take steps toward the reappearance alive of the disappeared is a subversive act, and measures will be adopted to deal with it.
— GENERAL OSCAR MEJIA VICTORES,
PRESIDENT OF GUATEMALA

In the Palace of the President this morning,
The General is gripped by the suspicion
That those who were disappeared will be returning
In a subversive act of resurrection.

Why do you worry? The disappeared can never
Be brought back from wherever they were taken;
The age of miracles is gone forever;
These are not sleeping, nor will they awaken.

And if some tell you Christ once reappeared
Alive, one Easter morning, that he was seen —
Give them the lie, for who today can find him?

He is perhaps with those who were disappeared,
Broken and killed, flung into some ravine
With his arms safely wired up behind him.

Nor is Martin uncritical of American government and society. With a great deal of poise and humor, he writes in "E.S.L.," a poem about teaching English to recent immigrants to America, that his students want to learn to write English in order to participate in the American Dream. The "New World they would enter" turns out to be chiefly a consumeristic fiction invented by advertisers:

> ...Suburban Paradise, the endless shopping center
> Where one may browse for hours before one chooses
> Some new necessity — gold-flecked magenta
>   Wallpaper to re-do the spare
>   Bath no one uses,
>
>   Or a machine which can,
>   In seven seconds, crush
> A newborn calf into such seamless mush
> As a *mousse* might be made of...

This is hardly what one would term "yuppie poetry."

In a healthy state of American letters, such skill and humanity as is displayed in the work of many of the new formalists would be recognized and given their due. Instead, we waste time in fruitless debates about whether formal poetry is American or conservative; whether such poetic resources as meter and rhyme are worth teaching our younger poets in university writing programs. A truly liberal poetics would recall that one of the primary meanings of the word *liberal* is freedom to choose, and how can young poets choose what they have not been taught or exposed to? We must begin to recognize that although Whitman is certainly one of our high watermarks in American poetry, one of our indispensable guides, the English language did not begin with him, and that this century has produced great poets other than Williams, who are just as truly American as he. To ignore their examples and limit our poetic resources to the "American speech patterns" of Williams' verse is to unnecessarily restrict them.

As long as American poets speak English, it is foolish to talk of an exclusively American poetry. American poets must be permitted and encouraged to practice not only a visual prosody based on the space bars of their typewriters and the white space they produce on the printed page, but also to use those older, pretechnological devices — meter, stress and syllable count, rhyme — which are rooted in our linguistic history and, I am quite sure, in our physiologies as well. Perhaps there can even be said to exist an ecology of linguistic and poetic resources which the new free verse poetics, bred by our new technologies, have threatened with extinction. Rather than let whole species of poetry disappear, we should encourage their preservation. The new formalists are bringing a new vitality to American poetry by doing just that. A liberal criticism would recognize and reward their growing achievements.

TRADITION AND REVOLUTION:
THE MODERN MOVEMENT
AND FREE VERSE

⤲⧫⤳

Timothy Steele

Free verse is possibly the most significant legacy of the revolution in poetry which occurred in the first quarter of this century.
A kind of free verse had existed earlier; in our language, the
King James Psalms and the "stave-prose poetry" (to use George
Saintsbury's term) of James Macpherson, William Blake, Martin
Tupper, and Walt Whitman can be adduced as examples of proto-
vers libre. But it was in this century that the theory and practice of Ford Madox Ford, Ezra Pound, T. S. Eliot, and others
made free verse a dominant medium for English and American
poetry. In an interview in *Antaeus* in 1978, Stanley Kunitz
remarks of contemporary poetry: "Non-metrical verse has swept
the field, so that there is no longer any real adversary from the
metricians." Though Kunitz may be overstating the case, his

AUTHOR'S NOTE: For this essay, I have used standard editions of
the writers discussed, the Loeb Classical Library editions in the case
of most of the ancient writers. I have consulted W. B. Stanford's edition
of *The Frogs* (London: MacMillan, 1958) and C. O. Brink's edition
of the *Ars Poetica* (Cambridge: Cambridge University Press, 1971),
and I would like to acknowledge particular debts to both these editors,
not only for the careful texts they prepared, but for the lively and
illuminating commentaries that accompany the texts.

First published in *The Southwest Review*, Summer, 1985, Vol. 70 No. 3, Copyright ©
1988 by Timothy Steele. Reprinted with permission of the author and publisher.

assessment of prevailing practice is accurate: most verse published today is not in meter. And we have the early modernists, and the success of their revolution, to bless or curse for this situation.

Having now some distance on the revolution, we would do well to examine the ideas with which its leaders explained it and free verse. One of the most crucial of these ideas is that the modern revolution is essentially like earlier revolutions. The modern movement's leaders commonly argue, that is, that theirs is a rebellion against an antiquated idiom and is, as such, precisely the rebellion that "modernists" of all ages have had to undertake to keep poetry vitally engaged with the speech and life of its time. Free verse, according to this argument, does not represent a rejection of traditional poetic discipline, but is rather an innovation of the sort which inevitably accompanies changes in style and taste.

In one respect, this argument is valid. Poetic conventions evolve, flourish, and eventually turn stale with use. When their art suffers a period of decline, it is only right that poets should try to revive it. This is what good poets have always done; this is what Ford, Pound, Eliot, and their followers were doing when they urged that the styles of Victorian verse had grown creaky and run-down and needed to be replaced by an idiom more genuinely equipped to treat modern life.

In another respect, however, the argument is not so sound. In its advocacy of non-metrical poetry, the modern revolution differed from former revolutions. It differed from that which Euripides led against Aeschylean style and from that which Horace led against the literary excesses of his day; and it differed from — to speak of Eliot's favorite examples — the revolution which Dryden led against Cleveland and the metaphysicals and the revolution which Wordsworth led against the neoclassicists.

To be sure, earlier revolutions frequently entailed the elevation of certain verse forms at the expense of once-prominent ones. Wordsworth and the romantics, for instance, cultivated the sonnet, ballad stanzas, and blank verse—forms relatively neglected by the previous age—and generally shunned the balanced couplet, in which so much of the poetry of the previous age had been composed. Yet Wordsworth did not argue, as the modernists of this century did, that non-metrical verse was a suitable means of reforming the faults of predecessors. Indeed, historically considered, non-metrical verse is nothing if not singular, in that, until this century, virtually all Western poetry is informed by the distinction, enunciated as far back as Gorgias (*Helen*, 9) and Aristotle (*Rhetoric*, 3.8.1–3), that prose is organized in the general patterns and periods of rhythm (*rhythmos*) and poetry in the specifically and regularly ordered rhythmical units of meter (*metron*).

The modern movement's leaders seem not to have comprehended or admitted the singularity of non-metrical verse, nor has its singularity been sufficiently appreciated by subsequent poets and critics. Our primary aim in the remarks that follow will be to clarify the nature of the modern movement and free verse and to establish their relationship to previous literary revolutions; and we will do this by examining what Ford, Pound, and Eliot said about the modern movement in general and free verse in particular, and by examining evidence from relevant earlier literary history. Secondarily, we will try to set forth some of the reasons why non-metrical verse became the vehicle by which the modern movement was carried forward, and will sketch, by way of conclusion, some of the implications of the modern movement and free verse for current poetic practice.

                              *   *   *

We may begin with Eliot. Though anticipated and influenced in various ways by Ford and Pound, Eliot became the most public and prestigious spokesman for the modern movement, and he consequently received opportunity and encouragement to expound the movement in a more systematic fashion than his co-revolutionaries. Eliot's views of the modern movement and free verse appear most tellingly in two lectures delivered in the forties, "The Music of Poetry" and the second of his Milton papers, to the pertinent passages of which we should now look.

In the Milton lecture, Eliot deals with the modern revolution in general, sounding the theme that it is like the earlier revolutions effected by Dryden and Wordsworth and involves an effort to empty poetry of hot air and to relate poetry meaningfully to contemporary speech:

> I have on several occasions suggested, that the important changes in the idiom of English verse which are represented by the names of Dryden and Wordsworth, may be characterized as successful attempts to escape from a poetic idiom which has ceased to have a relation to contemporary speech. This is the sense of Wordsworth's Prefaces. By the beginning of the present century another revolution in idiom — and such revolutions bring with them an alteration of metric, a new appeal to the ear — was due.

It is important to note here two things. First, Eliot associates "idiom" with "metric." Second, he asserts that, in literary revolutions, an alteration of the former entails an alteration of the latter. Eliot's association of idiom and metric is itself questionable. Though what a poet says is always related to the way in which he says it, idiom and metric are different things. Idiom

is immediate and fluid; it changes from generation to generation and can even vary greatly among different groups of contemporaries speaking the same language. Meter, on the other
hand, is much less local. It is an abstraction; it comprises a
measure or measures by means of which speech can be organized
into particular rhythmical patterns. Poets working in entirely
different times and idioms can use the same meter; Shakespeare
and Wordsworth, though of different eras and outlooks, both
employ the iambic pentameter. Indeed, entirely different languages can share the same meters, as, for instance, Greek and
Latin share the dactylic hexameter or as Russian and German
and English share the iambic tetrameter.

As for Eliot's assertion that alterations of idiom inevitably
bring alterations of metric, the assertion is simply not borne
out by the testimony of literary history, certainly not by the
testimony Eliot himself cites. Wordsworth, throughout the
revolution he led, defended the virtues of conventional meter
as earnestly as he decried the vices of "poetic diction." Whereas
Wordsworth tried to reform poetry by bringing to metrical composition a more vital language than was in fashion at the time,
Eliot endeavored to reform poetry, at least in part, by abandoning conventional meter.

To put the matter more comprehensively and to anticipate
an issue we will discuss later in greater detail, we may say this
of the leaders of the modern literary revolution. With the best
of motives and intentions, they objected to the diction and
attendant subject matter of Victorian verse. Yet they identified
the vague and over-decorative lyricality of Victorian poetry with
the metrical system which the Victorians had used but which
was not itself Victorian, having been used for centuries by a
variety of poets working in a variety of styles. Consequently, the

moderns' argument that Victorian diction was outmoded came
to include the argument that traditional meter was outmoded.
And because the general formal quality of standard meter
became identified with the particular stylistic excesses of Victorian verse, an attack on the latter led to an attack on the
former. In view of the general soupiness of late Victorian verse,
the moderns' conflation of diction and meter is, in one sense
at least, perfectly understandable. At the same time, the conflation represents a fundamental confusion and mixing-together
of properties that have been, for most of literary history, considered and treated as distinguishable. And unless we understand this point, we will not understand why the modern
revolution, which began as a protest against the deficiencies
of nineteenth-century verse, developed into a movement directed
(in many cases contrary to its own intentions) against traditional
poetic technique.

Discussing the objectives he and his early associates enter-
tained, Eliot goes on to say, in his Milton lecture, that they
wanted to create a poetry which spoke unaffectedly. They wanted
to create poetry, Eliot recalls, which possessed the immediacy
of good prose and which took its subjects and vocabulary not
from dated canons of taste, but straight from modern life and
speech, regardless of their evidently "non-poetic" qualities:

> It was one of our tenets that verse should have the virtues
> of prose, that diction should become assimilated to cul-
> tivated contemporary speech, before aspiring to the eleva-
> tion of poetry. Another tenet was that the subject-matter
> and the imagery of poetry should be extended to topics
> and objects related to the life of a modern man or woman;
> that we were to seek the non-poetic, to seek even material
> refractory to transmutation into poetry, and words and
> phrases which had not been used in poetry before.

In "The Music of Poetry," Eliot advances arguments much like those he advances in his Milton paper. Here, too, Eliot characterizes the modern movement as "a period of search for a proper modern colloquial idiom," and contends that the modern revolution is identical to the revolutions led by Dryden and Wordsworth: "Every revolution in poetry is apt to be, and sometimes to announce itself to be a return to common speech. That is the revolution which Wordsworth announced in his prefaces, and he was right: but the same revolution had been carried out a century before by Oldham, Waller, Denham and Dryden; and the same revolution was due again something over a century later."

In addition to speaking of the modern movements in general, Eliot speaks in this essay of free verse in particular, and, with regard to the latter, he makes two points which are of special interest. One point is that the free verse he and his fellow experimentalists wrote was in essence simply a natural expression of a desire for poetic reform. Free verse embodied, Eliot says, not a rejection of poetic discipline, but a dissatisfaction with moribund procedures. "Only a bad poet could welcome free verse as a liberation from form," Eliot affirms. "It was a revolt against dead form, and a preparation for new form or for the renewal of the old."

A second point Eliot urges is that those who question the legitimacy of free verse are misguided. They are misguided, contends Eliot, not only to the extent that they see free verse as an expression of a wish to escape poetic restraint rather than as a revolt against dead form; they are also misguided to the extent that they fail to see that the distinction between metrical and non-metrical verse is basically trivial compared to the more profound distinction between good writing and bad: "As for free verse,' I expressed my view twenty-five years ago by saying that no verse is free for the man who wants to do a good job. No one has better cause to know than I, that a great deal of bad prose has been written under the name of free verse; though whether its authors wrote bad prose or bad verse, or bad verse in one style or in another, seems to me a matter of indifference."

In speaking as he does, Eliot embodies attitudes also held by other leaders of the modern movement. These attitudes are especially evident in the literary criticism of Ford Madox Ford, who, though mainly remembered today for his novels, began writing free verse in the nineties and who in the first quarter of this century could rightly claim to be, as he puts it in his *Thus to Revisit*, a volume of reminiscences published in 1921, "the doyen of living writers of *Vers Libre* in English."

Ford's views about the modern movement and free verse appear most clearly in his preface to his *Collected Poems* of 1911, in a long essay entitled "The Battle of the Poets" in *Thus to Revisit*, and in some notes for a lecture on vers libre which he delivered in the twenties in New York City and which Frank MacShane has preserved in his *Critical Writings of Ford Madox Ford*. Ford emphasizes, as Eliot does, that the modern revolution in general was a protest against the outmoded idiom of Victorian verse. In his preface to his *Collected Poems*, Ford discusses the literary revolt which began with his generation and says: "What worried and exasperated us in the poems of the late Lord Tennyson, the late Lewis Morris, the late William Morris, the late — well, whom you like — is not their choice of subject, it is their imitative handling of matter, of words, it is their derivative attitude." Ford develops this theme in *Thus to Revisit*, in which he tells us that, when as a young writer he analyzed the Victorians, he came to the conclusion that their faults in part resulted from lofty attitudinizing and that poetry, if it was to recover from these faults, had to be brought back down to earth and into touch with the solid, workmanlike qualities of good prose. "I had to make for myself the discovery that verse must be at least as well written as prose if it is to be poetry," Ford remarks. "The Victorians killed the verse side of poetry because, intent on the contemplation of their own moral importance, they allowed their sentences to become intolerably long, backboneless, and without construction."

For Ford, as for Eliot, the importance of prose qualities in verse extends to specific issues of diction and subject. Not only must poetry achieve a clarity of meaning and structure comparable to that of prose; poetry must also speak in contemporary terms and address contemporary material, even if such terms and such material are not customarily believed to be "poetic." In *Thus to Revisit*, Ford says that by 1898 he had worked out a "formula" for writing poems, and some of the features of his formula will strike our ears as being very similar to the "tenets" Eliot discusses in his Milton essay. The individual articles of the formula, Ford writes, were

> that a poem must be compounded of observation of the everyday life that surrounded us; that it must be written in exactly the same vocabulary as that which one used for one's prose; that, if it were to be in verse, it must attack some subject that needed a slightly more marmoreal treatment than is expedient for the paragraph of a novel; that, if it were to be rhymed, the rhyme must never lead to the introduction of unnecessary thought; and lastly, that no exigency of meter must interfere with the personal cadence of the writer's mind or the pressure of the recorded emotion.

The faith which Ford attached to these articles is obvious

in his preface to his *Collected Poems*, in which he characterizes his verse as having "one unflinching aim — to register my own times in terms of my own time." And Ford significantly relates this "unflinching aim" to earlier poetic revolutions, arguing, no less forcefully than Eliot, that he and poets like him are thus performing a function good poets have always performed, to wit, connecting poetry to the real life of its era: "I would rather read a picture in verse of the emotions and environment of a Goodge Street anarchist than recapture what songs the sirens sang. That after all was what Françoise Villon was doing for the life of his day."

About free verse in particular, Ford makes points much like those Eliot makes about the subject. In *Thus to Revisit*, for instance, Ford speaks of imagism (of which he was one of the eleven charter members represented in Pound's *Des Imagistes* anthology of 1914), and he urges that imagistic vers libre is a rebellion not against poetic rigor, but against the rhetorical vices of the Victorians. "The work is free," Ford says of the imagists' poems, "of the polysyllabic, honey-dripping and derivitive adjectives that, distinguishing the works of most of their contemporaries, makes nineteenth-century poetry as a whole seem greasy and 'close,' like the air of a room." Ford also argues, in his lecture on vers libre, that free verse is a natural expression of the desire for (to return to Eliot's phrase) "a proper modern colloquial idiom." Perhaps recalling Wordsworth's definition of a Poet as "a man speaking to men," Ford asserts that "if a man cannot talk like an educated gentleman about things that matter in direct and simple English let him hold his tongue." Ford then cites Wordsworth's pentameter, "Shine, Poet! in thy place, and be content," and comments: "That is really what vers libre is. It is an attempt to let personalities express themselves more genuinely than they have lately done."

Many of the ideas we find in Eliot and Ford are to be found as well in Pound. For Pound, too, the modern revolution represents an overthrowing of lax style, and shows, in this regard, a healthy resemblance to earlier revolutions. In his "A Retrospect" essay, published in *Pavannes and Divisions* in 1918 but incorporating some materials which had appeared earlier in periodicals, Pound looks back on the beginnings of imagism and free verse, and suggests that they were a salutary protest against the poetry of the nineteenth century, a period he describes as being "a rather blurry, messy sort of a period, a rather sentimentalistic, mannerish sort of a period." Pound tells us that when he and H. D. and Richard Aldington decided in 1912 to form a group dedicated to revitalizing poetry, they adopted as their first principle, "Direct treatment of the 'thing' whether subjective or objective"; and in Pound's mind, this is exactly the principle earlier poets embraced when they forged new styles. "In the art of Daniel and Cavalcanti," Pound says in the same essay, "I have seen that precision which I miss in the Victorians, that explicit rendering, be it of external nature or of emotion. Their testimony is of the eyewitness, their symptoms are first hand." Speaking generally of the modern movement, Pound adds: "As to Twentieth century poetry, and the poetry which I expect to see written during the next decade or so, it will, I think, move against poppy-cock, it will be harder and saner...At least for myself, I want it so, austere, direct, free from emotional slither."

In his 1913 essay, "The Serious Artist," Pound sounds similar themes. Alluding to Stendhal's remark that prose (specifically, the prose of the serious novelist) "is concerned with giving a clear and precise idea of the movements of the spirit," Pound urges that modern poetry must adopt the same objective. In advocating this "new sort" of poetry, Pound tells us, he is really doing nothing except advocating an "old sort," a poetry with the requisite sharpness and immediacy to engage a worthy audience:

> And if we cannot attain to such a poetry, noi altri poeti, for God's sake let us shut up. Let us 'Give up, go down,' etcetera; let us acknowledge that our art, like the art of dancing in armour, is out of date and out of fashion. Or let us go to our ignominious ends knowing that we have strained at the cords, that we have spent our strength in trying to pave the way for a new sort of poetic art — it is not a new sort but an old sort — but let us know that we have tried to make it more nearly possible for our successors to recapture this art. To write a poetry that can be carried as a communication between intelligent men.

Pound also stresses, with Eliot and Ford, that poetry will not recover from its Victorian maladies unless it secures the virtues of good prose. This emphasis is evident in "The Serious Artist" and in his 1929 "How to Read" essay, in both of which Pound observes that, as he puts it in the latter essay, in the nineteenth century "the serious art of writing 'went over to prose.'" The modern poet must in consequence emulate, Pound urges, the scrupulosity and careful workmanship of the modern novelist if poetry is to recover a central position in imaginative literature. No less emphatic on this subject is Pound's 1914 article for *Poetry* on Ford's verse. Here, Pound praises Ford for trying to bring the language of verse up to date and argues that, if modern poets wish to refresh their art, they would do well to follow Ford's attempt to integrate real speech and real life into poetry. Pound hails Ford's "On Heaven" as the "best poem yet written in 'the twentieth century fashion,'" and concludes his consideration of Ford by saying: "I find him significant and revolutionary because of his insistence upon clarity and precision, upon the prose tradition; in brief, upon efficient writing—even in verse."

With respect to free verse, Pound presents ideas that are similar to those presented by Eliot and Ford. Indeed, the clearest portion of the "Re Vers Libre" section of Pound's "Retrospect" essay is a one-sentence paragraph which runs: "Eliot has said the thing very well when he said, "No *vers* is *libre* for the man who wants to do a good job.'" Pound also cites Eliot's dictum in his review of *Prufrock and Other Observations* for *Poetry* in 1917, and here Pound suggests, as does Eliot himself, that distinctions between formal and free verse are not especially significant when compared to distinctions between good and bad writing. "A conviction as to the rightness or wrongness of *vers libre*," says Pound at the start of that section of his review specifically devoted to Eliot's versification, "is no guarantee of a poet." This notion in turn appears to underlie the "Credo" secton of the "Retrospect" essay, in which Pound affirms, evidently referring to formal and free verse: "I believe in technique as the test of a man's sincerity; in law when it is ascertainable; in the trampling down of every convention that impedes or obscures the determination of the law, or the precise rendering of the impulse."

* * *

Most literary revolutions are led, as the modern one was, by poets who feel that poetry has grown pompous and must be refashioned so that it can speak directly and truly of life. Yet the suggestion that an abandonment of meter is a suitable means of reforming poetry is a particular feature of the modern literary revolution. To establish these points more securely—to establish both the way the modern revolution resembled earlier revolutions and the way it differed from them in its identification of diction with meter and in its advocacy of a poetry "free" of conventional versification—we should now turn to the two ancient literary innovators mentioned above, Euripides and Horace, and to the two English ones to whom Eliot appeals, Dryden and Wordsworth.

Though Euripides did not formally engage (as far as we know) in literary criticism, the fact that he consciously revolutionized tragedy at the end of the fifth century B.C. is borne out in the testimony of subsequent ancient writers. It is equally apparent that the two traits that most marked his innovations are traits we associate with the modernists of our time. First, Euripides objected to the heroic model of previous tragedy and insisted on presenting his characters and their world in a "realistic" manner, however much such a presentation involved what traditionalists considered to be qualities wholly inappropriate to tragic drama. Second, he rejected the elevated rhetoric that had characterized tragic style since Aeschylus' time and wrote rather in a style incorporating the ordinary speech of his day. The first of these traits is noted by, among others, Dio Chrysostom (*Oration*, 52) and Diogenes Laertius (*Lives*, 4.5.6 [*Crantor*]), and is noted as well by Aristotle (*Poetics*, 1460b33–34), who records that "Sophocles said that he portrayed people as they ought to be and Euripides portrayed them as they are." The second of these traits, the colloquial novelty of Euripides' diction, receives comment from Quintilian (*Institutiones Oratoriae*, 10.1.68) and Longinus (*On the Sublime*, 40.2), and from Aristotle (*Rhetoric*, 3.2.5) in his discussion of art-which-hides-art: "Art is cleverly concealed when the speaker chooses his words from ordinary language (*eiothyias dialektou*) and puts them together like Euripides, who was the first to show the way."

Even if we lacked the evidence of such commentators, we would still have ample testimony about Euripides' innovations and about the controversy they excited. This additional testimony is supplied by Aristophanes' *The Frogs*, which provides perhaps the earliest extended examination of a literary revolution and several lines of which, interestingly, Ford uses as an epigraph to "The Battle of the Poets" essay in *Thus to Revisit*. It will be recalled that the second half of *The Frogs* consists of a formal debate, with Dionysus serving as judge, between Aeschylus and Euripides — the former cast in the role of the somewhat stodgy defender of older conventions, the latter cast in the role of the wily and newfangled parvenu. The debate takes place at Pluto's palace in Hades, where Aeschylus, who has long occupied the honorary Chair of Tragedy, finds his tenureship challenged by the arrival of the recently deceased Euripides — (Aristophanes' play was first staged in 405 B.C., the year after Euripides' death); and the charges which Euripides levels at the older Aeschylus, and the terms with which Euripides justifies his own innovations, strikingly resemble statements made by the modernists of our time.

For example, Euripides criticizes Aeschylus as bombastic *(kompophakelorremona*, "boast-bundle-phrased") (839) and argues that Aeschylus' tragedies are works of an overly poetical impostor *(alazon)* (907 ff.). So wildly inflated is Aeschylus' style, Euripides says (926), that it is at times downright unintelligible *(agnota)*, and, with a colorful metaphor, he alleges that, under Aeschylus' influence, tragedy itself grew into a state of sickly bloating *(oidousan)*, which, however, has since been happily alleviated by strong doses of modernity (939 ff.). "When I took over Tragedy from you," Euripides' remarks run in David Barrett's recent translation, "the poor creature was in a dreadful state. Fatty degeneration of the Art. All swollen up with high-falutin' diction. I soon got her weight down, though: put her on a diet of particles, with a little finely chopped logic (taken peripatetically), and special decoction of dialectic, cooked up from books and strained to facilitate digestion."

As for his own "new" style, Euripides boasts that he did not rely on the grandiose and fabulous (959). Instead, "I wrote about familiar things *(oikeia pragmat' eisagon)*, things the audience knew about." Nor did he, he adds, bludgeon the audience with big words or befuddle them with resonant obscurities; no, he spoke in "human terms" *(phrazein anthropeios*, "language man to man")* (1058). Euripides further argues that he avoided inane ornament or "padding" *(stoiben)* (1178) and that his writing was "clear" and "accurate"— *saphes* and *leptos* being the words used in several places to denote these qualities. And, indeed, when Euripides speaks of the way he "reduced" tragedy (941), the term he employs, *ischnana*, indicates not only "spare," but suggests the *ischnos charakter* of the classical plain style itself, of which Euripides was one of the founders. That Euripides ultimately loses the debate — Dionysus favoring Aeschylus because he is a sounder ethical guide than his more stylistically sophisticated rival — does not concern us here. What is important is simply the similarity between Euripides' ideas and innovations and those of the leaders of the modern movement in our century.

Issues like those raised by Euripides' work appear in Horace's literary epistles. It would be wrong to call Horace a Euripidean figure, for Horace repeatedly urges that poetry should feature both moral concern and technical finesse, and seeks to heal the kinds of breaches between ethics and aesthetics depicted in *The Frogs*. Nevertheless, Horace is staunchly opposed to the literary conservatism of his day, and in his epistle to Augustus, he writes:

"I am impatient that any work is censured, not because it is thought to be coarse or inelegant in style, but because it is modern *nuper*) . . . If novelty *(novitas)* had been as offensive to the Greeks as it is to us, what in these days would be ancient?" *(Epistles,* 2.1.76–77; 90–91). Horace, moreover, persistently objects to the notion that poetic diction is a static and time-hallowed dialect and persistently urges that the language of verse should be meaningfully related to the speech of real men and women.

In the earliest of his literary epistles, Horace discusses the nature of satire, a genre that, he argues, could be much improved if the deficiencies of its originator, Lucilius, were recognized and corrected. Though Horace respects and praises Lucilius, he also says that Lucilius' writing is often "harsh" *(durus)*, "turbid" *(lutulentus)*, "verbose" *(garrulus)* and generally "slapdash" or "lazy" *(piger)* *(Satires,* 1.4.8–12). "You need terseness *(brevitate)*," Horace urges, recommending an antidote to Lucilius' shortcomings, "that the thought may run on, and not become entangled in verbiage that weighs upon wearied ears" *(Satires,* 1.10.9–10). Concerning his own satires, Horace announces that they are "akin to prose" *(sermoni propriora)* *(Satires,* 1.4.42) and adds that so different in general is the diction of satire from what is commonly considered poetic speech that, were one to deprive satirical verses of their "regular beat and rhythm" *(tempora certa modosque)*, they would scarcely retain any poetic features whatever (56ff.). And Horace in fact goes so far as to say that in writing satire he does not view himself as a poet (38–44) and to raise the question of whether satire itself can be deemed verse, so humble and plain is the speech in which it is written (63–65).

There is, however, patently an element of irony in such self-deprecation, and it is clear that Horace is poking fun at those who require that verse always be pitched in the grand manner.

Moreover, the points Horace facetiously offers in his early literary epistles reappear in the more serious setting of his later *Art of Poetry*. Here, Horace argues in several contexts that, if plain diction is adroitly managed, if it is characterized by *iunctura* (a skillful weaving together of words), *calliditas* (an artful dexterity of arrangement), and *urbanitas* (an engaging refinement of manner), it is far preferable to a continually elevated style. Such plain diction, Horace furthermore contends, has the advantage of being able to deal, without exaggeration or affectation, with life as it is really lived. With respect to dramatic writing, Horace advises that the poet who has mastered the tools of his trade should then "look to life and manners for a model, and draw from thence living words *(vivas voces)*." Such a poetry may seem "without force and art" *(sine pondere et arte)*, but it nevertheless "gives the people more delight and holds them better than verses void of thought, and sonorous trifles *(versus inopes rerum nugaeque canorae)*" (318–323). And discussing, in another passage, the quality of *iunctura*, Horace makes much the same argument in a broader and more personal manner: "My aim shall be poetry," he tells us, "so moulded from the familiar that anybody may hope for the same success, may sweat much and yet toil in vain when attempting the same: such is the power of order and connexion, such the beauty that may crown the commonplace" (240–243).

Horace's insistence that poetry should deal with the commonplace as well as the lofty, and his insistence that the poet should draw his speech and matter directly from life, are related to his belief that the language of verse is not an artificial vocabulary, but is derived from and governed by normal usage. Like the modernists of our time, he objects to the coterie styles of his day and to the tendency of many poets to isolate themselves in a rarefied linguistic autonomy. "All mortal things shall perish," Horace cautions in *The Art of Poetry*, "much less shall the glory and glamour of speech endure and live. Many terms that have fallen out of use shall be born again, and those shall fall that are now in repute, if Usage so will it *(si volet usus)*, in whose hands lies the judgment, the right and the rule of speech" (68–72). This argument is in turn related to Horace's contention that, as usage changes, the poet has the right to bring into verse what Eliot refers to, in his Milton essay, as "words and phrases which had not been used in poetry before." As Horace sums up the issue, "If haply one must betoken abstruse things by novel terms, you will have a chance to fashion words never heard of by the kilted Cethegi [ancient Romans], and license will be granted, if used with modesty; while words, though new and of recent make, will win acceptance, if they spring from a Greek fount and are drawn therefrom but sparingly" (48–53). And in the same way that Eliot urges in his early essay on Swinburne that a poet should be free to seek language "to digest and express new objects, new groups of objects, new feelings, new aspects," so Horace urges that a poet always should be allowed to import into his work novel terms to treat novel subjects in contemporary life. "And why should I be grudged the right of adding, if I can," Horace asks, "my little fund, when the tongue of Cato and of Ennius has enriched our mother-speech and brought to light new terms for things? It has ever been, and ever will be, permitted to issue words stamped with the mint-mark of the day" (55–59).

Dryden, too, stresses that verse should be written in an unaffected and contemporary idiom. Indeed, this aspect of Dryden provides the governing theme of the three BBC lectures on Dryden that Eliot delivered in 1931 and in which Eliot observed:

"What Dryden did, in fact, was to reform the language, and devise a natural, conversational style of speech in verse in place of an artificial and decadent one . . . He restored English verse to the condition of speech." Dryden's emphasis on naturalness is evident in much of his writing, perhaps nowhere more so than in two of his earliest and best-known critical pieces, his 1664 dedication of *The Rival Ladies* to the Earl of Orrery and his *Essay of Dramatic Poesy*, which was composed in 1665/66 and published in 1668.

The dedication to *The Rival Ladies* is of particular importance to our concerns, because Dryden explicitly advocates in his remarks to his patron a poetry which has "the elegance of prose." Dryden is using the term "negligence," we should note, not in the sense of "carelessness," but in the sense in which Cicero uses the word in his definition of the plain style — in the sense of "directly and uncosmetically attractive." "There is such a thing even as a careful negligence *(neglegentia),"* writes Cicero. "Just as some women are said to be handsomer when unadorned — this very lack of ornament becomes them — so this plain style gives pleasure even when unembellished: there is something in both cases which lends greater charm, but without showing itself" *(Orator,* 78). Inasmuch as *The Rival Ladies* is not only in meter, but in rhyme, and inasmuch as some critics of Dryden's day were arguing that rhyme in dramatic verse produced an inevitably stilted quality, Dryden is particularly interested in making the point that rhyme can be harmonized with, as he puts it, "ordinary speaking." Infelicities may occur, Dryden concedes, when a poet uses rhyme ineptly; by the same token, however, when rhyme is expertly employed "the first word in the verse seems to beget the second, and that the next, till that becomes the last word in the line which, in the negligence of prose, would be so." And when used in this happy manner, Dryden continues, "rhyme has all the advantages of prose besides its own."

The virtues of natural style are discussed at greater length in the *Essay of Dramatic Poesy*. Among the many topics the four disputants in the dialogue examine are the condition of English verse in the immediately preceding age and the direction in which contemporary verse might profitably move. And Eugenius, one of the two characters who voice Dryden's own views, makes a number of statements resembling those made by Eliot, Ford, and Pound. For one thing, Eugenius argues that the metaphysical poetry so popular with the previous generation is hopelessly stiff and false. Speaking of John Cleveland's work in particular, Eugenius suggests that using words in an odd or distorted manner may be permissible on occasion, but "to do this always, and never be able to write a line without it, though it may be admired by some few pedants, will not pass" with discriminating readers. Eugenius then contrasts truly fine writing, which speaks "easily" (without peculiarity or strain) to a wide audience, with the type of poetry represented by Cleveland: "Wit is best conveyed to us in the most easy language; and is most to be admired when a great thought comes dressed in words so commonly received that it is understood by the meanest apprehensions, as the best meat is the most easily digested: but we cannot read a verse of Cleveland's without making a face at it, as if every word were a pill to swallow: he gives us many times a hard nut to break our teeth, without a kernel for our pains."

In another section of the dialogue, Eugenius takes a position which is not unlike that which Pound takes in his "Retrospect" essay and which involves the argument that the innovations of newer writers like Waller and Denham are in no way seditious assaults on the art of poetry, but are instead a healthy reaction against the vices of a worn-out mode; and it is noteworthy that at this juncture no one else in the dialogue, not even the hide-bound and cantankerous Crites, opposes Eugenius. On the contrary, Dryden reports, "every one was willing to acknowledge how much our poesy is improved by the happiness of some writers yet living, who first taught us to mould our thoughts into easy and significant words, to retrench the superfluities of expression, and to make our rhyme so properly a part of the verse that it should never mislead the sense, but itself be led and governed by it."

We should also observe that, as well as recommending naturalness of style and (to use Pound's phrase) "efficient writing" in verse, Dryden is in general a champion of the literature of his nation and his time. Much of the *Essay of Dramatic Poesy* concerns the Quarrel of the Ancients and the Moderns, which had begun in Italy in the fifteenth century and which continued in England and France down into the eighteenth, and Dryden, though respectful of the achievements of the Greeks and Romans, stoutly defends the claims of the moderns. Modern English dramatists especially, Dryden feels, deserve credit for the originality of their plots and the "just and lively image of human nature" they present. Eugenius and his ally (for the most part) Neander make the points that the ancients tended to recycle the same stories again and again in their plays, and did not present the entertaining and realistic varieties of mood found in many modern dramas. And if it would be an exaggeration to portray Dryden's views in terms of the Poundian programme of "Make It New," it is nevertheless the case that he is interested in, and values, the contemporary in many of the same ways that Pound and Eliot and Ford do.

Before moving to the final section of our essay, we may briefly consider Wordsworth, in whom we find many of the ideas we discovered in the other poets we have examined. In the preface to the second edition of *Lyrical Ballads*, Wordsworth announces that his work is a reaction against "the gaudiness and inane phraseology of many modern writers" and against "POETIC DICTION," which he characterizes as "arbitrary and capricious habits of expression." Such habits, he suggests, are connected with another literary vice, this being the turning aside from real experience in order "to trick out or to elevate nature." Of his own poetry, Wordsworth avows that his object in writing it was "to choose incidents and situations from common life, and to relate or describe them, throughout, as far as was possible in a selection of language really used by men." Wordsworth also informs us that his verse involves a belief that "ordinary things should be presented to the mind," and the poet should not dwell, Wordsworth adds, in a private lexicon and among a circumscribed set of "poetical" subjects; rather, the poet's work should partake of a "general sympathy," and the poet must remember that "Poets do not write for Poets alone, but for men."

Like earlier and later poetic innovators, Wordsworth also contends that the language of poetry should be vitally related to the language of fine prose. For instance, in his preface, he asserts of verse that "the language, though naturally arranged, and according to the strict laws of metre, does not differ from that of prose." He furthermore argues "that not only the language of a large portion of every good poem, even of the most elevated character, must necessarily, except with reference to the metre, in no respect differ from that of good prose, but likewise that some of the most interesting parts of the best poems will be found to be strictly the language of prose when prose is well written." And toward the end of this part of his preface, he remarks: "We will go further. It may be safely affirmed, that there neither is, nor can be, any *essential* difference between the language of prose and metrical composition."

As is the situation with other innovators at whom we have been looking, Wordsworth wants to write directly and freshly, and he says of his verse overall: "I have at all times endeavoured to look steadily at my subject; consequently, there is I hope in these Poems little falsehood of description, and my ideas are expressed in language fitted to their respective importance." The aim is true speech, a poetry that communicates itself to its readers with clarity and energy, a style free of mannerism and literary posturing.

* * *

If a reader of Roman poetry had fallen asleep in 45 B.C. and had awakened twenty-five years later to find Horace's *Odes* on his chest, he might well have been astonished on unrolling the scroll. The poet's material and presentation of it, in any event, would have seemed most unusual. Yet the reader, at least the educated one, would have recognized the verse forms, and if he had wished, he could have traced in his mind their continuity all the way back to the misty beginnings of Greek lyric. Similarly, if an English reader had fallen asleep in 1775 and had awakened a quarter of a century later to find the *Lyrical Ballads* at his bedside, he might well have been startled by the subject and manner of "Tintern Abbey" or "Her Eyes Are Wild." He would, however, have had no difficulty determining that the first was in conventional blank verse and the second in conventional rhymed iambic tetrameters. If a reader had fallen asleep in 1900

and had awakened in 1925 to find Ford's *To All the Dead,* Eliot's
The Waste Land, and Pound's *A Draft of XVI Cantos,* it is
unlikely he would have had the slightest idea of what to make
of the versification of the poems.

This is the singularity of the modern movement. It broke with
traditional versification. It did not involve, to recall Eliot's phrase,
"an alteration of metric"—a change from one clear set of principles to another—but rather an escape from metric. Like earlier
revolutionaries, those of this century urged that poetry should
embody the virtues of lively colloquial speech and genuine
thought and feeling; but earlier revolutionaries did not urge,
to cite Ford once more, "that no exigency of meter must inter-
fere with the personal cadence of the writer's mind or the
pressure of the recorded emotion." Euripides' metrical virtuosity
is legendary; and though his choruses were sometimes accused
of licentiousness, this charge appears to have been brought
against their dance and musical elements as much as their
rhythmical character. Horace, however innovative in his treatment of his subject matter, is a master of conventional craft.
"My own delight," he says, "is to shut up words in feet" *(me
pedibus delectat claudere verba) (Satires,* 2.1.28). To speak a
moment of Villon, whom Ford and Pound both refer to as a
model, he is shockingly original; yet he writes in metrical forms,
ballades and *rondeaux,* which are extremely strict and which
had been bequeathed to him by earlier poets like Deschamps
and Machaut.

The same circumstance applies to Dryden and Wordsworth.
Though a defender of modern practices, Dryden throughout
his criticism emphasizes the value of metrical composition. In
fact, one of the common themes of his essays, dedications, and
prefaces is that those who have difficulty writing naturally in

verse should blame themselves and not their medium. In his dedication to *The Rival Ladies*, Dryden admits that rhyme can result in awkwardnesses, but adds that it does so only, "when the poet either makes a vicious choice of words, or places them, for rhyme sake, so unnaturally as no man would in ordinary speaking." This argument appears as well in the *Essay of Dramatic Poesy*, in which Neander comments at one point that "the necessity of a rhyme never forces any but bad or lazy writers to say what they would not otherwise." The fact that Dryden himself, later in his career, abandoned the use of rhyme in his dramatic works, is not of consequence in the present context, for he makes much the same arguments about unrhymed metrical composition that he makes about rhymed metrical composition. For instance, in the section of the *Essay* in which Neander discusses rhyme, he also cites a line of blank verse containing two clumsy inversions, "I heaven invoke, and strong resistance make," and remarks: "You would think me very ridiculous if I should accuse the stubbornness of blank verse for this, and not rather the stiffness of the poet." And generally Dryden's attitude about meter seems summarized in a statement he makes in the last paragraph of a *Defense* which he wrote of his *Essay* in the wake of Robert Howard's attack on it. "I have observed," says Dryden, "that none have been violent against verse, but such only as have not attempted it, or have succeeded ill in their attempt."

   Wordsworth, too, is a strong defender of meter, and his preface to *Lyrical Ballads* has an eloquent explanation of its values. Indeed, Wordsworth carefully distinguishes the conventions of meter from the conventions of "POETIC DICTION"— arguing that the latter create a harmful barrier between reader and poet, but that the former establish a healthy and necessary bond between the two.

> The distinction of metre is regular and uniform, and not, like that which is produced by what is usually called POETIC DICTION, arbitrary, and subject to infinite caprices upon which no calculation whatever can be made. In the one case, the Reader is utterly at the mercy of the Poet, respecting what imagery or diction he may choose to connect with the passion; whereas, in the other, the metre obeys certain laws, to which the Poet and Reader both willingly submit because they are certain, and because no interference is made by them with the passion, but such as the concurring testimony of ages has shown to heighten and improve the pleasure which co-exists with it.

Wordsworth continues by exploring the nature of meter itself and "the charm which, by the consent of all nations, is acknowledged to exist in metrical language." He speaks of the happy effect of meter for the reader — of the "small, but continual and regular impulses of pleasureable surprise from the metrical arrangement" and of "the pleasure which the mind derives from the perception of similitude in dissimilitude." And Wordsworth speaks as well of the fundamental and wonderful paradox of successful metrical composition: it is speech which is natural, yet which, at the same time, is ordered within and played off against the norm of a fixed line: "Now the music of harmonious metrical language, the sense of difficulty overcome, and the blind association of pleasure which has been previously received from works of rhyme or metre of the same or similar construction, an indistinct perception perpetually renewed of language closely resembling that of real life, and yet, in the circumstance of metre, differing from it so widely — all these imperceptibly make up a complex feeling of delight."

In view of the statements of Dryden and Wordsworth, we may

find it hard to comprehend how Eliot could repeatedly justify vers libre by appealing to their authority. In a broader sense, we may find it difficult to comprehend how the modernists of our time could in general argue so forcefully that their revolution, which developed and expressed itself—practically speaking—through non-metrical poems, was just like earlier literary revolutions. Admittedly, the modernists' enterprise was, at least in its initial stages, polemical: they wanted first and foremost their views heard and their verse published and read. And, like all polemicists, they may have tended to avail themselves of evidence which supported their cause and to have suppressed evidence that did not. Yet this is neither a complete nor a fair explanation of their use of the past and their desire, which was without doubt sincere, to reform poetry. We must therefore surmise that there were factors in the cultural life of their times which did not in earlier periods exist or exert a determining power, but which did exist in the modern period and helped to give rise to the concept of non-metrical verse. Before we conclude, it behooves us to take note of several of these factors and the manner in which they have shaped the poetry of our time.

One important factor is the influence of the modern physical sciences on our culture. Though evident as early as the seventeenth century, the influence does not really become pervasive until the technological triumphs of the nineteenth century. And increasingly in that century, one comes across the idea that art is not making the kinds of advances science is and that art should model its methods on those of science so that it, too, can achieve a kind of demonstrable, quantitative "progress." This idea is in turn productive of the notion that art should be "experimental" and that the artist should aspire to "breakthroughs" and "discoveries." Insofar as many of the advances of the modern physical sciences were results of inventions of or refinements of apparatus, artists of the late nineteenth and early twentieth century came to be more and more tempted to seek novelties of technique. Pound in particular reflects the influence of the modern physical sciences, in that his literary criticism is saturated with scientific and pseudo-scientific terminology. "THE IDEOGRAMMIC METHOD OR THE METHOD OF SCIENCE" is, for instance, the rallying cry in his *ABC of Reading*, and he appears to have believed that, in heaping together the miscellaneous materials of his *Cantos*, he was following the procedure of a biologist collecting data. Art, of course, is always and necessarily capable of novelty, but traditionally its novelty has resided in its subject matter — the ever-changing manners and morals of human beings and their societies. Then, too, art has always and necessarily shared certain values — clearsightedness, rigor, honesty — with science. However, the tendency to model art on science and to assert that each generation of artists should do something technically new is a feature distinctly of our time. It is also a feature that would naturally encourage poets to try unprecedented procedures, such as writing verse without meter.

Another factor which helped to shape and give sanction to non-metrical verse is the development of "Aesthetics." We use the term today in discussing issues throughout literary history; we have used the term, in fact, in these remarks in a comparison of Horace and Euripides. But the term, however widely useful its applications, did not even exist until Baumgarten coined it in 1750. And not until the end of the eighteenth century, when Kant elaborated his system of three Critiques — isolating thereby the Beautiful (Judgment) from the True (Pure Reason) and the

Good (Practical Reason)—was there a philosophical schema within which art could claim independence from reason and ethics, and from, by extension, its own history. One argument Eliot, Ford, and Pound all make about their movement is that it involved, as Eliot says in his music essay, "an insistence upon the inner unity which is unique to every poem, against the outer unity which is typical." If every poem is to be regarded, as Eliot suggests, as an object with a unique inner unity or autonomy, it follows that every poem can have or create, so to speak, its own individual prosody.

Aestheticism also encouraged the development of non-metrical verse in another respect. In elevating music as the "purest" of the arts, writers in the aesthetic tradition helped produce a climate of opinion in which literary and visual artists aspired to musicality. The central idea of Eliot's music essay is that poetry has or can have a musical structure and that such a structure is in some fashion superior to a metrical structure. As for Ford and Pound, they both explain vers libre in terms of music, actually construing the vers libre line with eighth-notes, quarter-notes, and half-notes—Ford doing this in his preface to his *Collected Poems* and Pound in his "Tradition" essay. In this regard, Pound's famous remark that the poet should "compose in the sequence of the musical phrase, not in sequence of a metronome" is doubly significant. First, it indicates the degree to which music has, in Pound's mind anyway, supplanted meter as the measure of verse, and, second, it suggests the degree to which meter (the root word of *metronome*) has come to be viewed as something monotonous and inferior.

Another factor which contributed to the development of non-metrical verse is the rise and triumph of the modern novel. Though people have always told stories, and though traditions of prose fiction go back at least as far as Aesop, from the time of Homer to the eighteenth century, the fiction of prestige is virtually all metrical. Not until the nineteenth century do we, when thinking of the finest fiction writers of the age, think to a great extent of prose writers. A constant theme of the modern poets of our time is that verse has lost a lot of its material to prose fiction and that if poetry is to recover the material, it must assimilate elements and characteristsics of the novel. In this context, Ford and Pound's assertion that verse must be at least as well-written as prose could be readily translated into the notion that verse should be written as the novel is written —without meter.

We should mention as well a point the late J. V. Cunningham raises in an interview in a forthcoming issue of *The Iowa Review*. In one respect, the modernists of our time did not understand traditional meter and confused meter with a convention of reading and scanning that developed in the schools in the nineteenth century. This convention, which is still reflected in some textbooks, involves speaking lines of verse in a heavily artificial and sing-song way to bring out their metrical identity:

> Of *man's* first *disobedience, and* the *fruit*

Such reading clarified the metrical norm of the line, but it totally obliterates natural degrees of relative strees within the line. It sounds awful, to boot, and can easily lead, as Cunningham suggests it did lead, to the feeling that meter is something stiff and wooden.

This certainly appears to have happened with Pound. His remarks about the metronome, and his related imperative, "Don't chop your stuff into separate *iambs,*" are salutary in that they remind the poet that it is incumbent on him to give his verse rhythmical life. At the same time, these remarks exhibit a startling ignorance of English metrical practice, as does his characterization, in "Treatise on Metre" in the *ABC of Reading*, of the iambic pentameter as "ti tum ti tum ti tum ti tum ti tum . . . from which every departure is treated as an exception." Good poets do not compose foot by foot; and, given the fact that any complete articulation in English has one and only one primarily stressed syllable and a number of syllables receiving greater or lesser degrees of secondary stress, it would actually be rather difficult to write a "metronomic" line in English, a line, that is, of light and heavy syllables of perfectly equivalent alternating weight. Pound's ti-tumming accounts for the metrical norm of the pentameter line and for the way a student might scan or read the line to bring out its metrical identity, but the ti-tumming does not account for the infinite varieties of rhythmical contour (and they are not "exceptions") that can be struck across the conventional pentameter. Here, for example, are pentameters from poems of Shakespeare, Dryden, Jane Austen, Robert Frost, and Thom Gunn:

> Prosperity's the very bond of love
>
> Thou last great prophet of tautology
>
> The day commemorative of my birth
>
> Snow falling and night falling fast, oh, fast
>
> Resisting, by embracing, nothingness

Each of these lines is orthodox, yet each has, within the context of that orthodoxy, a personal rhythm. The method of reading and scanning to which Cunningham refers, however, obscures this quality of English meter, and Cunningham is no doubt correct in observing that the understandable hostility to the method or convention came to be directed at meter itself.

We have come to our conclusion. Whether one feels pro or con about the movement Eliot, Ford, and Pound led, one probably should be, if one cares about poetry as a living art — an art existing not simply in texts and anthologies, but practiced by women and men today — troubled by this aspect of the movement: new forms were, it was hoped, to emerge from the experiments with non-metrical verse, or the old forms were supposed to revive. This has not happened. Rather, in the wake of the triumph of the modern revolution, several generations of poets have merely continued to write non-metrically. It is on this point that we should be most skeptical of Eliot's contention that metrical considerations are negligible when compared with the broader question of good and bad writing. As true as it is that meter alone will never produce a fine poem, even a bad poet who writes in meter keeps alive the traditions of metrical composition. When, however, good and bad poets alike devote themselves to non-metrical verse, it is possible that all sense of meter — and of the memorability and symmetry and surprise it can give listeners and readers — will be lost.

This danger, interestingly enough, was evident to Eliot late in his career. At the end of the Milton essay of 1947, he remarks: "We cannot, in literature, any more than in the rest of life, live in a perpetual state of revolution"; and warning against "a progressive deterioration" in poetry, he asks his audience to reflect that "a monotony of unscannable verse fatigues the attention even more quickly than a monotony of exact feet." Were Eliot alive today, he might well feel the same unease expressed in these comments. He and his co-revolutionaries had a valid quarrel with the nineteenth century and rebelled with specific goals in view. Whatever one thinks of their experiments with non-metrical verse, the experiements at least had a purpose. Now, however, the styles and attitudes of the nineteenth century have long since vanished, and the great majority of contemporary poets seem merely following, by rote and habit, a procedure of writing, and breaking up into lines, predictably mannered prose.

NOTES ON THE NEW FORMALISM

Dana Gioia

1.

Twenty years ago it was a truth universally acknowledged that a young poet in possession of a good ear would want to write free verse. Today one faces more complex and problematic choices. While the overwhelming majority of new poetry published in the U.S. continues to be in "open" forms, for the first time in two generations there is a major revival of formal verse among young poets. The first signs of this revival emerged at the tail end of the 'Seventies, long after the more knowing critics had declared rhyme and meter permanently defunct. First a few good formal books by young poets like Charles Martin's *Room For Error* (1978) and Timothy Steele's *Uncertainties and Rest* (1979) appeared but went almost completely unreviewed. Then magazines, like *Paris Review* which hadn't published a rhyming poem in anyone's memory, suddenly began featuring sonnets, villanelles, and syllabics. Changes in literary taste make good copy, and the sharper reviewers quickly took note. Soon some of the most lavishly praised debuts like Brad Leithauser's *Hundreds of Fireflies* (1983) and Vikram Seth's *The Golden Gate* (1986) were by poets working entirely in form.

Literature not only changes; it must change to keep its force and vitality. There will always be groups advocating new types of poetry, some of it genuine, just as there will always be

First published in *The Hudson Review*, Autumn 1987, Copyright © 1987 by The Hudson Review, Inc. Reprinted with permission of the author and publisher.

conservative opposing forces trying to maintain the conventional models. The revival of rhyme and meter among some young poets creates an unprecedented situation in American poetry. The new formalists put free verse poets in the ironic and unprepared position of being the *status quo*. Free verse, the creation of an older literary revolution, is now the long-established, ruling orthodoxy; formal poetry the unexpected challenge.

There is currently a great deal of private controversy about these new formalists, some of which occasionally spills over into print. Significantly, these discussions often contain many odd misconceptions about poetic form, most of them threadbare clichés which somehow still survive from the 'Sixties. Form, we are told authoritatively, is artificial, elitist, retrogressive, right-wing, and (my favorite) un-American. None of these arguments can withstand critical scrutiny, but nevertheless, they continue to be made so regularly that one can only assume they provide some emotional comfort to their advocates. Obviously, for many writers the discussion of formal and free verse has become an encoded political debate.

When the language of poetic criticism has become so distorted, it becomes important to make some fundamental distinctions. Formal verse, like free verse, is neither bad nor good. The terms are strictly descriptive not evaluative. They define distinct sets of techniques rather than rank the quality or nature of poetic performance. Nor do these techniques automatically carry with them social, political, or even, in most cases, aesthetic values. (It would, for example, be very easy for a poet to do automatic writing in meter. One might even argue that surrealism is best realized in formal verse since the regular rhythms of the words in meter hypnotically release the unconscious.) However obvious these distinctions should be, few poets or critics seem to be making them. Is it any wonder then that so much current writing on poetry is either opaque or irrelevant? What serious discussion can develop when such primary critical definitions fail to be made with accuracy?

2.

Meter is an ancient, indeed primitive, technique that marks the beginning of literature in virtually every culture. It dates back to a time, so different from our specialized modern era, when there was little, if any, distinction between poetry, religion, history, music, and magic. All were performed in a sacred, ritual language separated from everyday speech by its incantatory metrical form. Meter is also essentially a pre-literate technology, a way of making language memorable before the invention of writing. Trained poet-singers took the events and ideas a culture wanted to preserve—be they tribal histories or magic ceremonies —formulated them in meter, and committed these formulas to memory. Before writing, the poet and the poem were inseparable, and both represented the collective memory of their culture.

Meter is therefore an aural technique. It assumes a speaker and a listener, who for the duration of the poem are intertwined. Even in later literary cultures meter has always insisted on the primacy of the physical sound of language. Unlike prose, which can be read silently with full enjoyment, poetry demands to be recited, heard, even memorized for its true appreciation. Shaping the words in one's mouth is as much a part of the pleasure as hearing the sounds in the air. Until recently educa-tion in poetry always emphasized memorization and recitation. This traditional method stressed the immediately communicable and communal pleasures of the art. Certainly a major reason for the decline in poetry's popular audience stems directly from the abandonment of this aural education for the joylessly intellectual approach of critical analysis.

Free verse is a much more modern technique that presupposes the existence of written texts. While it does not abandon the aural imagination — no real poetry can — most free verse plays with the way poetic language is arranged on a page and articulates the visual rhythm of a poem in a way earlier metrical verse rarely bothered to. Even the earliest known free verse, the Hebrew Psalms (which actually inhabit a middle ground between free and formal verse since they follow a principle of syntactic but not metrical symmetry) were created by "the people of the Book" in a culture uniquely concerned with limiting the improvisatory freedom of the bard for the fixed message of the text.

Most often one first notices the visual orientation of free verse in trivial ways (the lack of initial capitals at the beginning of lines, the use of typographical symbols like "&" and "7," the arbitrary use of upper or lower case letters). e. e. cummings spent his life exploiting these tricks trying to create a visual vocabulary for modern poetry. Eventually, however, one sees how the visual field of the page is essential to the organization of sound in free verse. Printed as run-on lines of prose, a free verse poem reads radically differently from how it does printed as verse (whereas most metrical verse still retains its basic rhythmic design and symmetry). This visual artifice separates free verse from speech. Technological innovation affects art, and it is probably not accidental that the broadscale development of free verse came from the first generation of writers trained from childhood on the shift-key typewriter introduced in 1878. This new device allowed writers to predict accurately for the first time the *look* of their words on the printed page rather than just their sound.

All free verse deals with the fundamental question of how and when to end lines of poetry when there is no regular meter to measure them out. The earliest free-verse matched the line with some syntactic unit of sense (in Hebrew poetry, for instance, the line was most often a double unit of parallel syntactic sense):

1 Except the Lord build the house, they labor in
   vain that build it:
   Except the Lord keep the city, the watchman
   waketh but in vain.

2 It is vain for you to rise up early, to sit up late,
   To eat the bread of sorrows: for so he giveth his
   beloved sleep.

                                         (Psalm 127)

Once free verse leaves the strict symmetry of sacred Hebrew poetry, there is no way for the ear to judge accurately from the sounds alone the metrical structure of a poem (unless the reader exaggerates the line breaks). Sometimes one wonders if even the poet hears the purely aural pattern of his words. Most critics do not. For instance, it has never been noted that the most famous American free verse poem of the twentieth century, William Carlos Williams' "The Red Wheelbarrow," is not only free verse but also two rather undistinguished lines of blank verse:

so much depends upon a red wheel barrow
glazed with rain water beside the white chickens.

One reason that these lines have proved so memorable is that they are familiarly metrical — very similar in rhythm to another famous passage of blank verse, even down to the "feminine" endings of the lines:

To be or not to be, that is the question:
Whether 'tis nobler in the mind to suffer...

That Williams wrote blank verse while thinking he was
pioneering new trails in prosody doesn't necessarily invalidate
his theories (though it may lead one to examine them with a
certain skepticism). This discrepancy, however, does suggest two
points. First, even among its adversaries, metrical language
exercises a primitive power, even if it is frequently an unconscious
one. Second, the organizing principle of Williams' free verse is
visual. What makes "The Red Wheelbarrow" free verse is not
the sound alone, which is highly regular, but the visual placement of those sounds on the page.

> so much depends
> upon
>
> a red wheel
> barrow
>
> glazed with rain
> water
>
> beside the white
> chickens.

Here words achieve a new symmetry, alien to the ear, but
no less genuine. The way Williams arranges the poem into
brief lines and stanzas slows the language until every word
acquires an unusual weight. This deliberate visual placement
twists a lackluster blank verse couplet into a provocatively
original free verse lyric which challenges the reader's definition
of what constitutes a poem. Much of the poem's impact comes
from catching the reader off guard and forcing him to reread
it in search of what he has missed because nothing of what
Williams has said comprises a satisfactory poem in a conventional sense. The element of surprise makes this type of poem

a difficult trick to repeat and may explain why so much of the minimalist poetry written in the Williams tradition is so dull. The poetic experience comes in the rereading as the reader consciously revises his own superficial first impression and sees the real importance of Williams' seemingly mundane images. Just as Williams' imagery works by challenging the reader to see the despoiled modern world as charged with a new kind of beauty, so too does his prosody operate by making everyday words acquire a new weight by their unexpectedly bold placement on the page. No aural poem could work in this way.

3.

The current moment is a fortunate one for poets interested in traditional form. Two generations now of younger writers have largely ignored rhyme and meter, and most of the older poets, who worked originally in form (such as Louis Simpson and Adrienne Rich) have abandoned it entirely for more than a quarter of a century. Literary journalism has long declared it defunct, and most current anthologies present no work in traditional forms by Americans written after 1960. The British may have continued using rhyme and meter in their quaint, old-fashioned way and the Irish in their primitive, bardic manner, but for up-to-date Americans it becomes the province of the old, the eccentric, and the Anglophilic. It was a style that dared not speak its name, except in light verse. Even the tri-nominate, blue-haired lady laureates now wrote in free verse.*

---

*The editors of *The Hudson Review* ask, as perhaps they should, if this statement is a sexist stereotype. I offer it rather as investigative journalism based on painful, first-hand knowledge of the work of such

By 1980 there had been such a decisive break with the literary past that in America for the first time in the history of modern English most published young poets could not write with minimal competence in traditional meters (not that this failing bothered anyone). Whether this was an unprecedented cultural catastrophe or a glorious revolution is immaterial to this discussion. What matters is that most of the craft of traditional English versification has been forgotten.

Since 1960 there has also been relatively little formal innovation done by the mainstream either in metrical or free verse. Radical experimentation like concrete poetry or language poetry has been pushed off to the fringes of the literary culture where it either has been ignored by the mainstream or declared irrelevant. At the same time most mainstream poets have done little of the more focused (and less radical) experimentation with meters or verse forms that open up new possibilities for poetic language. Since 1960 the only new verse forms to have entered the mainstream of American poetry have been two miniatures: the double dactyl and the ghazal, the latter usually in a dilute unrhymed version of the Persian original.

Indeed, the most influential form in American poetry over this quarter century has been the prose poem, which strictly speaking is not a verse form at all but a stylistic alternative to verse as the medium for poetry. In theory the prose poem is the most protean form of free verse in which all line breaks

---

important contemporary poets as Sudie Stuart Hager, Winifred Hamrick Farrar, Maggie Culver Fry, Helen von Kolnitz Hyer, Louise McNeill Pease, and the late Peggy Simpson Curry (the official poet laureates of Idaho, Mississippi, Oklahoma, South Carolina, West Virginia, and Wyoming respectively). When such poets write in free verse, how can that style not be said to belong to the establishment?

disappear as a highly-charged lyric poem achieves the ultimate organic form. In recent American practice, however, it has
mostly become a kind of absurdist parable having more to do
with the prose tradition of Kafka or Borges than the poetic
tradition of Baudelaire or Rimbaud. As poetry literally became written in prose, was it any wonder that verse technique
suffered?

Likewise, although the past quarter century has witnessed
an explosion of poetic translation, this boom has almost
exclusively produced translations of a formally vague and colorless sort. Compared to most earlier translation, these contemporary American versions make no effort whatsoever to
reproduce the prosodic features of their originals. One can now
read most of Dante or Villon, Rilke or Mandelstam, Lorca or
even Petrarch in English without any sense of the poem's original
form. Sometimes these versions brilliantly convey the theme
or tone of the originals, but more often they sound stylistically
impoverished and anonymous. All of the past blurs together
into a familiar tune. Unrhymed, unmetered, and unshaped,
Petrarch and Rilke sound misleadingly alike.

This method of translating foreign poetry into an already
available contemporary style also brings less to the language
than the more difficult attempt to recreate a foreign form in
English (as Sir Thomas Wyatt did for the Italian sonnet or the
anonymous translators of the King James Bible did for the
Hebrew Psalms). New verse forms and meters can have a
liberating effect on poetry. They allow writers to say things that
have never worked in poetry before or else to restate familiar
things in original ways. Many of the most important forms in
our language were once exotic imports—the sonnet, sestina,
ballade, villanelle, triolet, terza rima, pantoum, rubaiyt, haiku,

ottava rima, free verse, even the prose poem. Recent translation has done little to expand the formal resources of American poetry. Ironically it may have done more to deaden the native ear by translating all poetry of all ages into the same homogenous style. Studying great poetry in such neutralized versions, one gets little sense of how the forms adopted or invented by great writers are inseparable from their art. Not only the subtleties are lost but even the general scheme.

This assessment does not maintain that metrical innovation is necessary to write good poetry, that successful poetic translation must always follow the verse forms of the original or that prose is an impossible medium for poetry. It merely examines some current literary trends and speculates on both their origins and consequences. It also suggests that the recent dearth of formal poetry opens interesting possibilities for young poets to match an unexploited contemporary idiom with traditional or experimental forms. Indeed the current moment may even offer poets an opportunity for formal innovation and expansion unprecedented in the language since the end of the eighteenth century, for no age since then has been so metrically narrow or formally orthodox as our own.

4.

For the arts at least there truly is a *Zeitgeist*, especially at moments of decisive change when they move together with amazing synchronization. We are now living at one such moment to which critics have applied the epithet "postmodern," an attractive term the meaning of which no two writers can agree on precisely because it does not yet have one. The dialectic of history is still moving too fast, and events still unforseen will probably define this moment in ways equally unexpected.

One day cultural historians will elucidate the connections between the current revival of formal and narrative poetry with this broader shift of sensibility in the arts. The return to tonality in serious music, to representation in painting, to decorative detail and non-functional design in architecture will link with poetry's reaffirmation of song and story as the most pervasive development of the American arts towards the end of this century.

No one today can accurately judge all of the deeper social, economic, and cultural forces driving this revival, but at least one central motivation seems clear. All of these revivals of traditional technique (whether linked or not to traditional aesthetics) both reject the specialization and intellectualization of the arts in the academy over the past forty years and affirm the need for a broader popular audience. The modern movement, which began this century in bohemia, is now ending it in the university, an institution dedicated at least as much to the specialization of knowledge as to its propogation. Ultimately the mission of the university has little to do with the mission of the arts, and this long cohabitation has had an ennervating effect on all the arts but especially on poetry and music. With the best of intentions the university has intellectualized the arts to a point where they have been cut off from the vulgar vitality of popular traditions and, as a result, their public has shrunk to groups of academic specialists and a captive audience of students, both of whom refer to everything beyond the university as "the real world." Mainly poets read contemporary poetry, and only professional musicians and composers attend concerts of new music.

Like the new tonal composers, the young poets now working in form reject the split between their art and its traditional audience. They seek to reaffirm poetry's broader cultural role and restore its parity with fiction and drama. The poet, Wade Newman, has already linked the revival of form with the return to narrative and grouped these new writers as an "expansive movement" dedicated to reversing poetry's declining importance to the culture. These young poets, Newman claims, seek to engage their audience not by simplifying their work but by making it more relevant and accessible. They are also "expansive" in that they have expanded their technical and thematic concerns beyond the confines of the short, autobiographical free verse lyric which so dominates contemporary poetry. Obviously, the return to form and narrative are not the only possible ways of establishing the connection between the poet and the broader public, but it does represent one means of renewal, and if this particular "expansive movement" works, American poetry will end this, its most distinguished century, with more promise to its future than one sees today.

5.

One of the more interesting developments of the last five years has been the emergence of pseudo-formal verse. This sort of writing began appearing broadly a few years ago shortly after critics started advertising the revival of form. Pseudo-formal verse bears the same relationship to formal poetry as the storefronts on a Hollywood backlot do to a real city street. They both look vaguely the same from a distance. In pseudo-formal verse the lines run to more or less the same length on the page. Stanzas are neatly symmetrical. The syllable count is roughly regular line by line, and there may even be a few rhymes thrown in, usually in an irregular pattern.

Trying to open the window on a Hollywood facade, one soon discovers it won't budge. The architectural design has no structural function. Psuedo-formal verse operates on the same principle. It displays no firm concept of how meters operate in English to shape the rhythm of a poem. Though arranged in neat visual patterns, the words jump between incompatible rhythmic systems from line to line. The rhythms lack the spontaneity of free verse without ever achieving the focused energy of formal poetry. They grope towards a regular rhythmic shape but never reach it. Ultimately, there is little, if any, structural connection between the look and the sound of the poem.

There are two kinds of pseudo-formal poems. The first type is more sophisticated. It appears regularly metrical. The first line usually scans according to some common meter, but thereafter problems occur. The poet cannot sustain the pattern of sounds he or she has chosen and soon begins to make substitutions line by line, which may look consistent with the underlying form but actually organize the rhythms in incompatible ways. What results technically is usually neither good free verse nor formal verse. Here, for example, is the opening of a poem by a young writer widely praised as an accomplished formalist. (Most poetry reviewers call any poem which looks vaguely regular "formal.") This passage wants to be blank verse, but despite a few regular lines, it never sustains a consistent rhythm long enough to establish a metrical base:

> From this unpardoned perch, a kitchen table
> In a sunless walk-up in a city
> Of tangled boulevards, he tested
> The old, unwieldy nemesis — namelessness.
> Forgetting (he knew) couldn't be remedied
> But these gestures of identity (he liked to think)
> Rankled the equanimities of time:
> A conceit, of course, but preferable to

> The quarrels of the ego, the canter of
> Description or discoveries of the avant-garde.

At first glance this passage appears to be in blank verse. The poem's first line unfolds as regular iambic pentameter (with a feminine ending). The second line has ten syllables, too, but it scans metrically either as awkward trochees or pure syllabics. A regular iambic rhythm appears again in line three, but now it falls decisively one foot short. Line four begins as regular blank verse but then abruptly loses its rhythm in word play between "nemesis" and "namelessness." Line five can only be construed as free verse. After a vague start line six plays with a regular iambic movement but dissipates itself over thirteen syllables. And so it continues awkwardly till the end. Good blank verse can be full of substitutions, but the variations always play off of a clearly established pattern. They help the overall meter build a syntactic intensity. Here the poem never established a clear rhythmic direction. The lines never quite become blank verse. They only allude to it.

The second type of pseudo-formal poem is more common because it is easier to write. It doesn't even try to make a regular pattern of sound, however awkwardly. It only wants to look regular. The lines have no auditory integrity, as free or formal verse. Their integrity is merely visual — in a gross and uninteresting sense. The same issue of *The Agni Review*, which published the previous example, also contains a poem in quatrains which has these representative stanzas:

> When at odd moments, business and pleasure
> pale, and I think I'm staring into space,
> I catch myself gazing at a notecard propped
> on my desk, "The Waves at Matsushima."

. . . .

> and wider than the impossible journey
> from island to island so sheerly
> undercut by waves that no boat could find
> a landing, nor a shipwrecked couple
>
> rest beneath those scrubby pines at the top
> that could be overgrown heads of broccoli,
> even if they could survive the surf, tall
> combers, more like a field plowed by a maniac . . .

These line lengths seem determined mainly by their typographic width. Why else does the author break the lines between "pleasure" and "pale" or "tall" and "combers"? The apparently regular line breaks fall without any real rhythmic relation either to the meter or the syntax. As Truman Capote once said, "That's not writing — it's typing." There is no rhythmic integrity, only incompatible, provisional judgements shifting pointlessly line by line. The resulting poems remind me of a standard gag in improvisational comedy where the performers pretend to speak a foreign language by imitating its approximate sound. Making noises that resemble Swedish, Russian, Italian or French, they hold impassioned conversations on the stage. What makes it all so funny is that the actors, as everyone in the audience knows, are only mouthing nonsense.

The metrical incompetence of pseudo-formal verse is the most cogent evidence of our literature's break with tradition and the lingering consequences. These poets are not without talent. Aside from its rhythmic ineptitude, their verse often exhibits many of the other qualities that distinguish good poetry. Even their desire to try traditional forms speaks well of their ambition and artistic curiosity. How then do these promising authors, most of whom not only have graduate training in writing or literature but also work as professional teachers of writing, not hear the confusing rhythms of their own verse? How can they believe their expertise in a style whose basic principles they so obviously misunderstand? That these writers by virtue of their training and position represent America's poetic intelligentsia makes their performance deeply unnerving—rather like hearing a conservatory trained pianist rapturously play the notes of a Chopin waltz in 2/4 time.

These young poets have grown up in a literary culture so removed from the predominently oral traditions of metrical verse that they can no longer hear it accurately. Their training in reading and writing has been overwhelmingly visual not aural, and they have never learned to hear the musical design a poem executes. For them poems exist as words on a page rather than sounds in the mouth and ear. While they have often analyzed poems, they have rarely memorized and recited them. Nor have they studied and learned poems by heart in foreign languages where sound patterns are more obvious to non-native speakers. Their often extensive critical training in textual analysis never included scansion, and their knowledge of even the fundamentals of prosody is haphazard (though theory is less important than practice in mastering the craft of versification). Consequently, they have neither much practical nor theoretical training in the way sounds are organized in poetry. Ironically this very lack of training makes them deaf to their own ineptitude. Full of confidence, they rely on instincts they have never developed. Magisterially they take liberties with forms whose rudimentary principles they misconstrue. Every poem reveals some basic confusion about its own medium. Some misconceptions ultimately prove profitable for art. Not this one.

6.

In my own poetry I have always worked in both fixed and open forms. Each mode opened up possibilities of style, subject, music, and development the other did not suggest, at least at that moment. Likewise experience in each mode provided an illuminating perspective on the other. Working in free verse helped keep the language of my formal poems varied and contemporary, just as writing in form helped keep my free verse more focused and precise. I find it puzzling therefore that so many poets see these modes as opposing aesthetics rather than as complimentary techniques. Why shouldn't a poet explore the full resources the English language offers?

I suspect that ten years from now the real debate among poets and concerned critics will not be about poetic form in the narrow technical sense of metrical versus non-metrical verse. That is already a tired argument, and only the uninformed or biased can fail to recognize that genuine poetry can be created in both modes. How obvious it should be that no technique precludes poetic achievement just as none automatically assures it (though admittedly some techniques may be more difficult to use at certain moments in history). Soon, I believe, the central debate will focus on form in the wider, more elusive sense of poetic structure. How does a poet best shape words, images, and ideas into meaning? How much compression is needed to transform versified lines — be they metrical or free — into genuine poetry? The important arguments will not be about technique in isolation but about the fundamental aesthetic assumptions of writing and judging poetry.

At that point the real issues presented by American poetry in the 'Eighties will become clearer: the debasement of poetic

language; the prolixity of the lyric; the bankruptcy of the confessional mode; the inability to establish a meaningful aesthetic
for new poetic narrative; and the denial of musical texture in
the contemporary poem. The revival of traditional forms will
be seen then as only one response to this troubling situation.
There will undoubtedly be others. Only time will prove which
responses were the most persuasive.

EMACIATED POETRY

c⸲❀⸲ɔ

Wyatt Prunty

1.

Since the early 1960s American poetry has constituted
something quite different from the high modernist work of Eliot,
Tate, the early Lowell, and others. Two of the most prominent
practitioners of this new poetry are Robert Creeley and A. R.
Ammons. The first characteristic you notice about the change
to which Creeley and Ammons have contributed is a shrinkage
in margins that has produced a stylish, highly marketable thin-
ness. For two decades one of the most publishable forms for
poetry seems to have been the lyric broken into lines that would
fit in a newspaper column. Editors are always cramped for room
to include everything they would like to publish, but more than
a question of space is involved here. At the same time its margins
have narrowed, this poetry has been restricted in other ways.
It is thin in more senses than one.

The publication of *Life Studies* in 1959 announced that
something drastic in American poetry had happened. At a time
when the influence of existentialism had led to a premium's being
placed upon authenticity, Lowell deserted the traditionalism
of T. S. Eliot for the immediacy of William Carlos Williams.
A general change in poetry was under way. Haut bourgeois was
out, déclassé in. The rigors of poetic form amounted, it was
now thought, to an inauthentic treatment of experience that,

First published in *The Sewanee Review*, Winter, 1985, Copyright © 1985 by Wyatt
Prunty. Reprinted with permission of the author and publisher.

understood existentially, had to stand outside conventions as a unique moment. The isolated poet now set traditional categories of thought aside; the scales were removed from the shaman's eyes, and poems about one's return to origins (which, like victims, are always innocent and good) proliferated. Moments from one's formative childhood and from dreams were accompanied by primitive objects, stones, bones, caves, and other items that seemed irreducible and thus appeared as the indices of the unconscious, the essential man. What could be less ordered therefore more existentially authentic than the unconscious? Like a caveman's experience it was free of the clutterings of intellect and culture that stood between the eye and its object. The primitive, representing the unconscious, became a means for projection downward to dramatize human meaning much as religious belief and the traditional use of allegory had been an upward projection for transcendent meaning.

A change in poetic style is always connected to a change in thought. I have argued elsewhere that just as existentialism reached full stride Lowell's personal experience seemed to parallel much that Sartre and others were saying. Lowell's disillusionment over the allied bombing of civilian targets during World War II, the loss of his parents, his own mental difficulties, his departure from the church, his divorce from Jean Stafford (who also was a Catholic), and his marriage to Elizabeth Hardwick (who was not religious) — all of these events contributed to a shift in Lowell's thinking which in turn was reflected by a change in his poetic style. From the 1940s until the end of his life Lowell was a highly celebrated poet, and the scaled-down poetry of *Life Studies* significantly affected other poets. What Lowell's example urged was that poets should cease using classical and

Christian allusions to constitute meaning, especially through
the use of allegory, and should turn instead to experience.
Having left the church and faced his own dark world of the
unconscious, Lowell began writing out of personal experience,
his family's experience, and the history of New England. The
Christian myth, a basis for timeless meaning, had been replaced
by mundane history and personal dislocation.

The urgency, however, to make experience intelligible in a
time-ridden era (whether one should use myth, as Eliot suggested, reason, as Yvor Winters urged, or Jungian depth imagery)
did not change with the shift in style that Lowell and others
undertook. On the surface the classroom virtues of irony,
paradox, and ambiguity taught by Cleanth Brooks and other
influential critics half a generation earlier seemed to have been
set aside. Beneath that surface, in fact, the problems the Brooksian categories addressed did not disappear; and poetry continued to respond to them. Whether one was concerned with
religious experience (as Eliot was), with "preternatural" experience (as Winters said at times he was), or with the unconscious
mind, poetry's task continued to be that of ferreting order out
of apparent disorder. What actually happened was that a poor
man's version of irony, paradox, and ambiguity sprouted as part
of an excessive reliance upon enjambment. An abbreviated version of the Brooksian virtues appeared as the result of the use
of excessively short lines, and it did so in the poetry of those
who had rejected the New Criticism. We are familiar with the
Brooks version; here is a variation on it:

> As I sd to my
> friend, because I am
> always talking,—John, I

> sd, which was not his
> name, the darkness sur-
> rounds us, what
>
> can we do against
> it, or else, shall we &
> why not, buy a goddamn big car,
>
> drive, he sd, for
> christ's sake, look
> out where yr going.

This is Robert Creeley's "I Know a Man." It presents us with a speaker worrying about one's movement through the dark, the unintelligible. For Brooks and the New Critics words are linked with their particular bits of cultural baggage, and out of the various torsions that these words generate as a group a greater, more complex meaning is construed. Irony, paradox, and ambiguity are the results of a building up, of putting words in tension with one another. In contrast Creeley's wry method in "I Know a Man" is to break down. Ambiguity is created because the poem's foreshortened lines frustrate the reader's syntactical expectations. A mechanical substitution is offered for an intellectual problem. The lines are so short they cannot function as run-on lines, only as syntactical interruptions. The reader teeters between the end of one line and the beginning of another with the vague feeling that things are ambiguous, ironical, or paradoxical because the units of language to which he is accustomed have been interrupted. Rather than irony, paradox, and ambiguity existing as a nexus of meaning, one is given the *impression* of these elements. Being a physical disruption rather than an intellectual complication, the trick is similar to the surprise generated by the home movie that is reversed just after a child dives into a swimming pool.

Creeley's excessive line breaks leave the reader struggling to get through the poem. Line breaks separate subjects from their verbs, interrupt phrases, and split individual words into lesser parts. The reader's pace is slowed to such a extent that what would be recognized as a commonplace when confronted at ordinary mental speed sounds oracular at this halting pace. Robert Creeley speaks with as much facility as anyone — when he is not reading a poem. Give him a poem, however, one of his poems, and he stammers as though so fraught with emotion he can barely get the words over his lower teeth. Someone only casually familiar with poetry may think he has heard a great primal truth pulled from so deep within that the poet is barely capable of utterance. Actually he has heard an affectation made possible by foreshortened lines.

Here is another poem by Creeley, "Quick-Step":

> More gaily, dance
> with such ladies make
> a circumstance of dancing.
>
> Let them lead
> around and around, all
> awkwardness apart.
>
> There is
> an easy grace gained
> from falling forward
>
> in time, in
> simple time to
> all their graces.

This poem might well never have been written had William

Carlos Williams not already written "The Dance," particularly the phrase "they go round and / around." There are some nice moments in "Quick-Step," though it is at best a wistful lyric. It creates the clear impression, however, of being much more than wistful. As an individual's exaggeration in dress and movement will hold our attention and suspend our ordinary goings-about-our-business, the truncated lines in this poem work against the forward pressure of what the poem says as it moves at an exaggeratedly halting pace. We are briefly arrested, slowed, and charmed more by the slowing than by what we are told. A major element in Creeley's method is to call greater attention to what is visual in the poem than we would normally grant it. Stumbling over line-break after line-break, you tend only to picture things that have been named because so little is being said about them. In "Quick-Step" the act of dancing seems more vivid because so little else is there to compete with it, not even the momentum of the poem's own language.

Here is the same poem put into conventional lines:

> More gaily, dance with such ladies
> make a circumstance of dancing.
> Let them lead around and around,
> all awkwardness apart.
> There is an easy grace gained
> from falling forward in time,
> in simple time to all their graces

Given breadth, the language in "Quick-Step" demonstrates the same accented-unaccented alternation that has been with us since "Beowulf." Yet Creeley's use of foreshortened lines means that he was not seeking this sort of rhythm when he wrote the poem. The lines Creeley settled upon are too short for rhythm to work. But it exists in the language, whether the poet hears it or not.

Though greater momentum is generated by the use of conventional line lengths in "Quick-Step," the poem still produces a very ordinary event. Nothing can be done about what Creeley's enjambed method of composition did to the poem's content, particularly its overreliance upon that which is visual. There is a question as to how one should read the poem at the end of the first line because punctuation is needed there. (Creeley would say the point is that punctuation should not be there. He is interrupting our syntactical expectations with the absence of punctuation as well as with line-breaks.) Generally, however, the reader can move through the regularized version of the poem at a speed close to that at which we normally think. Doing so demonstrates the poem's essential slightness, in content as well as form.

Written with the oracular effect that excessive enjambment creates as an organizing principle, "Quick-Step" presents us with a characteristic trick in the first line; "such ladies" pretends to a specificity that does not exist. In addition the final word in the poem, "graces," is made to carry more significance than it can bear. The preceding words "awkwardness," "grace," and "falling" do not create a context for the ladies' "graces" to close the poem with anything definite enough to be meaningful. One is reminded of a vague, unrealistic, and high-handed male attitude that recent feminists have been so quick to identify. Creeley's poem is an unfocused wish directed toward an indefinite object. It is sentimental.

Creeley's use of enjambment disguises much that is objectionable in the poem because his line-breaks disturb the reader with a serious problem—the reliability of language to provide both a rational and truthful approximation of what is real. Initially you may not feel that Creeley's poem is simplistic because Creeley has skewed his writing so that the *way* he says things becomes the object of contention rather than *what* he says. Often the way a poem says what it means is nearly as important as what it does say, but in such situations the manner of statement, or suggestion, does not take the place of meaning. Creeley's willingness to expose himself to linguistic chance in his poetry is a source not of strength but of weakness. Too often what his truncated lines create is an unjustified multiplication of a passing wistful thought, an oracular leap from the commonplace to the commonplace squared. He is a master of the emaciated poem.

II

Amidst many variations there are two distinguishing marks in poetry written since the late fifties: Assumed primitivism in style and content, and an overreliance on the image that results in abandoning poetry as an auditory art. Much of the attraction these characteristics hold for poets stems from their desire to ferret meanings from what they consider to be their unconscious. . The influence of psychology has led us to a new sort of allegory (though there are other instances of the allegorical impulse, science fiction and children's literature for example). Poems now bridge the gap between the conscious and unconscious mind rather than that between a physical and metaphysical world. The world of dreams is generally a silent one, thus the exclusion of auditory concerns in poetry; it is primitive, and it is usually experienced visually— thus the excessive reliance upon imagery.

W. H. Auden's lines from "In Praise of Limestone" provide an appropriate comment here: "The poet, / Admired for his earnest habit of calling / The sun the sun, his mind Puzzle."

Auden is acknowledging the openness and capacity for wonder that are essential if one is to write poetry, whether the poet is open to reason, belief, the unconscious, or all of these. He is not urging ignorance as the basis for authenticity, however. The worst result of the poetic shift being considered has been the shamanism of poets like Allen Ginsberg, Robert Bly, and (too often) Robert Creeley. The best result of this shift has been the adjustments made by poets like Auden, who have stood ready on the one hand to exploit conventional poetic modes and ready on the other hand to accept the mind as "Puzzle" and to regard experience from a position outside accepted categories of thought, causality for example. Along with a number of others, Anthony Hecht, Howard Nemerov, and Richard Wilbur have been quite successful at practicing this kind of poetry.

Yvor Winters faulted Allen Tate for an excessive use of enjambment. Though he had accurately identified a departure from end-stopped lines that was soon to be taken to an extreme, Winters was too scrupulous where Tate was concerned. As with Robert Lowell's early work, Tate's poetry grew out of a sustained rhetoric that overran the boundaries of end-stopped lines as a natural result of its own momentum. The headlong pace of such rhetoric compounded meaning almost as quickly as a cluster of images might, though with one important difference. Where an image conveys a nexus of meaning immediately, as with Pound's "black bough" or Williams's "red wheel/barrow," the use of rhetoric in a poem requires time as meaning is built synthetically from moment to moment.

Rather than seeing the truth as though it were projected on a screen, the way Milton's angels were supposed to have done, Tate, Lowell, and others generated meaning out of the ongoingness of their own language. In part we have a distinction between poetry that generates meaning synchronically, with imagery, and poetry that operates diachronically, with rhetoric. The latter uses images also, but they are only part of the recipe. The rest of the formula includes statements, questions, all sorts of syntactical units. It also exploits the rhythms inherent in our language in a way that is discussed most successfully with the aid of phonetics.

Another element in the synthetic poetry of Tate and Lowell should be mentioned. The emotional thrust of the headlong pace of such poetry contributes greatly to the way that it affects the reader. As Winters knew, the rhythm in a poem reinforces meaning on an emotional level. What Winters saw toward the end of his life, however, was the growth of a poetry devoid of rhythm. Thin, usually very brief poems populating the pages of various periodicals ignored the rhythmical possibilities in language, relying instead upon imagery. Their lines were too short for effective movement to be established, the voice having no chance to gain momentum. What these lines did establish was the dominance of enjambment. End-stopped lines were the norm that gave significance to the reservation Winters made about Tate's and, indirectly, Lowell's use of enjambment, as they have been an essential part of poetry for centuries. But with the general turn made by poets to foreshortened lines enjambment was taken to such an extreme that its use was no longer significant. The rhythm to which it contributed could no longer be heard.

The momentum of language enables a poem's ending to stand on the ground of immediate conviction. The systematic disruption of that momentum by line-breaks, however, can leave a poem standing on the ground of immediate doubt. For us doubt is a familiar condition. But is the disruption of language that occurs in the poems discussed here a significant expression of doubt, or is it simply the incongruent exertion of an individual will? Showing that there are gaps in language is meaningful only if one's over-all purpose is to close them in some way. Language is self-sealing, and to a remarkable degree naming gaps seems to close them. In contrast the excessive use of enjambment makes you feel there are empty spaces in language, but that feeling names nothing, discloses nothing. It is the result of contrivance rather than an honest attempt to articulate a linguistic short-fall and correct it.

Irony, paradox, and ambiguity are intellectual answers to various linguistic shortfalls. They do not provide a complete solution to the problem of meaning, but they contribute to one. And they do so, finally, in an additive manner. As modes of thought they depend upon the extensiveness of meaning contained in language. The overuse of enjambed foreshortened lines for syntactical disruption is a physical response not grounded in the extensiveness of meaning but dependent upon the reader's expectations and the writer's will, the momentary surprise created by that will. Both methods are skeptical responses to experience. But the Brooksian formula proceeds additively on the assumption that language works, that it grasps what is really before us. The second formula proceeds subalternately on the assumption that reasoned language is arbitrary and inauthentic.

Here is a poem by A.R. Ammons, "Loss":

> When the sun
> falls behind the sumac
> thicket the
> wild
> yellow daisies
> in diffuse evening shade

> lose their
> rigorous attention
> and
> half-wild with loss
> turn
> any way the wind does
> and lift their
> petals up
> to float
> off their stems
> and go

Though it is quite different from the poetry of Eliot, Tate, and early Lowell, the method used in this poem is not new. On the one hand we are provided an example of the pathetic fallacy, a phrase invented by Ruskin; on the other hand "Loss" is reminiscent of what the Imagists were doing more than sixty years ago, and in some ways the Decadents before that. In a Paterian mood Lionel Johnson would say what he said when defining English decadence in *The Century Guild Hobby Horse* — that Ammons is trying "to catch the precise aspect of a thing, as you see or feel it." The most striking characteristic in Ammons's poetry is that he restricts himself to literal imagery almost all the way through a poem, reserving only one or two moments when he breaks out into figurative imagery. His previous restraint makes this shift all the more effective, though his reliance upon this method is one reason his poems are not successful when read aloud. In fact the shift from literal imagery to figurative imagery is a mode of thought that seems suited to painting, and Ammons has turned to painting in recent years. Poetry's affinity with painting is a matter of long standing. If we look no farther than the pre-Raphaelites, "Loss" reminds us of Dante Gabriel Rossetti's "The Woodspurge." In other ways, however, it is much closer to an imagist poem, particularly in avoiding conventional rhythms through using foreshortened enjambed lines.

As in Creeley's poems, the fragmentation of normal syntactical units in "Loss" gives priority to the poem's imagery. Greater amounts of time are created for smaller units of language as the reader is encouraged to meet experience visually with hierarchies, categories, or presuppositions set aside. "Loss" is primarily an artistic exercise in nominalism. Forcing us to focus on the particulars of nature more than on its patterns, the approach Ammons uses is skeptical, particularly because of its minimal expectations. As part of this skeptical or minimal point of view sentimentality creeps in, "daisies . . . half-wild with loss." In fact not much is being lost here. Though in part we are provided a play on the daisies' wildness mentioned earlier in the poem, the emotion of this statement outstrips its meaning.

Rather than finding a matrix for meaning in an image, "Loss" dramatizes the incoherence that will always result when we fix upon a thing subject to process. In this circumstance Ammons has dramatized a few moments in an isolated consciousness that happens to be looking at daisies. The poem generates a self-fulfilling prophecy for that consciouness: it uses imagery to give permanence within its own boundaries to daisies that, we are told, are nevertheless subject to time. A sense of loss is inevitable if not trustworthy.

Eliot's contention that the use of myth can make modern experience intelligible is based on assumptions about permanence similar to those made by Ammons and others where imagery is concerned. In both cases a spatial priority is established for what is being said, but with an important difference. We should not confuse the synchronic impulse to freeze predicaments spatially by using an image with a nevertheless similar tendency that occurs in the use of myth. Freezing a temporal predicament through the use of myth is a different matter because myths are stories and thus have duration: they carry histories. Images are often extensive, parts in networks of meaning, but characteristically their significance is not born of the past or of a supposed past. When an allusion is made to a myth, the reader familiar with that myth suddenly recalls a chain of events: time is gathered. When an image is used, relations rather than events are invoked. The projection of a temporal predicament into an atemporal image, which is the method Ammons and many others use, voids the problem of time rather than addressing it. The reader is offered a mechanical solution for an intellectual problem that is basic to our process-minded era. In "Loss" the disruption of our syntactical expectations through enjambment and the overreliance upon imagery operates on the basis of the same trick in timing that one finds in Creeley's "I Know a Man" and "Quick-Step." These poems are written to be read much the way Burma Shave signs were placed to greet travelers along the highway.

A wide range of excellent poetry has been written over the last thirty years, some of the best of it in free verse. In the restrictiveness of its short lines, however, the emaciated poem is not free but rigid. The lines are not long enough for rhythm to be established. I suspect that Creeley and Ammons would say that their thin poems are honest and authentic and that Eliot, Tate, and company wrote poetry that was self-consciously learned and bulky, thus posed and inauthentic. The question of authenticity, however, is predicated upon doubt, the same uncertainty about oneself and the world one inhabits that caused Robert Lowell's poetic shift. Though the most influential recent episode

has been the existentialists' alertness to the absurd, there is
nothing new about doubt in our thought. Using the cogito,
we have turned our predicament into our method: uncertainty has become our most reliable means for certainty as
we have learned to rely upon the self-sealing character of
language, which by allowing us to name a problem allows us
in some way to move beyond that problem. Since we begin with
uncertainty rather than belief, we must emphasize existence
rather than essence. Because of the self's precarious position,
as an entity standing in a world of process which dissolves
entities, misshapen exertions of the will are inevitable, the most
common of these being a very old and familiar exertion —
sentimentality.

III

Writing an emaciated poem is not the only way to slow a reader
and emphasize images. Reversing the rhythm in a line or plac-
ing a caesura in a line or both — these are common ways to
achieve the same effect and to do so without creating an interrupted surface that distracts the reader from what is being said.
Here is the first stanza of "Painting a Mountain Stream" by
Howard Nemerov:

> Running and standing still at once
> is the whole truth. Raveled or combed,
> wrinkled or clear, it gets its force
> from losing force. Going it stays.

Opening with the bold statement of a paradox, rather than a
vague feeling of contradiction created by truncated lines, this
is an ambitious poem. It entails the mutual dependence of
apparent opposites. We think of a stream as nominal; thus we

try to paint it. The real nature of that stream, however, is its ongoingness, which defies being fixed in a painting within a frame. Nemerov's answer to the intellectual problem of forcing something that is diachronic into synchronic terms in order to understand it is to say "paint this rhythm, not this thing." In other words the narrow thingness of Dr. Williams's red wheelbarrow is quickly exhausted, and we must move up to a level of abstraction — namely to the process within which wheelbarrows, boughs, daisies, and streams exist, in order to understand what we see. Having made such a move, we are capable of making more satisfactory statements. Having made a statement, Nemerov succeeds where Ammons fails. As a quiet part of what he is telling us, Nemerov sets up metrical reversals: they appear throughout the second line, in the first half of the third line, and in the second half of the fourth line. Anyone who wishes can break this poem into truncated lines, but doing so is unnecessary and would be cumbersome. Nemerov has already satisfied his poem's need for reversals, and has done so in a way that directs you to the meaning he intends rather than distracting you with syntactical interruptions.

For those intent on other ways of creating pauses here is an even quieter use of the caesura, taken from Nemerov's "The Blue Swallows":

> Across the millstream below the bridge
> Seven blue swallows divide the air
> In shapes invisible and evanescent,
> Kaleidoscopic beyond the mind's
> Or memory's power to keep them there.

The first, second, and fourth lines have an extra unstressed syllable each, placed after the second foot as a vestigial caesura.

An interruption or slowing occurs, but its force does not exceed the surprise created by what is being said. Line-breaks substituted for Nemerov's caesuras not only would sacrifice the convincingness created by the poem's rhythm: being heavy-handed, they would be the first step toward sentimentality, the emotional force given the statement exceeding the significance of that statement. "The Blue Swallows" ends with a Kantian answer to the sort of position Pater took in the "Conclusion" to *The Renaissance* — that nothing external to the mind has any meaning other than what is provided it by the mind, because meaning is completely subjective, even imprisoning. Rather than making experience the object of his poetry, as Creeley and Ammons do in a way resembling Pater and the Decadents, Nemerov has relation as his object. Acknowledging external patterns (and their vast multiplicity) as well as internal ones, Nemerov is concerned finally with appropriateness — the appropriate relation between mind and thing, or things. Consistent with this concern, his poem demonstrates an appropriate balance between perception and articulation.

With the exception of Lowell and Roethke the most talented (if not as a group the most influential) poets writing since World War II have continued to write poetry that takes advantage of traditional modes, a poetry that is successful auditorially as well as visually. Consider Louise Bogan, Edgar Bowers, J.V. Cunningham, Anthony Hecht, John Hollander, A.D. Hope, Elizabeth Jennings, Donald Justice, Maxine Kumin, James Merrill, Howard Nemerov, Robert Pack, Mona Van Duyn, Derek Walcott, Margaret Walker, Richard Wilbur, Reed Whittemore, and Judith Wright. Rather than using one poetic technique to the exclusion of others, these poets have been quick to exploit a wide range of tools traditionally available to poetry — rhyme, assonance, consonance, rhythm regular enough to function as rhythm, lines long enough to allow that rhythm to work, images, even symbols. In addition, these poets have been likely to be interested more in ideas about relations than in the "precise aspect" or nominalistic detail of an isolated experience.

There are variations on the shift in poetry I have described. Some poets write lines not shortened but elongated to the point that one seems to be reading prose — for example Whitman's windy descendant Allen Ginsberg. The existence of "poetic prose" is one truism among many that have been used to break down the altogether real distinction between poetry and prose. The prose poem, the one-word poem (which is four words), the concrete poem, and the emaciated poem have all resulted from half-truths. Though most often the image has been the basis, first one then another characteristic of poetry has been taken, to the exclusion of the rest of what constitutes poetry, and expanded to make a poetics. Because the method is easy to use, its results are easy to find.

Linked with the role the image plays in these variations is a question of talent that partly originates in the influence painting has had on the poetry of this century. In its silence and spatial fixity painting is vastly different from poetry, which is auditory and, like music, exists first in time. Seeking a quantity of output that reminds one of manufacturing, many poets writing emaciated poems are geared to the visual in poetry because the image is easy to use, as a visit to the typical workshop will demonstrate. At the same time poets writing overly thin poems have failed to employ some of the most effective poetic tools the language provides. And their poetry has suffered accordingly. Everyone recognizes the limitations of a painter who is color-blind. What about a poet who is tone-deaf or who lacks a sense of rhythm? For too many poets publishing today, creating the kind of poetry that Nemerov, Wilbur, and the others have written is not a realistic possibility. These poets will argue that what they are doing is the authentic thing to do. For those who have no choice, of course it is.

Special acknowledgment: "I Know a Man" and "Quick-Step" from *The Collected Poems of Robert Creeley 1945–1975* are reproduced by permission of the publisher, the University of California Press. Copyright 1962, 1967 by Robert Creeley; copyright 1982 by the Regents of the University of California.

"Loss" is reprinted from *The Collected Poems: 1951–1971*, by A. R. Ammons, by permission of W.W. Norton & Company, Inc. Copyright © 1977, 1975, 1974, 1972, 1971, 1970, 1966, 1965, 1964, 1955 by A. R. Ammons.

WHAT'S NEW ABOUT THE
NEW FORMALISM?

Robert McPhillips

The reflorescence of formal poetry in the United States in the 1980s has caught the comfortably-tenured corps of the "free verse revolution" by surprise. Predictably, many of these middle-aged poet professors have launched blanket attacks on this diverse new movement, attempting to reduce it to something at best trivial, at worst downright dangerous. Such critical assaults have labeled these new formal poems as the products of "yuppie" poets for whom a poem is mere artifice, something to be valued as a material object; or, more perniciously, as the product of a neo-conservative *Zeitgeist*. There is, they further claim, nothing "new" about these poems at all. Rather than being perceived as innovative, these new formal poems of the 80s are dismissed as derivative, as retreats to the allegedly stale and stodgily "academic" formal poetry of the 50s against whose strictures the Beat, Confessional and Deep Image poets emerged. Such claims are simply untrue.

While there were many anthologies that showcased the formalist poets of the 50s, the most influential in establishing the identity of the movement was *New Poets of England and America* (1957), edited by Donald Hall, Robert Pack and Louis Simpson, and given its imprimatur by Robert Frost's introduction. It was this volume that first collected the group one now

First published in *Crosscurrents*, A Quarterly, Vol. 8, No. 2, 1988. Copyright © by Robert McPhillips. Reprinted with permission of the author and publisher.

identifies as the 50s formalist poets, a group that includes Edgar
Bowers, Anthony Hecht, John Hollander, Donald Justice,
Robert Lowell, William Meredith, James Merrill, Howard Moss,
Howard Nemerov, Adrienne Rich, Louis Simpson, William Jay
Smith, W. D. Snodgrass and Richard Wilbur. When one contem-
plates the American poets gathered in this seminal anthology,
a certain composite poem emerges that defines their shared
aesthetic assumptions. This collective poem is characteristically
ironic, emphasizing the poet's distance from his subject. Quite
frequently, it focuses upon a cultural artifact, usually a European one. Similarly, it routinely abounds in classical allusions
and sometimes boasts a foreign-language title reflecting a cultural
pedigree often backed up by an ornately baroque diction. It rarely
displays strong emotions directly, even—indeed, most
conspicuously—if it is a love poem. In short, the 50s formal
poem is elegant and learned and makes little attempt to communicate with readers who are otherwise.

The most ostentatiously academic of the 50s formalists is John
Hollander, a poet whose artistic development has been crippled
by his abundant intellect. In his early poems printed in *New
Poets*, one witnesses his penchant for the elitism of high culture.
Two of the four poems representing Hollander's early work contain titles in French and Latin: *"Paysage Moralisè"* and *"Horas
Tempestatis Quoque Enumero*: The Sundial." The former places
the mythical figures of Daphnis and Chloe in its "moralized
landscape," Chloe's resistance to Daphnis's erotic advances
yielding the poem's concluding epigrammatic moral:

> Under a soupy tree
> Mopes Daphnis, joined by all
> The brown surrounding landscape:

> Even in Arcady
> Ego needs must spoil
> Such a beautiful friendship.

Hollander's use here of myth and the abstract, the pseudo-Freudian lingo, ironically juxtaposed to cliché, distances the poet from the potentially personal subject of erotic frustration, unrequited love.

"Horas Tempestatis Quoque Enumero: The Sundial" is a perfect example of the 50s formal poem that uses elevated diction to leisurely and elaborately describe an art object, in this case a sundial with a Latin inscription. Hollander's refusal to provide a translation of this inscription in his title (which could be rendered "I Too Reckon Up the Hours of the Season") suggests both the assumptions he makes about his audience and the heightened approach he will take to his subject. His description of a rainstorm in the third of the poem's long, baroquely elegant stanzas serves as a particularly extreme example of Hollander's ornate rhetoric:

> The sundial and birdbath (which is which now?) run
> Over into the lawn, and bubbling puddles
> Drop down the steps. Neglected, by a wall,
> Two marble *putti* weep as they are bathed,
> Still leering through the rusty stains about
> Their mouths. The ruin and the summerhouse
> Are empty, but through the trumpeting downpour,
>   somewhere,
> Inside the long windows, Leopoldine is playing
> Her *Gradus ad Parnassum*, while nearby
> A Chinese philosopher on a silk screen shrinks
> From the thunder he has always held to be
> The ultimate disorder, as the wind
> Wrinkles a painted heron on the bank
>   Barely suggested behind him.

While one responds to the lushness of Hollander's language and the effortless music of some of the lines, one is put off by the aloof description, as if objects existed merely to be translated into, well "poetry." Only in the second half of this stanza, almost halfway through the poem, does one sense a human drama being introduced, albeit obliquely, and only then at the seeming excuse to write elegantly. The mellifluously named Leopoldine, struggling at her piano exercises, remains part of Hollander's flowing catalogue of cultural artifacts, as if there was no distinction between her and her *Gradus ad Parnassum*, or the silk screen of the Chinese philosopher behind her. The human significance of this scene is postponed until the poem's final two stanzas set at some point in the future. But this drama comes so late, and is itself so obscure, that it fails to redeem one's suspicion that, for all his technical skill, much of Hollander's writing is elegant but empty.

From the beginning, Anthony Hecht has shown an awareness of the tragic nature of human life. "The Vow," the first of his poems in the *New Poets* volume, is a powerful presentation of a father's vow to a miscarried fetus to love the children he and his wife have in the future all the more because of this loss. Nevertheless, Hecht began as, and continues to be, a highly *literary* poet. From the onset, one of Hecht's primary concerns has been to display how urbane, how highly cultured American literature has become since the days of Eliot and James.

This theme is central to Hecht's often-anthologized "La Condition Botanique." Once again the title of a major poem by a 50s academic formalist is in French. The poem is a lengthy, ornate, but brilliantly sustained description of the Brooklyn Botanical Garden. Yet, like Hollander, Hecht is leisurely and indirect in his approach to his true subject. By way of introduction, Hecht digresses, describing European landscapes before finally, in his third stanza, proceeding with his description of the garden. Hecht's intention here is to claim for American culture a site of aesthetic refuge analogous to the Ischian health spa he describes in his first stanza. But Hecht's heightened poetic diction emphasizes that his poem is meant to be itself such a cultural oasis. One sees this immediately in the diction and baroque form of Hecht's opening stanza:

> Romans, rheumatic, gouty, came
>   To bathe in Ischian springs where water steamed,
> Puffed and enlarged their bold imperial thoughts,
>   and which
> Later Madame Curie declared to be so rich
>   In radioactive content as she deemed
>   Should win them everlasting fame.

One is most immediately impressed here by Hecht's heavy consonance ("Romans, rheumatic, gouty, came" reads almost like Hopkins) and smooth assonance, the ease with which he manipulates a complex verse form and set rhyme scheme, and the range of the stanza's cultural references. The language is lush and the allusions sophisticated. But one can't imagine a person speaking these lines or singing them. "La Condition Botanique" is a literary *tour de force*, an elegant verbal construct that recreates, with Biblical, classical and literary allusions—the poem merits no fewer than sixteen footnotes in *The Norton Anthology of Modern Poetry*— a landscape of aesthetic perfection far removed from the ordinary world, from the Brooklyn outside the haven of the botanical garden.

Even Richard Wilbur, one of our finest living poets, is drawn to indirection, exotic words and cultural elitism. Hence his poem on crickets is not entitled "Crickets" or "Cicadas" but "Cigales."

And he cannot resist writing "A Baroque Wall-Fountain in the Villa Sciara," a poem whose title tells its story. These poems are hardly without their virtues. But it is worth noting that they are the virtues of a genteel cultural elite, their breeding ground the English Departments of the 50s with their Fulbright overseas scholarships and their zealous approbation of wit, irony and complexity, the legacy of the New Critics.

These are not the values and virtues of the 80s formalist poets who are as likely to be found in the business world as they are in the university, and whose inspiration derives not from the academy but from the quotidian world and the desire to write about emotion directly and memorably. As yet, there is no anthology similar to that of *New Poets of England and America* to give the New Formalists a representative group identity. Still, a survey of dozens of volumes of poetry published in the last decade or so by younger poets experimenting with traditional forms does allow for significant generalizations.

Characteristically, the diction of the New Formalist poem is colloquial rather than elevated. If the poem concerns cultural objects, they are likely to be from popular culture and to be indiginously American. This is not to say that they aspire to the flat, affectless realism of the practitioners — Frederick Barthelme, Ann Beattie, the late Raymond Carver, et al. — of minimalist fiction. In general, the New Formalists differ from the academic formalists in the ease with which they accept their own cultural tradition as firmly established — for which, of course, they are indebted to their more self-consciously cultural formalist predecessors. Hence, in the poems of such numerous and widely diverse poets as Dick Allen, Tom Disch, Frederick Feirstein, Dana Gioia, Emily Grosholz, Rachel Hadas, Paul Lake, Brad Leithauser, Charles Martin, Molly Peacock, Robert Phillips,

Mary Jo Salter, Gjertrud Schnackenberg, Robert Shaw, Timothy Steele and Henry Taylor, we find a variety of subjects quite distinct from those of the poems in *New Poets of England and America*. These subjects range from a Joycean account of a day in the life of an ordinary New Yorker to encounters with flying saucers, from the jazz musician Bix Beiderbecke to the twentieth-century saint Simone Weil, from masturbation to marriage, from the streets of Brooklyn and Buffalo to the farms of rural Virginia and the parched hills of California, from the fiction of Chandler and Cheever to the films of Bertolucci and Godard. There are also a more significant number of women poets in the 80s writing formal poems directly addressing distinctly female experience—sexuality, abortion, child-rearing—than was true of the 50s when the notable exception was Adrienne Rich, ironically one of the few poets from that group to make a fully successful shift from formal to free verse.

   If the lives and the culture that these poems derive from are less elevated than their 50s counterparts, rooted unself-consciously in the middle class rather than in a real or aspired to aristocracy, these are hardly brand-name poems in the way that Frederick Barthelme and Bret Easton Ellis's stories and novels are, reducing the quality of human life to the surface level of the detritus of the shopping malls and fast food chains, the chic nightclubs and MTV, that have become the tacky furniture of much of our contemporary existence. When Dana Gioia invokes an unnamed Beach Boys song in his autobiographical lyric "Cruising with the Beach Boys," the occasion of the poet's hearing a song on the radio while on a business trip in an unfamiliar landscape prompts him to reflect on his late adolescence in Southern California and to reexperience the sense of vulnerability and self-pity he thought he had outgrown.

One cannot imagine Hecht, Hollander or Wilbur ever daring to face such direct and potentially sentimental emotion in their poems.

Timothy Steele seems the most closely derivative from the academic formalists. Tellingly, however, it is less from the overly-baroque and erudite elements in that poetry than from the more modest, benignly pastoral side of Wilbur that he springs. In his most recent volume, *Sapphics Against Anger* (1986), Steele is not below naming a meditative poem "Chanson Philosophique" or writing on Biblical or historical subjects, as in "In the King's Rooms" and "1816." But neither is he above celebrating the ethnic vitality of the streets of Los Angeles ("Near Olympic") nor the exuberance of rollar skaters at a California beach ("At Will Rogers Beach").

In "Timothy," Steele translates a kind of grass bearing his name into an emblem of himself, uniquely personalizing a poem of pastoral description. "Timothy," strongly reminiscent of two early Frost poems, "Mowing" and "The Tuft of Flowers," describes the harvesting of the grass for hay with the poet-harvester modestly taking "pleasure in the thought / The fresh hay's name was mine as well." The "soothing, rhythmic ache" of cutting the grass with a scythe becomes analogous to the poet's own labor at writing a poem, an idea elaborated on in the poem's final two quatrains:

> Pumping a handpump's iron arm,
> I washed myself as best I could,
> Then watched the acres of the farm
> Draw lengthening shadows from the wood
> Across the grass, which seemed a thing
> In which the lonely and concealed

> Had risen from its sorrowing
> And flourished in the open field.

There is little of the strain here of a metaphysical conceit, or the ornateness of diction or heaviness of wit characteristic of so much 50s formalism. Steele's strict adherence to metrics and rhyme (he is as much derived from Yvor Winters as from Wilbur) distinguishes his verse from most of his contemporaries; yet the simplicity of his language and the easy musical flow of his lines detracts attention from the artifice of his rhyme pattern. Steele, as craftsman, "washe[s]" himself after the "sorrowing" of his labor, leaving the reader with an effortless poem that gracefully reveals what was previously "lonely and concealed" "in the open field" of his paradoxically metrically closed poem. Steele has, then, written a decidedly literary poem, recalling a tradition from Marvell to Wordsworth to Frost and Wilbur, without being in the least academic.

Charles Martin is a more eclectic poet. The poems from his two books, *Room for Error* (1978) and *Steal the Bacon* (1987), are set in Brooklyn, Buffalo and Vermont, and his subjects encompass everything from graffiti to Latin American politics to Dracula, from *Robinson Crusoe* to flying saucers. Martin's Brooklyn poems — "Sharks at the New York Aquarium" and "Poem in Brooklyn," for example — differ radically from Hecht's "La Condition Botanique." The former, a sonnet, focuses on the aquarium at Coney Island with an economy of words rarely encountered in Hecht. Similarly, it is not told from the perspective of a cultured aesthete but from that of a speaker possessed of childlike wonder confronted with the spectacle of the "simple lives" of the nonetheless exotic fish. Yet Martin's persona remains firmly rooted in the real world of Brooklyn, where he finds himself, at the poem's conclusion, "again, outside the tank, / Uneasily wrapped in our atmosphere!," one in which "Children almost never tap on the glass."

But this sense of childlike wonder yields almost to one of religious yearning in "Taken Up," the final poem in Martin's unduly neglected first volume. This poem postulates a group of people "Tired of earth" who long for some means of transcendence. They find this in the form of a flying saucer, a "disc descended, / That glowing wheel of lights whose coming ended / All waiting and watching...." In the poem's — and the volume's — final stanzas of rhymed tercets, Martin freshly presents an image of the desire to seek an entirely new culture, a desire for the possible transformations of the future rather than a nostalgic yearning for the classical European cultural past. The people gathered on a hill to greet the saucer respond thus to the aliens on board:

> Light was their speech, spanning mind to mind:
> *We came here not believing what we find —*
> *Can it be your desire to leave behind*
>
> *The earth, which even these angels bless,*
> *Exchanging amplitude for emptiness?*
> And in a single voice they answered *Yes,*
>
> Discord of human melodies all bent
> To the unearthly strain of their assent.
> *Come then,* the Strangers said, and those who were
>   taken went.

Having paid tribute, earlier in this volume, to the Latin poet Calvus, as well as to Melville, Dante, Robert Duncan, Milton Avery, Theodore Roethke and Godard, Martin here seemingly tips his hat to Steven Spielberg. But what is more notable is

Martin's unusual ability to write in clear, unadorned langauge, making each of his subjects memorable through his graceful, unobtrusive use of rhyme. In "Taken Up," Martin extends the range of contemporary poetry to include the resources of science fiction, as have Dick Allen and Frederick Turner. He does so in such a quiet yet skillful manner, mingling awe and muted humor — reminiscent, perhaps, in an odd way of some of Emily Dickinson's oblique and irreverently theological meditations on death — as to transform it into a distinctly contemporary form of religious verse.

Dana Gioia's first collection of poetry, *Daily Horoscope* (1986), could, in itself, constitute the central document establishing the most pertinent distinctions between the 50s and the New Formalists of the 80s. Gioia has perfected a quiet, colloquial, genuinely human voice in his personal lyrics that is alien to the irony of the academic formalists and the frequent hysteria of the Confessional poets.

This intimate voice underlies Gioia's elegiac and decorously poised love poems as well as his numerous poems which eschew the personal, poems that range in subject matter from jazz to pornography, from the lives of the great composers to that of businessmen after work. The landscapes vary widely — and are quite distinct from the landscapes of the earlier formalist poets: Southern California, Westchester County, the expansive parking lot of a suburban corporation. They extend as well, in Steven's phrase, to "an Italy of the mind" rather than of the guidebooks, not to that symbol of the pinnacle of European culture but the the impoverished country from which the poet's family emigrated to the United States.

Some of Gioia's best poems remain uncollected. In "Equations of the Light," published in *The New Yorker* in 1986, seven blank

verse quatrains recreate the unexpected excitement and tran-
sience of a love affair. In this lyric notable for its intricate narrative structure, the poet contrasts the quotidian demands of
life with the brief luminous moments afforded by an unexpected
encounter:

> Turning the corner, we discovered it
> just as the old wrought-iron lamps went on —
> a quiet, tree-lined street, only one block long,
> resting between the noisy avenues.
>
> The street lamps splashed the shadow of the leaves
> across the whitewashed brick, and each tall window,
> glowing through the ivy-decked façade,
> promised lives as perfect as the light.

These lines are as elegant as any by Hecht or Wilbur, but their
elegance doesn't rely on elevated diction, literary allusions, or
an exotic setting. Instead, the poem achieves its effect upon the
reader through its reenactment of the poet and his companion's
experience of encountering this idyllic street with its promise
of perfection wholly unawares. Likewise, it conveys the physical
beauty of that street captured at just that magical moment which
"lingered like a ghost," transforming it into the ideal objective
correlative for this evanescently passionate meeting.

  But to say that Gioia's language is plain is not to say that
the emotion he evokes is simple. After feeling so at home in
this discovered environment that the poet feels "we could have
opened any door / entered any room the evening offered," he
goes on to question such certainty:

> Or were we so deluded by the strange
> equations of the light, the vagrant wind
> searching the trees, we believed this brief
> conjunction of our separate lives was real?

Whereas a poet like John Ashbery might push such a question
so far as to disintegrate whatever image of epiphanic beauty his
poem seemed to be building toward, or a Hollander use it to
distance himself ironically from speaking directly about love,
Gioia makes such a question an integral part of what constitutes
both the beauty and fragility of love.

In these brief remarks I have tried to examine, in broad terms,
what is *new* about the poems of the New Formalists by examining the differences between the formalists who emerged after
the Second World War and those who, in the late 70s and early
80s, have tried to regain for poetry some of the ground lost to
it — not merely rhyme and meter, but more importantly a sense
of common human experience as opposed to solipsistically
unique "experiences"— by the free verse poets who understand-
ably rebelled against what they perceived to be the overly
academic, ironic, refined formal poems of the 50s.

Attention to form has allowed a significant number of younger
poets to think and communicate clearly about their sense of
what is of most human value — love, beauty, mortality. They
address themselves primarily neither to the academy nor to other
poets. Instead, they seem interested in reestablishing an audience
of common readers, transcending sexual or ideological alle-
giances, tapping into a potential openness to the verities and
music available exclusively in the aesthetic realm of poetry. The
New Formalists speak clearly and eloquently about our shared
human experience. But at their best they do more. In the words
of Dana Gioia, they remind us that even in the course of

everyday life there come rare moments of luminosity when:

> . . . only briefly then,
> You touch, you see, you press against
> The surface of impenetrable things.

THE NEURAL LYRE:
POETIC METER, THE BRAIN, AND TIME

⚜

Frederick Turner and Ernst Pöppel

This essay brings together an old subject, a new body of knowledge, and a new scientific paradigm which have not previously been associated with one another. The subject is poetic meter, a universal human activity, which despite its universality and obvious importance in most human cultures, has received very little attention from humanists, except for the studies of a few literary prosodists, and virtually none at all from science. The new body of knowledge consists in the findings of that intense study of the human brain which has taken place in the last few decades; the new scientific paradigm has been developed by the International Society for the Study of Time. Its major postulates are: that an understanding of time is fundamental to an understanding of the real world; that time is not simple, but composite; that time is a hierarchy of more and more complex temporalities; that the more complex temporalities evolved as part of the general evolution of the universe, and in a sense the evolution of time *constitutes* the evolution of the universe; and that the hierarchical character of time as we know it reflects and embodies the various stages of its evolution.[1]

The radically interdisciplinary nature of this essay is not simply a consequence of the need to seek explanations across the boundaries of different fields. It represents also a commitment and a belief on the part of its authors. We are convinced not only that this type of study will cast light on its specific subject (poetic meter), but also that the scientific material will be reciprocally enhanced in value, taking its place within a framework which gives it greater predictive power; and we further believe that "understanding" itself consists in just such a union of detailed knowledge with global significance.

At this point it might be helpful to review the major characteristics of human cortical information-processing, as it has been provisionally determined by studies in perceptual psychology, brain-chemistry, psychology, brain evolution, brain development, ethology, and cultural anthropology.[2] Individually, the characteristics of human brain-activity which are listed below are commonplace and uncontroversial for the most part; collectively, they constitute a new picture of the human mind. This new picture replaces older, simpler models of it, such as the unextended rational substance of Descartes, the association-matrix of Locke, the *tabula rasa* of Hume, the passive, reinforcement-driven animal of Skinner, and the genetically hard-wired robot of the sociobiologists, though it does include the elements which led those writers to construct their models.

Human information-processing is, on the crude level of individual neurons, *procrustean*. That is, it reduces the information it gets from the outside world to its own categories, and accepts reality's answers only if they directly address its own set of questions. In the macrocosm, our perception of electromagnetic radiation cuts out all but heat and the visible spectrum; in the microcosm, a given neuron in the visual cortex will fire only if certain characteristics — say, a moving vertical light contrast — are met by the retinal image, and will ignore all others. We possess, as it were, a certain domineering and arrogant quality in our dealings with sensory information, and our brain will "listen" only to replies to its own inquiries. In quantum physics the familiar procrustean questions — Waves or particles? Which slit did the photon pass through? Is this ray of light polarized north-south or east-west? — force reality into a certainty and definiteness which it did not naturally possess: and this insistence on unambiguity is rooted in our neurons themselves.

Thus we may say that human information processing is, secondly, *determinative*: that is, it insists on certainty and unambiguity, and is thus at war with the probabilistic and indeterminate nature of the most primitive and archaic components of the universe. This insistence on definiteness, however, is in a grand tradition: matter itself is a condition of energy which severely limits the probabilistic waywardness of its elementary particles; large clumps of organized matter, like crystals, have overcome much of the vagueness and unpredictability of their primary constituents (though they pay for their certainty by becoming liable to entropic decay). Indeed, the replication of living matter could be said to be another stage in the suppression of physical ambiguity, for it implies an exact continuity and stability of structure which survives even the matter of which it is composed. Thus the human neural insistence on determinateness is in line with a general tendency of nature, and is related to the syllogistic proposition that homeostatic systems tend to endure and survive.

Third, and in contrast to the "conservative" tendency we have just described, the human nervous system seems designed to register differences. It is *habituative*. That is, it tends to ignore repeated and expected stimuli, and respond only to the new and unexpected. Though it asks the questions, it is more interested in odd answers than ordinary ones. Temporally it hears changes and sees movements; spatially it sees contrasts and borderlines. Deprived of its saccades, the eye sees nothing, for it sees no differences.

Fourth, human nervous activity is fundamentally *synthetic* in its aim. It seeks gestalts even when they are not there: and there is a serious ontological question as to whether they do in fact come to exist when we find them there.

It is (5) *active* rather than passive: it constructs scenarios to be tested by reality, vigorously seeks confirmation of them, and painfully reconstructs them if they are deconfirmed. The brain is at least as much an organ of action as it is an organ of knowledge.

It is thus (6) *predictive:* the patterns it extrapolates or invents are patterns which involve specific expectations of what will happen next, and in the more distant future, expectations which await satisfaction and are tested by the senses. Dreaming—it would seem from the testimony of Shakespeare, Descartes, Kékulé, and Freud—is the formative stage of pattern-creation: out of dreams come *A Midsummer Night's Dream*, skeptical philosophy, the benzene ring, and a viable ego. So dominant is the human adaptation for predictive calculation that it might be said that the human senses exist as a check on our predictions rather than, as in most other animals, triggers for appropriate behavior.

The whole matter of prediction is very complex. One of us (Pöppel) has pointed out the relationship between prediction and memory; indeed, he says, the adaptive function of memory *is* prediction.[3] Memory, however, would be useless in an entirely random and indeterminate universe: therefore the very fact that the metabolically expensive neural machinery of memory evolved and proved adaptive is a kind of odd proof that the universe is at least locally predictable, to justify such an investment.

But, on the other hand, an entirely deterministic and predictable universe would have no use for memory, either. The *Umwelt* of the lower animals, as determined by their affectors and receptors, is so limited that, to the extent that organisms survive, such an *Umwelt* constitutes a predictable universe; therefore, they possess no memories but only fixed action patterns triggered by appropriate stimuli. Memory only makes sense in a world of many possible futures, a world not fully determined: otherwise we could be programmed to perform an automatic and invariable set of behaviors which would exactly fit our adaptive needs. All futures share a common past: and thus memory gives us a handle on any possible future.

It has been objected, however, that the universe is indeed deterministic and predictable, but so complex that no animal can exactly predict its behavior, and that the very complex nervous systems of the higher animals developed precisely in order to improve their predictive powers. Such an argument produces an interesting dialectic, which might be worth following. It could be replied to the objection that the nervous systems of human beings are many orders of magnitude more complex than the physical universe they are, it is claimed, designed to predict. There are billions of times more possible brain-states in a single human brain than there are particles in the physical cosmos: the relations of the brain's parts carry usable information, whereas the relations between particles in the physical world do not.

There might, however, be a rejoinder to *this* argument, in turn. Human brains are part of the universe, and they merely make the job of predicting it more difficult without altering, by their presence, its actual determinateness. The fact that a major function of human brains is to predict the complex behaviors of each other, in no way weakens the proposition that the world is predictable.

But even this argument can be countered. For it implicitly yields the point that the world is *in practice* unpredictable, because any mechanism complex enough to predict events outside itself would also be so complex as to pose an insuperable problem to another predicting-mechanism, unless that other mechanism were in turn more complex still. It would not, moreover, be able to predict its own behavior. If Apollo gives prophesies, we should perhaps believe him, because he knows the mysteries of things and all human thoughts. But if Zeus, who also knows what Appollo is thinking, and who thus knows what Apollo will do, makes a contrary prophesy, we should believe Zeus instead. But Zeus does not know what Zeus will do, so perhaps we should not even believe Zeus after all.

Our original objector might still be able to argue that the predictability of events is only theoretical, not practical. But this argument must fail, too; for when we are dealing with the whole universe, the practical *is* the theoretical: if something is practically impossible for the whole universe, that is a way of saying it is theoretically impossible.

Finally, our antagonist might fall back to the position that future events are *determined* but not *predictable*. But since predictability would be the only conceivable scientific *test* of determinateness, such a statement would be semantically empty. A system whose complexity is increasing faster than any theoretical prediction-system could operate would therefore not be fully determined. In such a universe free choice based on memory would be a powerful survival strategy.

The peculiar logical form of this digression — which uses the infinite regress as a way of proving a negative proposition by means of a *reductio ad absurdum* — illustrates the peculiar predicament that the human brain at once evolved to handle and at the same time helped to create for itself. The very structure of the thinking process itself reflects the increasing levels of complexity the brain was called upon to deal with.

Human information processing is, therefore, (7) *hierarchical* in its organization. In the columns of neurons in the sensory cortex a plausible reconstruction of the world is created by a hierarchy of cells, the ones at the base responding to very simple stimuli and passing on their findings to cells progammed to respond to successively more complex stimuli. Likewise, motor decisions are passed down a long command-chain of simpler and simpler neural servomechanisms.

The co-ordination of these hierarchical systems in which many kinds of disparate information must be integrated, some requiring more processing-time and some requiring less, requires a neural pulse within which all relevant information is brought together as a whole. For instance, in the visual system many levels of detail — frequency, color, and depth must all be synchronized, or we would not be able to associate the various features of a visual scene.[4] Thus brain processing is (8) essentially *rhythmic*. That these rhythms can be "driven" or reinforced by repeated photic or auditory stimuli, to produce peculiar subjective states, is already well known.

More controversial in detail, but in general widely accepted, is the proposition that the brain's activities are (9) *self-rewarding*. The brain possesses built-in sites for the reception of opioid peptides such as enkephalin — the endorphins — and also other pleasure-associated neurohumors such as the catecholamines. It also controls the manufacture and release of these chemicals, and it has been shown that behavior can be reinforced by their use as a reward. The brain, therefore, is able to *reward itself* for certain activities which are, presumably, preferred for their adaptive utility. Clearly if this system of self-reward is the major motivating agent of the brain, any external technique for calibrating and controlling it would result in an enormously enhanced mental efficiency: we would, so to speak, be able to harness all our intellectual and emotional resources to a given task. (Indeed, we will argue later that this is exactly what an esthetic education, including an early introduction to metered verse in the form of nursery rhymes, can do.) It is, we believe, precisely this autonomous and reflexive reward system which underlies the whole realm of human values, ultimate purposes, and ideals such as truth, beauty, and goodness.

Associated with the brain's capacity for self-reward is (10) that it is characteristically *reflexive*. It is within broad limits self-calibrating (partly because of the habituation response). And it seems, unlike a computer, to have a more or less general capacity to convert software into hardware—short-term memory into long-term memory, for example—and vice-versa, to examine by introspection its own operations, so that its hardware can become its input or even its program. In the brain the observer problem becomes most acute: in fact we might define consciousness itself *as* the continuous irresolvable disparity between the brain as observer of itself and the brain as the object of observation. The coincidence between the words for consciousness and conscience in many languages points, incidentally, to the relationship between self-awareness and self-reward.

The human nervous system, we know now, cannot be separated

from the human cultural system it was designed to serve. Its operations are (11) essentially *social*. It is not only specific skills and communicative competences that are learnt in a social context, but also the fundamental capacities of arousal, orientation, attention, and motivation. Clearly we possess genetic proclivities to learn speech, elementary mathematical calculation, and so on; but equally clearly we require a socio-cultural context to release that potential. On the other hand, human society itself can be profoundly changed by the development of new ways of using the brain: take, for instance, the enormous socio-cultural effects of the invention of the written word. In a sense, reading is a sort of new synthetic instinct, input which becomes a program and which in turn crystallizes into neural hardware, and which incorporates a cultural loop into the human nervous circuit. This "new instinct" in turn profoundly changes the environment within which young human brains are programmed. In the early stages of human evolution such new instincts (speech must have been one) had to wait for their full development while sexual selection established the necessary elaborate vocal circuitry in the cortex. Later on we were able to use our technology, which required much less time to develop, as a sort of supplementary external nervous system. A book is a sort of R.O.M. chip we can plug in to our heads.

One of the most exciting propositions of the new brain science is that human information processing is (12) *hemispherically specialized*. Here some important distinctions must be made. There are strong logical objections to the popular and prevailing view that the right brain is emotional while the left brain is rational, and that artistic capacities, being emotional, are located in the right brain. Both sides of the brain are capable of rational calculation: it is surely just as rational to "see" a geometric proof—which is the function of the right brain—as to analyze a logical proposition—which would be done on the left. And both sides of the brain respond to the presence of brain chemicals, and thus both must be said to be "emotional" in this crude sense. The right brain may be better able to recognize and report emotions, but this capacity is surely a cognitive one in itself, and does not necessarily imply a judgment about whether it *feels* emotions more or less than the left. Above all, art is quite as much a rational activity as it is an emotional one: so the location of art on the "emotional" right is surely the result of a misunderstanding of the nature of art. More plausible is the position of Jerre Levy, who characterizes the relationship between right and left as a complementarity of cognitive capacities.[5] She has stated in a brilliant aphorism that the left brain maps spatial information into a temporal order, while the right brain maps temporal information onto a spatial order. In a sense understanding largely *consists* in the translation of information to and fro between a temporal ordering and a spatial one—resulting in a sort of stereoscopic depth-cognition. In Levy's view, the two "brains" alternate in the treatment of information, according to a rhythm determined by the general brain state, and pass, each time, their accumulated findings on to each other. The fact that experienced musicians use their left brain just as much as their right in listening to music shows that their higher understanding of music is the result of the collaboration of both "brains," the music having been translated first from temporal sequence to spatial pattern, and then "read," as it were, back into a temporal movement. The neurobiologist Günther Baumgartner suggests that the fore-brain acts as the integrating agent between specialized left and right functions, and it is in this integrative process that we would locate the essentially creative capacities of the brain, whether artistic or scientific. The apparent superiority of the isolated right brain in emotional matters may well reflect simply the fact that emotions, like music, are temporal in nature and their articulation requires the sort of temporal-on-spatial mapping that is the specialty of the right.

Finally, human information-processing can be described as (13) *kalogenetic* (Turner), a word coined from the Greek KALOS, for beauty, goodness, rightness; and GENESIS: begetting, productive cause, origin, source.[6] Another word for this characteristic, coined in jest as an etymological chimera by Pöppel, is *mono-causotaxophilia*, the love of single causes that explain everything. William James called it "the will to believe." Laughlin and d'Aquili use the term "the cognitive imperative," or the "what is it?" syndrome, while Zollinger has identified it in the scientific urge to confirm and affirm a given hypothesis, rather than to deconfirm it (as Karl Popper would have us do). Baumgartner's notion of the integrative function of the forebrain also partakes of the same idea. The human nervous system has a strong drive to construct affirmative, plausible, coherent, consistent, parsimonious, and predictively powerful models of the world, in which all events are explained by and take their place in a system which is at once rich in implications beyond its existing data and at the same time governed by as few principles or axioms as possible. The words that scientists use for such a system are "elegant," "powerful," and, often, "beautiful"; artists and philosophers use the same terms and also "appropriate," "fitting," "correct," "right," all of which can translate the Greek KALOS.

If this tendency *is* a true drive, then according to the theory of reinforcement, it is an activity for which the brain rewards itself; and if there were techniques by which the endogenous reward system could be stimulated and sensitized, then those techniques would enable us to greatly enhance the integrative powers of our minds.

*

Any candidate for identification as such a technique would have to meet certain qualifications. First, it would probably be culturally universal, since it would be based on neural and biochemical features common to all human beings.[7] Second, it would be very archaic, identifiable as an element of the most ancient and the most primitive cultures. Third, it would be likely to be regarded by its indigenous practitioners as the locus of an almost magical inspiration and as a source of wisdom; it would have the reputation of having significantly contributed to the efficiency and adaptiveness of the societies in which it is practiced. Fourth, it would be associated with those social and cultural activities which demand the highest powers of original thought and complex calculation, such as education, the organization of large-scale projects like war and co-operative agriculture, and the rituals which digest for social uses the dangerous and valuable energies implicit in sexuality, birth, death, sickness, and the like.

Metered poetry, the use of rule-governed rhythmic measures in the production of a heightened and intensified form of linguistic expression, nicely fulfills these requirements. Jerome Rothenberg's collection of ancient and "primitive" poetry, *Technicians of the Sacred*,[8] contains poems or excerpts from poems from about eighty different cultures, past and present, in Africa, North and South America, Asia, and Oceania; W. K.

Wimsatt's excellent collection of essays, *Versification: Major Language Types*, describes the metrical features of Chinese, Japanese, Hebrew, Greek, Latin, Slavic, Uralic, Germanic, Celtic, Italian, Spanish, French, Old English and Modern English, and apologizes (p. 17) for omitting the Vedic-Indic verse system, the Arabic, including Swahili, and the Persian.[9] Metered poetry is a highly complex activity which is culturally universal. One of us (Turner) has heard poetry recited by Ndembu spirit-doctors in Zambia and has, with the anthropologist Wulf Schiefenhövel, translated Eipo poetry from Central New Guinea.[10] He reports, as a poet, that the meter of Eipo poetry, when reproduced in English, has much the same emotional effect as it does in the original. Such a minute correspondence between poets in such widely different cultures surely points to an identical neurophysiological mechanism.

In nearly all cultures, metered poetry is used in the crucial religious and social (and often economic) rituals, and has the reputation of containing mysterious wisdom; the learning of major poetic texts is central to the process of education in nearly all literate traditions. Much work—farming, herding, hunting, war, ship-handling, even mining—has its own body of poetry and song.

It may be objected, however, that we have simply lumped together many different uses of language under an artificial category of poetry. This objection is strongly negated by the fact that poets themselves, who ought to know, can recognize the work of their alien colleagues as poetry, despite cultural differences. But we do not have to rely only on the reports of qualified native informants. Objective and universal and specific traits can be identified across the whole range of poetic practice throughout the world and as far back into the past as we have records. From these universal characteristics we can construct a general definition of metered poetry which will hold good from the ancient Greeks to the Kwakiutl, and from Racine to Polynesia.

The fundamental unit of metered poetry is what we shall call the LINE. We distinguish it by capitalization from the normal use of the word, because some orthographic traditions do not conventionally write or print the LINE in a separate space as we do; and in other traditions there are examples of a long line divided by a caesura into two sections, which would, in terms of our classification, actually consitute a couplet of LINES. There are also examples of what we would call a single LINE divided in half on the page. The LINE is preceded and followed by a distinct pause (not necessarily a pause for breath), which, despite the presence of other pauses within the line, divides the verse into clearly identifiable pieces. Turner, for example, can readily recognize the LINE-divisions of poetry in languages he does not know, when it is read aloud. The LINE unit can contain from four to twenty syllables; but it usually contains between seven and seventeen in languages which do not use fixed lexical tones, or between four and eight syllables in tonal languages, like Chinese, in which the metrical syllable takes about twice as long to articulate. Most remarkable of all, this fundamental unit nearly always takes from two to four seconds to recite, with a strong peak in distribution between 2.5 and 3.5 seconds. A caesura will usually divide the LINES in the longer part of the range; sometimes (as with Greek and Latin epic dactylic hexameters), the unit will be four to six seconds long, but clearly divided by a caesura and constituting for our purposes two LINES.

Turner has recorded and measured Latin, Greek, English,

Chinese, Japanese, and French poetry, and Pöppel has done so for German. Less systematic measurements, by syllable-count, have revealed fully consistent results for Ndembu (Zambia), Eipo (New Guinea), Spanish, Italian, Hungarian, Uralic, Slavic, and Celtic. An average syllable in a non-tonal language takes about ¼ second to articulate, and in a tonal language about ½ second, though recitation traditions vary in this respect. The Ndembu LINE averages ten syllables; Eipo poetry favors an eight- or twelve-syllable line; in Spanish the epic line of the *Poema de Mio Cid* is about fourteen syllables, but most other poetry is octosyllabic or hendecasyllabic (eight or eleven); the classic Italian line is the eleven-syllable *endecasillabo*; Hungarian uses lines between six and twelve syllables long, with a preference for eights and twelves; Slavic has octosyllabics and decasyllabics, with an epic long line of fifteen to sixteen syllables; Celtic has sevens, eights, nines, and some longer-lined meters.[12]

Among the traditions we have measured more closely, the results are as follows, giving a range of different meters:

Japanese

Epic meter (a seven-syllable LINE followed by a five-syllable one) (average)	3.25 secs.
Waka (average)	2.75 secs.
Tanka (recited much faster than the epic, as 3 LINES of 5, 12, and 14 syllables) (average)	2.70 secs.

Chinese

Four-syllable line	2.20 secs.
Five-syllable line	3.00 secs.
Seven-syllable line	3.80 secs.

English

Pentameter	3.30 secs.
Seven-syllable trochaic line	2.50 secs.
Stanzas using different line	
lengths	3.00 secs., 3.10 secs.
Ballad meter (octosyllabic)	2.40 secs.

Ancient Greek

Dactylic hexameter (half-line)	2.80 secs.
Trochaic tetrameter (half-line)	2.90 secs.
Iambic trimeter[13]	4.40 secs.
Marching anapests	3.50 secs.
Anapestic tetrameter (half-line)	2.50 secs.

Latin

Alcaic strophe	3.90 secs.
Elegiac couplet	3.50 secs.
Dactylic hexameter (half-line)	2.80 secs.
Hendecasyllabic	3.80 secs.

French

Alexandrine (12-syllable)	3.80 secs.
Decasyllable with octosyllable	
(La Fontaine)	3.00 secs.

German
(Sample of 200 poems, collected by Pöppel)

LINE-length of under 2 seconds	3%
LINE-length of 2–3 seconds	73%
LINE-length of 3–4 seconds	7%
LINE-length between 4 and 5 seconds[14]	17%

This fundamental unit is nearly always a rhythmic, semantic, and syntactical unit, as well: a sentence, a colon, a clause,
or a phrase; or a completed group of them. Thus other linguistic

rhythms are entrained to the basic acoustic rhythm, producing that pleasing sensation of "fit" and inevitability which is
part of the delight of verse, and is so helpful to the memory.
Generally a short line is used to deal with light subjects, while
the long line is reserved for epic or tragic matters.

It is, we believe, highly significant that this analysis of the
fundamental LINE in human verse gives little or no significance
to breath, or "breath-units," as a determinant of the divisions
of human meter. Thus our commonsense observation that
breath in speech is largely under voluntary control, and that
one could speak anything from one syllable to about forty in
one breath, is vindicated. Systems of verse based on breath-
units, such as "projective verse" and many other free-verse
systems, therefore have no objective validity or physiological
foundation.[15]

The second universal characteristic of human verse meter is
that certain marked elements of the LINE or of groups of LINES
remain constant throughout the poem, and thus serve as indi-
cators of the repetition of a pattern. The 3-second cycle is not
merely marked by a pause, but by distinct resemblances between
the material in each cycle. Repetition is added to frequency to
emphasize the rhythm.

These constant elements can take many forms. Simplest of
all is a constant number of syllables per line, as in Hungarian
folk poetry; but here the strict grammatical integrity of each
line is insisted upon, as if to compensate for the absence of other
markers. Some verse forms (for instance, that of the *Poema de
Mio Cid)* have a fixed number of stressed syllables per line, with
an unfixed number of unstressed syllables. Other meters (most
European ones, for example) use small patterns of syllables,
distinguished by stress or length, to make feet, creating a line

out of a fixed number of feet. Tonal languages, like Chinese, distinguish between syllables of an unchanging tone and syllables which change tone, and construct meters out of repeated patterns of changing and unchanging syllables. Celtic poetry uses prescribed *cadences*; Old English uses systematic alliteration. Many languages use some system of assonance, especially rhyme, which usually marks very strongly the ending of a line, and thus forms a strong contrast-spike to divide off one line from the next. Hebrew poetry uses semantic and syntactical parallels between its pairs of half-lines. Often many of these devices will be used at once, some prescribed by the conventions of the poetic form, others left to the discretion and inspiration of the poet. No verse-convention prescribes *all* the characteristics of a line, so every poem contains an interplay between prescribed elements and free variation.[16]

Sometimes, as in the Spenserian stanza, or in the Greek or English ode, or in the invented stanzas of Donne or Yeats, a whole group of lines of different lengths will itself constitute a repeated element. When lines of different lengths are used together, as in Milton's *Lycidas*, the rhyme (which stresses the integrity of the line) and the foot are given especial emphasis to compensate for the variation in the fundamental pulse — as if to insist on the threshold dividing the carrier-wave from mere "noise." And in variable-lined verses there is usually a normal-length line which acts as an unconscious constant against which the exceptions are measured as such.

At this point, it should be indicated that some of the characteristics of metered poetry do not apply to songs and lyrics derived from a song tradition. Music has its own form of organization, which diminishes the importance of the line to the advantage of the musical phrase. But in those traditions where we can see poetry emerging from song, such as the Latin lyric, there is an interesting tendency, as the musical order is forgotten, toward the establishment of the characteristically poetic forms of organization: the regular line, with variations, the distinction between different types of syllable (long and short, stressed and unstressed, tonally changing or unchanging), and the rest. Thus the fact that songs do not conform to the limits of poetic meter is negative proof of the relation of language and meter.

The third universal characteristic of human metrical verse is *variation*, or, more precisely, a pseudolinguistic generativeness created by the imposition of rules, which makes possible significant perturbations of an expressive medium. Robert Frost put it very well, in a negative way, when he described poetry without meter as being like tennis without a net: the net introduces a restriction which is paradoxically fertile in the elaboration of groundstrokes which it demands, and significant in that it distinguishes legal from illegal shots.

Variation does not necessarily mean departure from the rules (Romantic and Modernist theories of art sometimes make this mistake). Variation does not occur *despite* the rules but *because* of them. Freedom never means a freedom *from* rules, but the freedom *of* rules. It is important here for us to distinguish our general position from that of sociobiological and other purists of the genetic-deterministic persuasion on one hand, and from the pure cultural relativists, behaviorists or otherwise, on the other. Genetic determinists would be likely to assume, once a human universal such as metrical verse is pointed out to them, that this behavior indicates the presence of a set of biological constraints which act as an outer envelope, restricting possible human behaviors within a given repertoire, large or small.

Cultural relativists would tend to deny the existence of such a human universal, or would be inclined to dismiss it as an analogous response to similar problems or stimuli, or as an artificial product of the investigator's definitional vocabulary and research method.

We would adopt a third position, which is already hinted by our use of the word "pseudolinguistic." For us, the similarities between metered verse in different cultures are real and do indeed indicate a shared biological underpinning; but unlike the genetic determinists we do not regard this shared inheritance as a constraint, nor as an outer envelope restricting human behavior to a certain range. Rather, we would regard it as a set of rules which, though derived from the structure of the human auditory cortex and the brain in general, does not restrict, but enormously increases, the range of possible human behavior.

At first glance, this position might appear paradoxical. How can the range of possibilities be *increased* by the imposition of rules governing their use? If rules are rules, then they must surely *deny* certain previously possible behaviors, and therefore decrease the total number of them.

The paradox is easily resolved. A mathematical analogy will help. Given four possible behaviors, A, B, C, and D, only four alternatives exist. If we now impose a rule, which is that these behaviors can only be performed two at a time, suddenly and strangely there are now not four but six alternatives: AB, BC, CD, AC, BD, AD. Of course, this is cheating, in a sense, because before we mentioned the rule we never hinted that behaviors might come in groups. It could be pointed out that if we are talking about *sets* of behaviors, in fact sixteen possibilities exist: the ten already mentioned, the four groups of three, the whole group together, and the null set. But this is precisely what the rule has done: it has created the *group* of behaviors as a significant entity, as a behavior in itself, and therefore expanded the repertoire from four to six. Furthermore, those six permitted combinations now stand in relation to ten non-permitted ones, and their correctness marks them out as valuable and special, as opposed to the "incorrect" permutations. Thus the rule as introduced a) a greater repertoire of behaviors than was previously possible and b) a marker of significance and value. All game-rules work in this way, creating possible scenarios and desired goals out of thin air.

The linguistic rules of phonology, grammar, and the lexicon work in a generally similar way. Linguistic rules are, to an extent, arbitrary and culture-bound: but Chomsky has shown certain invariant characteristics in the way in which human languages use syntactical subordination, which are no doubt biological in origin (and probably related to the *hierarchical* nature of human brain process). Meter, with its cultural variations in LINE-length, shows a similar interplay of cultural and genetic forces, and, more important, it produces a similar *increase* in the repertoire of behavior and a similar capacity to create significance.

In fact it is this general strategy by which the DNA molecule of life and the nervous systems of the higher animals attained greater complexities than the physical universe out of which they evolved; by making *permutations* of elements significant through highly restrictive "rules," and therefore increasing, as it were, the "cardinality" of the number of bits of information that the organism could hold. We find, for example, a similar interplay between genetic and cultural factors in the human recognition of colors: a rather restricted set of anatomically-determined color sensitivities is combined by culture into a large, and often idiosyncratic repertoire of tints and shades, many of them with strong ideological significance. The range, variety, and combinations of colored pigmentation used in animal ritual behavior attests to a corresponding extension and valorization of color distinctions among the higher animals.

Thus metrical variation can be seen as a code, or communicative device, and the various elements of meter can be neatly described in terms of information theory. The three-second LINE is the communicative medium or "carrier-wave," which must be distinguishable from mere "noise" or the random transmissions around it, by the recurrence of a pause at the LINE-ending, by the many regular metrical features — syllable-count, stress, quantity, tone, systematic assonance, etc. — that we have described, and by the coincidence of semantic, syntactic, and rhythmic units with the LINE unit. Metrical variation is the "message" which is transmitted upon the communicative medium — like a radio-transmission, it consists of a systematic distortion of a regular medium or wave, which nevertheless remains within the regular parameters of the medium so that at all times the transmission is distinguishable from random noise.

The "message" that metrical variation conveys, however, is rather mysterious. If it is a code, what kind of code is it? Metrical scholars have attempted to discover exact relationships between individual metrical variations and the semantic content of poetry.[17] But their conclusions have been disappointingly vague or arbitrary, reminiscent, in fact, of musicological attempts to assign fixed meanings to different musical keys, signatures, and variations, so as to make a symphony describe a scene or conduct an argument. Here the analogy between metrical and linguistic significance breaks down. Certainly a connection between metrical (or musical) and linguistic meaning exists, and in some cultural traditions (English Augustan poetry and European Romantic music, for instance) artists have developed a self-conscious repertoire of metrical or musical codes to convey specific meanings. But other traditions do not possess such codifications, or else use the same specific devices to convey entirely different ideas.

The predicament of the critic, in fact, can be likened to that of a viewer of a visual artifact who is so convinced that what he is looking at is a page of writing that he does not realize that the artifact is actually a *picture*. Perhaps it is a picture of something he has never seen (or even noticed), and thus his mistake is a natural one. But the attempt to extract a sort of linguistic meaning out of the planes, lines, corners, masses, and angles of a picture would be frustratingly arbitrary — especially if he had a whole series of paintings of different subjects, in which the same visual elements were used for entirely different purposes; the same curve for a face, a hillside, and the sail of a ship. Linguistic meaning and pictorial meaning are based on codes so fundamentally different that no code-cracking algorithm that would work on one could possibly work on the other. Their mutual intelligibilty cannot be sought in the direction of analysis, but only within the context of a synthetic whole which contains both of them.

What we are suggesting is that a linguistic type of analysis of meter, as of music (or painting, e.g., Chinese landscape painting), is likely to be fruitful *only* when the composer has arbitrarily *imposed* linguistic meaning on the elements of his composition; and that the meaning of metrical variation must be sought in a fashion much more like that of the recognition of a tune or the subject of a picture. That is, metrical variations are not significant in themselves, like sememes: but rather they form, together, a picture-like *Gestalt* which is a distinct representation of something that we can recognize; and thus, like pictorial representations, or music, they are much less culture-bound than linguistic codes. But here, excitingly, we encounter a paradox stemming from the gross structure of the human brain. Poetry, being an art of languge, is presumably processed by the left temporal lobe of the brain. But meter, we are suggesting, carries meaning in a fashion much more like that of a picture or a melody, in which the meaning inheres more in the whole than in the parts. There is no "lexicon" of metrical forms: they are not *signs* but elements of an analogical structure. And this kind of understanding is known to take place on the *right* side of the brain. If this hypothesis is accurate, meter is, in part, a way of introducing right-brain processes into the left-brain activity of understanding language; and in another sense, it is a way of connecting our much more culture-bound (and perhaps evolutionarily later) linguistic capacities with the relatively more "hardwired" spatial pattern-recognition faculties we share with the higher mammals.

*

It is in the context of this hypothesis that we wish to introduce the major finding of this essay, which explains, we believe, the extraordinary prevalence of the 3-second LINE in human poetry.

If we ask the question "what does the ear hear?" the obvious answer is "sound." What is sound? Mechanical waves in the air or other medium. But this answer is not very illuminating. We can, for instance, perceive mechanical waves by the sense of touch: it would be as inaccurate to say that a deaf man "heard" a vibrating handrail with his fingers, as it would be to say a blind man "saw" a fire with the skin of his face. What characterizes hearing as such is not that it senses mechanical waves but that it senses the distinctions between mechanical waves; just as what characterizes sight is not the perception of electromagnetic waves but the perception of distinctions between electromagnetic waves.

For the sense of sight those distinctions (except for color) are spatial ones; but for the sense of hearing they are mainly temporal. To put it directly: what the sense of hearing hears is essentially *time*. The recognition of differences of pitch involves a very pure (and highly accurate) comparative measurement of different frequencies into which time is divided. The perception of timbre, tone, sound texture, and so on consists in the recognition of combinations of frequencies; and the sense of rhythm and tempo carries the recognition of frequency into the realm of longer periods of time.

The sense of hearing is not only a marvellously accurate instrument for detecting differences between temporal periods; it is also an active organizer, arranging those different periods within a hierarchy as definite as that of the seconds, minutes, and hours of a clock, but one in which the different periodicities are also uniquely valorized. In the realm of pitch the structure of that hierarchy is embodied in the laws of harmony, and is well known (although it has not often been recognized that "sound" and "time" are virtually the same thing). New discoveries by Ernst Pöppel's group in Munich have begun to open up the role of the auditory time-hierarchy in the structure and function of the brain. Out of this investigation is coming a comprehensive understanding of the general scheduling-organization of the human sensory-motor system, and a fresh approach to the production and understanding of language. We shall first briefly outline the auditory hierarchy.

Events separated by periods of time shorter than about three

thousandths of a second are classified by the hearing system
as simultaneous. If a brief sound of one pitch is played to one
ear, and another of a different pitch is played to the other less
than .003 sec. later, the subject will experience only one sound.
If the sounds are a little more than .003 sec. apart, the subject
will experience two sounds. However, he will not be able to
tell which of the two sounds came first, nor will he until the
gap between them is increased ten times. Thus the lowest
category in the hierarchy of auditory time is *simultaneity*, and
the second lowest is mere temporal *separation*, without a preferred order or time. The most primary temporal experience is
timeless unity; next comes a spacelike recognition of difference —
spacelike because, unlike temporal positions, spatial positions
can be exchanged. One can go from New York to Berlin or from
Berlin to New York; but one can only go from 1980 to 1983,
not from 1983 to 1980. Likewise, the realm of "separation" is
a non-deterministic, acausal one: events happen in it, perhaps
in patterns or perhaps not, but they cannot be said to cause
one another, because we cannot say which came first.

When two sounds are about three hundredths of a second
apart, a subject can experience their *sequence*, accurately reporting which came first. This is the third category in the hierarchy of auditory time, subsuming separations and simultaneities
and organizing them rationally with respect to each other. But
at this stage the organsm is still a passive recipient of stimuli;
we can hear a sequence of two sounds one-tenth of a second
apart, but there is nothing we can do in response to the first
sound before the second sound comes along: we are helpless
to alter what will befall us, if the interval between the alert and
its sequel falls within this range. Unlike the world of temporal
separation, which is in a sense a realm of chance and pattern,

the world of sequence is a realm of fate and cause. Events follow each other, and their temporal connections can be recognized as necessary, if indeed they are; but there is nothing we can do about it.

Once the temporal interval is above about three-tenths of a second, however, we have entered a new temporal category, which we might call *response*. For three-tenths of a second (.3 sec.) is enough time for a human subject to react to an acoustic stimulus. If we play two sounds to our subject a second apart, the subject could in theory prepare to deal with the second sound in the time given him after hearing the first. The perceiver is no longer passive, and events can be treated by him as actions in *response* to which he can perform actions of his own and which he can modify before they happen if he understands their cause. For response to exist there must be simultaneities, a separation, and a further element which might be characterized as function or, in a primitive sense, purpose. The response to a given stimulus will differ according to the function of the responding organ and the purpose of the organism as a whole.

At several places in this analysis it has been pointed out that a given familiar temporal relation — chance, pattern, fate, cause, action, function, purpose — only becomes possible when there is enough time for it to exist in. The idea that an entity needs time to exist in has become commonplace recently: an electron, for instance, requires at least 10^{-20} sec. of time (its spin period) to exist in, just as surely as it requires 10^{-10} centimeters of space (its Compton wavelength). The corollary to this observation is that entities which consist only in spatio-temporal relations are not necessarily less real for that than material objects, for spatio-temporal relations are exactly what material objects consist of too. But though a given period of time may be sufficient for an example of given relation — chance, cause, function — to be recognized in, it is not enough for the concept of the relation to be formulated in. It takes much less time to recognize or speak a word once learned than it takes to learn the word in the first place. Many examples of the sequence or response relation between events must be compared before a causal or purposive order can be formulated and thus recognized in individual cases. But comparison requires discrete parcels of experience between which the comparison may be made, and since the entities being compared are themselves temporal in nature, these parcels of experience must consist in equal periods of time. In like fashion, the analysis of a picture (for transmission, reproduction, or identification of its details) might begin by dividing the picture up into "pixels" by means of a series of grids of various frequency; the highest-frequency grid representing the limit of the eye's activity, the lower ones increasingly concerned with complex relations between details. The next lowest time-division beyond the .3 second resonse-frequency must be sufficiently long to avoid falling into the range of the characteristic time-quanta required for the completion and recognition of the temporal relations to be compared. The comparison of experience takes more time than experience itself; the recognition of a melody takes more time than the hearing of the single notes.

This fundamental "parcel of experience" turns out to be about three seconds. The three-second period, roughly speaking, is the length of the human present moment. (At least it is for the auditory system, which possesses the sharpest temporal acuity of all the senses. The eye, for instance, is twice as slow as the ear in distinguishing temporal separation from simultaneity.) The philosophical notion of the "specious present" finds here its experimental embodiment.

A human speaker will pause for a few milliseconds every three seconds or so, and in that period decide on the precise syntax and lexicon of the next three seconds. A listener will absorb about three seconds of heard speech without pause or reflection, then stop listening briefly in order to integrate and make sense of what he has heard. (Speaker and hearer, however, are not necessarily "in phase" for this activity; this observation will be seen to be of importance later.)

To use a cybernetic metaphor, we possess an auditory information "buffer" whose capacity is three seconds' worth of information; at the end of three seconds the "buffer" is full, and it passes on its entire accumulated stock of information to the higher processing centers. In theory this stock could consist of about 1,000 simultaneities, 100 discrete temporal separations, and ten consecutive responses to stimuli. In practice the "buffer" has rather smaller capacity than this (about 60 separations); it seems to need a certain amount of "down-time."

It appears likely that another mechanism is involved here too. Different types of information take different amounts of time to be processed by the cortex. For instance, fine detail in the visual field takes more time to be identified by the cortex than coarse detail. (Indeed, the time taken to process detail seems to be used by the brain as a tag to label its visual frequency.)[18] Some sort of pulse is necessary so that all the information of different kinds will arrive at the higher processing centers as a bundle, correctly labelled as belonging together, and at the same time; the sensory cortex "waits" for the "slowest" information to catch up with the "fastest" so that it can all be sent off at once. And this 3-second period constitutes a "pulse."

Beyond the two horizons of this present moment exist the two

periods which together constitute *duration*, which is the highest
or "longest-frequency" integrative level of the human perception of time. Those two periods, the past and the future, memory
and planning, are the widest arena of human thought (unless
the religious or metaphysical category of "eternity" constitutes
an even wider one). It is within the realm of duration that what
we call freedom can exist, for it is within that realm that purposes and functions, the governors of response, can themselves
be compared and selected. The differences between past and
future, and the differences between possible futures, constitute
the field of *value*, and the relations between low-frequency
objects and the more primitive high-frequency objects of which
they are composed constitute the field of *quality*.

It is tempting to relate this foregoing hierarchical taxonomy
of temporal periodicities to the structure and evolution of the
physical universe itself. The temporal category of *simultaneity*
nicely corresponds to the atemporal *Umwelt* of the photon,
which reigned supreme in the first microsecond of the Big Bang.
The category of *separation* resembles the weak, acausal,
stochastic, spacelike temporality of quantum physics, within
which there is no preferred direction of time; a condition which
must have prevailed shortly after the origin of the universe, and
of which the quantum-mechanical organization of subatomic
particles is a living fossil. The category of *sequence* matches the
causal, deterministic, and entropic realm of classical hard science,
whose subject came into being some time after the origin of
the universe, once the primal explosion had cooled sufficiently
to permit the existence of organized, discrete, and enduring matter. With the category of *response* we are clearly within the
Umwelt of living matter, with its functions, purposes, and even
its primitive and temporary teleology, which began about ten

billion years after the Big Bang. Once we cross the horizon of the present we leave the world of animals and enter the realm of *duration,* which first came into being perhaps a million years ago (if it was roughly coeval with speech and with that development of the left brain which gave us the tenses of language). The evolution and hierarchical structure of the human hearing mechanism thus could be said to recapitulate the history and organization of the cosmos. The history of science has been the retracing of that path backwards by means of clocks of greater and greater acuity.

*

Cosmological speculation aside, it should already be obvious that a remarkable and suggestive correlation exists between the temporal organisation of poetic meter and the temporal function of the human hearing mechanism. Of general linguistic significance is the fact that the length of a syllable—about ⅓ second—corresponds to the minimum period within which a *response* to an auditory stimulus can take place: this is commonsense, really, as speech must, to be efficient, be as fast as it can be, while, to be controllable, it must be slow enough for a speaker or hearer to react to a syllable before the next one comes along.

Of more specific significance for our subject is the very exact correlation between the three-second LINE and the three-second "auditory present." The average number of syllables per LINE in human poetry seems to be about ten; so human poetic meter embodies the two lowest frequency rhythms in the human auditory system.

The independence of poetic meter from the mechanism of breathing, which we have already noted, is thus explained by the fact that the master-rhythm of human meter is not pulmonary but neural: we must seek the origins of poetry not among the lower regions of the human organism, but among the higher. The frequent practice in reading "free verse" aloud, of breathing at the end of the line—even when the line is highly variable in length and often broken quite without regard to syntax—is therefore not only grammatically confusing but deeply unnatural; for it forces a pause where neural processing would not normally put it.

But at least there was a clear, if erroneous, rationale for the doctrine of meter as made up of "breath-units." Without this rationale, how do we explain the cultural universality of meter? *Why* does verse embody the three-second neural "present"? What functions could be served by this artificial and external mimicry of an endogenous brain rhythm? Given the fact, already stated, that poetry fulfils many of the superficial conditions demanded of a brain-efficiency reward control system, how might the three-second rhythm serve that function? And what is the rôle of the other components of meter—the rhythmic parallelism between the LINES, and the information-bearing variations upon that parallelism?

One further batch of data will help guide our hypothesizing: the subjective reports of poets and readers of poetry about the effects and powers of poetic meter. Although these reports would be inadequate and ambiguous as the sole support of an argument, they may point us in the right direction and confirm conclusions arrived at by other means.

A brief and incomplete summary of these reports, with a few citations, should suggest to a reader educated in literature the scope of their general agreement. Robert Graves speaks of the shiver and the coldness in the spine, the hair rising on the head and body, as does Emily Dickinson. A profound muscular relaxation yet an intense alertness and concentration is also recorded. The heart feels squeezed and the stomach cramped. There is a tendency toward laughter or tears, or both; the taking of deep breaths; and a slightly intoxicated feeling (Samuel Taylor Coleridge compared it to the effects of a moderate amount of strong spirits upon a conversation). At the same time there is a cataract or avalanche of vigorous thought, in which new connections are made; Shakespeare's Prospero describes the sensation as a "beating mind" (the phrase is repeated three times in different places in the play). There is a sense of being on the edge of a precipice of insight — almost a vertigo — and the awareness of entirely new combinations of ideas taking concrete shape, together with feelings of strangeness and even terror. Some writers (Arnold, for instance) speak of an inner light or flame. Outside stimuli are often blanked out, so strong is the concentration. The imagery of the poem becomes so intense that it is almost like real sensory experience. Personal memories pleasant and unpleasant (and sometimes previously inaccessible) are strongly evoked; there is often an emotional re-experience of close personal ties, with family, friends, lovers, the dead. There is an intense valorization of the world and of human life, together with a strong sense of the reconciliation of opposites — joy and sorrow, life and death, good and evil, divine and human, reality and illusion, whole and part, comic and tragic, time and timelessness. The sensation is not a timeless one as such, but an experience of time so full of significance that stillness and sweeping motion are the same thing. There is a sense of power combined with effortlessness. The poet or reader rises above the world, as it were, on the "viewless wings of poetry," and sees it all in its fullness and completeness, but without loss of the quiddity and clarity of its details. There is an awareness of one's own physical nature, of one's birth and death, and of a curious transcendence of them; and, often, a strong feeling of universal and particular love, and communal solidarity.

Of course, not all these subjective sensations necessarily occur together in the experience of poetry, nor do they usually take their most intense form; but a poet or frequent reader of poetry will probably recognize most of them.

To this list, moreover, should be added a further property of metered poetry, which goes beyond the immediate experience of it: that is, its memorability. Part of this property is undoubtedly a merely technical convenience: the knowledge of the number of syllables in a line and the rhyme, for instance, limits the number of words and phrases which are possible in a forgotten line and helps us to logically reconstruct it. But introspection will reveal a deeper quality to this memorability: somehow the rhythm of the words is remembered even when the words themselves are lost to us; but the rhythm helps us to recover the mental state in which we first heard or read the poem, and then the gates of memory are opened and the words come to us at once.

Equipped with the general contemporary conception of brain-processing with which this essay began, with the temporal analysis of meter and its correlation to the hearing-system, and with the subjective reports of participants in the art, we may now begin to construct a plausible hypothesis of what goes on in the brain during the experience of poetry.

Here we can draw upon a relatively new and speculative field of scientific inquiry, which has been variously termed "neuro-physiology," "biocybernetics," and "biopsychology," and is associated with the names of such researchers as E. Bourguignon, E. D. Chapple, E. Gellhorn, A. Neher, and R. Ornstein.

Barbara Lex's essay "The Neurobiology of Ritual Trance,"[19] in which she summarizes and synthesizes much of their work, provides many of the materials by which we may build an explanatory bridge between the observed characteristics of human verse and the new findings of the Munich group about the hearing mechanism. Although Lex is concerned with the whole spectrum of methods by which altered states of consciousness may be attained—alcohol, hypnotic suggestion, breathing techniques, smoking, music, dancing, drugs, fasting, meditation, sensory deprivaton, photic driving, and auditory driving—and her focus is on ritual rather than the art of poetry, her general argument fits well with our own findings.

Essentially her position is that the various techniques listed above, and generalized as "driving behaviors," are designed to add to the linear, analytic, and verbal resources of the left brain the more intuitive and holistic understanding of the right brain; to tune the central nervous system and alleviate accumulated stress; and to invoke to the aid of social solidarity and cultural values the powerful somatic and emotional force mediated by the sympathetic and parasympathetic nervous systems, and the ergotropic and trophotropic responses they control.[20]

It has been known for many years that rhythmic photic and auditory stimulation can evoke epileptic symptoms in seizure-prone individuals, and can produce powerful involuntary reactions even in normal persons. The rhythmic stimulus entrains and then amplifies natural brain rhythms, especially if it is tuned to an important frequency such as the ten cycle-per-second alpha wave. It seems plausible to us that the three-second poetic LINE is similarly tuned to the three-second cycle of the auditory (and subjective-temporal) present. The metrical and assonantal devices of verse such as rhyme and stress, which create similarities

between the LINES, emphasize the repetition. The curious subjective effects of metered verse — relaxation, a holistic sense of
the world and so on — are no doubt attributable to a very mild
pseudotrance state induced by the auditory driving effect of this
repetition.

Auditory driving is known to affect the right brain much more
powerfully than the left: thus, where ordinary unmetered prose
comes to us in a "mono" mode, so to speak, affecting the left
brain predominantly, metered language comes to us in a "stereo"
mode, simultaneously calling on the verbal resources of the left
and the rhythmic potentials of the right.[21]

Of course, the matter is not as simple as this, even at this
level of discussion. The accurate scansion of poetry involves
a complex analysis of *grammatical* and *lexical* stress, which must
be continually integrated with a non-verbal right-brain
understanding of *metrical* stress. The delightful way in which
the rhythm of the sentence, as a semantic unit, counterpoints
the rhythm of the meter in poetry, is thus explained as the result
of a co-operation between left and right brain functions. The
"stereo" effect of verse is not merely one of simultaneous stimulation of two different brain areas, but also the result of a necessary
integrative collaboration and feedback between them. The
linguistic capacities of the left brain, which, as Levy says, provide a temporal order for spatial information, are forced into
a conversation with the rhythmic and musical capacities of the
right, which provide a spatial order for temporal information.

But the driving rhythm of the three-second LINE is not just
any rhythm. It is, as we have seen, tuned to the largest limited
unit of auditory time, its specious present, within which causal
sequences can be compared, and free decisions taken. A complete poem — which can be any length — is a duration, a realm of

values, systematically divided into presents, which are the realm of action. It therefore summarizes our most sophisticated and most uniquely human integrations of time.

There is, perhaps, still another effect at work on the cortical level. The various divinatory practices of humankind (another cultural universal, perhaps) all involve a common element: a process of very complex calculation which seems quite irrelevant to the kind of information sought by the diviner. A reader of the Tarot will analyze elaborate combinations of cards, an *I Ching* reader will arrive at his hexagram through a difficult process of mathematical figuring, a reader of the horoscope will resort to remarkable computations of astronomical position and time. (The common use of the word "reader" in these contexts is suggestive.) The work of scanning metered verse, especially when combined with the activity of recognizing allusions and symbolisms, and the combination of them into the correct patterns, seems analogous to these divinatory practices. The function of this demanding process of calculation may be to occupy the linear and rational faculties of the brain with a task which entirely distracts them from the matter to be decided—a diagnosis, a marriage, the future of an individual. Once the "loud voice" of the reductive logical intelligence is thus stilled by distance, the quieter whispering of a holistic intuition, which can integrate much larger quantities of much poorer-quality information in more multifarious ways—though with a probability of accuracy which is correspondingly much lower—can then be heard. The technique is something like that of the experienced stargazer, who can sometimes make out a very faint star by focussing a little to one side of it, thereby bringing to bear on it an area of the retina which, though inferior in acuity, is more sensitive to light. The vatic, prophetic, or divinatory powers traditionally attributed to poetry may be partly explained by the use of this technique. If the analogy is slightly unflattering to the work of some professional analytic critics of poetry — reducing their work, as it does, to the status of an elaborate decoy for the more literalistic proclivities of the brain — there is the compensation that it is after all a very necessary activity, indeed indispensable precisely because of its irrelevance.

On the cortical level, then, poetic meter serves a number of functions generally aimed at tuning up and enhancing the performance of the brain, by bringing to bear other faculties than the linguistic, which we can relate to the summary of healthy brain characteristics at the beginning of this paper. By ruling out certain rhythmic possibilities, meter satisfies the brain's procrustean demand for unambiguity and clear distinctions. By combining elements of repetition and isochrony on one hand with variation on the other, it nicely fulfils the brain's habituative need for controlled novelty. By giving the brain a system of rhythmic organization as well as a circumscribed set of semantic and syntactical possibilities, it encourages the brain in its synthetic and predictive activity of hypothesis-construction, and raises expectations which are pleasingly satisfied at once. In its content, poetry has often had a strongly prophetic character, an obvious indication of its predictive function; and the mythic elements of poetry afford more subtle models of the future by providing guides to conduct. Poetry presents to the brain a system which is temporally and rhythmically hierarchical, as well as linguistically so, and therefore matched to the hierarchical organization of the brain itself. It does much of the work that the brain must usually do for itself, in organizing information into rhythmic pulses, integrating different types of information — rhythmic, grammatical, lexical, acoustic — into easily assimilable parcels and labelling their contents as belonging together. Like intravenous nourishment, the information enters our system instantly, without a lengthy process of digestion. The pleasure of metered verse evidently comes from its ability to stimulate the brain's capacities of self-reward, and the traditional concern of verse with the deepest human *values*—truth, goodness, and beauty—is clearly associated with its involvement with the brain's own motivational system. Poetry seems to be a device the brain can use in reflexively calibrating itself, turning its software into hardware and its hardware into software: and accordingly poetry is traditionally concerned, on its semantic level, with consciousness and conscience. As a quintessentially cultural activity, poetry has been central to social learning and the synchronization of social activities (the sea-shanty or work-song is only the crudest and most obvious example). Poetry, as we have seen, enforces cooperation between left-brain temporal organization and right-brain spatial organization and helps to bring about that integrated stereoscopic view that we call true understanding. And poetry is, *par excellence*, "kalogenetic"—productive of beauty, or elegant, coherent, and predictively powerful models of the world.

It might be argued—and this is a traditional charge against poetry—that in doing all these things poetry deceives us, presenting to us an experience which, because it is so perfectly designed for the human brain, gives us a false impression of reality and separates us from the rough world in which we must survive. Much modern esthetic theory is in fact devoted to reversing this situation , and making poetry—and art in general—so disharmonious with our natural proclivities that it shocks us into awareness of the stark realities. Clearly a poetry which was too merely harmonious would be insipid—for it would disappoint the brain's habituative desire for novelty. But mere random change and the continuous disappointment of expectations is itself insipid; we are as capable of becoming habituated to meaningless flux as to mindless regularity.

Modernist esthetic theory may be ignoring the following possibility: that our species' special adaptation may in fact be to expect more order and meaning in the world than it can deliver; and that those expectations may constitute, paradoxically, an excellent survival strategy. We are strongly motivated to restore the equilibrium between reality and our expectations by altering reality so as to validate our models of it — to "make the world a better place," as we put it. The modernist attack on beauty in art would therefore constitute an attack on our very nature itself; and the modernist and post-modernist criticism of moral and philosophical idealism likewise flies in the face of the apparent facts about human neural organization. What William James called "the will to believe" is written in our genes; teleology is the best policy; and paradoxically, it is utopian to attempt to do battle against our natural idealism. Much more sensible to adjust reality to the ideal.

But our discussion of the effects of metered verse on the human brain has ignored, so far, the subcortical levels of brain activity. Let us substitute, as *pars pro toto*, "metered verse" for "rituals" in the following summary by Barbara Lex:

> The *raison d'être* of rituals is the readjustment of dysphasic biological and social rhythms by manipulation of neurophysiological structures under controlled conditions. Rituals properly executed promote a feeling of well-being and relief, not only because prolonged or intense stresses are alleviated, but also because the driving techniques employed in rituals are designed to sensitize

and "tune" the nervous system and thereby lessen inhibi-
tion of the right hemisphere and permit temporary right-
hemisphere dominance, as well as mixed trophotropic-
ergotropic excitation, to achieve synchronization of cortical rhythms in both hemispheres and evoke trophotropic
rebound.[22]

Lex maintains that the "driving" techniques of rhythmic
dances, chants, and so on can produce a simultaneous stimulation of both the ergotropic (arousal) and the trophotropic (rest)
systems of the lower nervous system, producing subjective effects
which she characterizes as follows: trance; ecstasy; meditative
and dreamlike states; possession; the "exhilaration accompanying
risk taking"; a sense of community; sacredness; a "process of
reviving the memory of a repressed unpleasant experience and
expressing in speech and actions the emotions related to it,
thereby relieving the personality of its influence"; alternate
laughing and crying; mystical experience and religious conver-
sion; experiences of unity, holism, and solidarity. Laughlin and
d'Aquili add to these effects a sense of union with a greater power,
an awareness that death is not to be feared, a feeling of harmony with the universe, and a mystical "conjunctio oppositorum"
or unity of opposites. This list closely resembles our earlier
enumeration of the experience of good metered verse as
described by literary people.

If Lex is right, we can add to the more specifically cortical
effects of metered verse the more generalized functions of a major
ritual driving technique: the promotion of biophysiological
stress-reduction (peace) and social solidarity (love). Meter clearly
synchronizes not only speaker with hearer, but hearers with
each other, so that each person's three-second "present" is in
phase with the others and a rhythmic community, which can

become a performative community, is generated.

Laughlin and d'Aquili connect the mythical mode of narrative with the driving techniques of ritual, pointing out that mythical thought expresses the "cognitive imperative," as they call it, or the desire for an elegant and meaningful explanation of the world;[23] and McManus argues that such practices are essential in the full development and education of children.[24] (Again we might point out that the modernist praise of mythical thought is misplaced; for it values the irrational element it discerns in myth, whereas true mythical thought, as Lévi-Strauss has shown, is deeply rational and has much in common with scientific hypothesis.)

The theory of the state-boundedness of memory might also explain the remarkable memorability of poetry. If meter evokes a peculiar brain state, and if each meter and each use of meter with its unique variations carries its own mood or brain-state signature, then it is not surprising that we can recall poetry so readily. The meter itself can evoke the brain-state in which we first heard the poem, and therefore make the verbal details immediately accessible to recall. Homer said that the muses were the daughters of memory, and this may be what he meant. By contrast, the modernist critic Chatman sneeringly dismisses the mnemonic function of metered poetry as being in common with that of advertising jingles. But if advertising jingles are left holding the field of human emotional persuasion, poetry has surely lost the battle—or the advertising jingles have become the only true poetry.

*

To sum up the general argument of this essay: metered poetry is a cultural universal, and its salient feature, the three-second present moment of the auditory information-processing system. By means of metrical variation, the musical and pictorial powers of the right brain are enlisted by meter to cooperate with the linguistic powers of the left; and by auditory driving effects, the lower levels of the nervous system are stimulated in such a way as to reinforce the cognitive functions of the poem, to improve the memory, and to promote physiological and social harmony. Metered poetry may play an important part in developing our more subtle understandings of time, and may thus act as a technique to concentrate and reinforce our uniquely human tendency to make sense of the world in terms of values like truth, beauty, and goodness. Meter breaks the confinement of linguistic expression and appreciation within two small regions of the left temporal lobe and brings to bear the energies of the whole brain.[25]

The consequences of this new understanding of poetic meter are very wide-ranging. This understanding would endorse the classical conception of poetry, as designed to "instruct by delighting," as Sir Philip Sidney put it.[26] It would suggest strongly that "free verse," when uncoupled from any kind of metrical regularity, is likely to forego the benefits of bringing the whole brain to bear. It would also predict that free verse would tend to become associated with views of the world in which the tense-structure has become very rudimentary and the more complex values, being time-dependent, have disappeared. A bureaucratic social system, requiring specialists rather than generalists, would tend to discourage reinforcement techniques such as metered verse, because such techniques put the whole brain to use and encourage world-views that might transcend the limited values of the bureaucratic system; and by the same token it would en-courage   activities   like   free   verse,   which   are highly specialized both neurologically and culturally. Prose, both because of its own syntactical rhythms and because of its traditional liberty of topic and vocabulary, is less highly specialized; though it is significant that bureaucratic prose tends toward being arhythmic and toward specialized vocabulary. The effect of free verse is to break down the syntactical rhythms of prose without replacing them by meter, and the tendency of free verse has been toward a narrow range of vocabulary, topic, and genre — mostly lyric descriptions of private and personal impressions. Thus free verse, like existentialist philosophy, is nicely adapted to the needs of the bureaucratic and even the totalitarian state, because of its confinement of human concern within narrow specialized limits where it will not be politically threatening.

The implications for education are very important. If we wish to develop the full powers of the minds of the young, early and continuous exposure to the best metered verse would be essential; for the higher human values, the cognitive abilities of generalization and pattern-recognition, the positive emotions such as love and peacefulness, and even a sophisticated sense of time and timing, are all developed by poetry. Furthermore, our ethnocentric bias may be partly overcome by the study of poetry in other languages, and the recognition of the underlying universals in poetic meter. Indeed, the pernicious custom of translating foreign metered verse originals into free verse may already have done some harm; it involves an essentially arrogant assumption of western modernist superiority over the general "vulgar" human love of regular verse.

It may well be that the rise of utilitarian education for the working and middle classes, together with a loss of traditional folk poetry, had a lot to do with the success of political and economic tyranny in our times. The masses, starved of the beautiful and complex rhythms of poetry, were only too susceptible to the brutal and simplistic rhythms of the totalitarian slogan or advertising jingle. An education in verse will tend to produce citizens capable of using their full brains coherently, able to unite rational thought and calculation with values and commitment.

NOTES

[1] This body of theory is developed in J. T. Fraser, *Of Time, Passion and Knowledge* (Braziller, 1975), and in J. T. Fraser *et al.*, eds., *The Study of Time*, vols. I, II, and III (Springer-Verlag, 1972, 1975, 1978).

[2] The following summary of characteristic human information processing strategies owes much to these sources of information:

The proceedings of the Werner Reimers Stiftung *Biological Aspects of Esthetics* Group.

C. D. Laughlin, Jr., and E. G. d'Aquili, *Biogenetic Structuralism* (Columbia University Press, 1974).

E. G. d'Aquili, C. D. Laughlin, Jr., and J. McManus, eds., *The Spectrum of Ritual: A Biogenetic Structural Analysis* (Columbia University Press, 1979).

D. E. Berlyne and K. B. Madsen, eds., *Pleasure, Reward, Preference: Their Nature, Determinants, and Role in Behavior*, (Academic Press, 1973).

A. Routtenberg, ed., *Biology of Reinforcement: Facets of Brain Stimulation Reward* (Academic Press, 1980).

J. Olds, *Drives and Reinforcements: Behavioral Studies of Hypothalamic Functions* (Raven Press, 1977).

C. Blakemore, *Mechanics of the Mind*, Cambridge University Press, 1977.

[3] E. Pöppel, "Erlebte Zeit — und die Zeit uberhaupt," paper given at the Werner Reimers Stiftung "Biological Aspects of Esthetics" conference, January, 1982.

[4] Private communications, I. Rentschler, 1981 and 1982.

[5] "Biological Aspects of Esthetics" meeting, January, 1982.

[6] F. Turner, "Verbal Creativity and the Meter of Love-Poetry," paper given at the "Biological Aspects of Esthetics" meeting, September, 1980.

[7] On cultural universals, see I. Eibl-Eibesfeldt, *Ethology* (Holt, Rinehart, 1970).

[8] J. Rothenberg, *Technicians of the Sacred* (Doubleday Anchor, 1968).

[9] W. K. Wimsatt, *Versification: Major Language Types*, New York University Press, 1972.

[10] Presented at the "Biological Aspects of Esthetics" meeting, April, 1981.

[11] For instance, in Yanomami contract-chants and Western advertising jingles.

[12] W. K. Wimsatt, *ibid.*

[13] This is a narrative meter, whose actual pauses do not necessarily fall upon the line-endings. In Aeschylus' *Agamemnon*, for example, an 11-line sample contained 15 pauses, and lasted 48 seconds. Thus in practice the LINE-length is about 3 seconds.

[14] Probably reflects the statistical effect of lines with a strong caesura.

[15] Charles Olson's *Projective Verse* (New York: Totem Press, 1959) is a good example of such free-verse theories.

[16] Wimsatt, *ibid.*

[17] There is an interesting account of various critical theories of meter in the introductory chapter of C. Chatman's *A Theory of Meter* (Mouton, 1965), but it is flawed by a bias against the possibility of biological foundations for metrical usage.

[18] Private communication, I. Rentschler, 1981.

[19] d'Aquili *et al.*, *The Spectrum of Ritual*, Ch. 4, pp. 117–51.

[20] "Ergotropic" refers to the whole pattern of connected behaviors and states that characterize the aroused state of the body, including an increased heart rate and blood flow to the skeletal muscles, wakefulness, alertness, and a hormone balance consistent with "fight or flight" activities.

"Trophotropic" refers to the corresponding system of rest, body maintenance, and relaxation: decreased heart rate, a flow of blood to the internal organs, an increase in the activity of the digestive process, drowsiness, and a hormone balance consistent with sleep, inactivity, or trance.

[21] John Frederick Nims makes exactly this point in his *Western Wind: An Introduction to Poetry* (Random House, 1983), p. 258.

[22] d'Aquili *et al.*, p. 144.

[23] *Ibid.*, Ch. 5, pp. 152–82.

[24] *Ibid.*, Ch. 6, pp. 183–215.

[25] Charles O. Hartman, in his *Free Verse: An Essay on Prosody* (Princeton University Press, 1980), like many free-verse theorists, argues against the isochronic theory of meter. But his strictures apply to the lengths of syllables and feet, not to the LINE: and part of his argument is based on the fact that much free verse does not fit any temporal schema. This would not be a problem for our argument, which does not consider such free verse to be poetry in the strict sense. His argument attempts to save free verse, and therefore defines verse in a hopelessly vague way; ours is content to abandon it *as verse* unless it consciously or unconsciously employs the human and universal grammar of meter. It may be an admirable kind of word play, and it might even be argued that it is a new art-form of our century. But it is not poetry; and if this sounds dogmatic, it should be remembered that dogmatism is only bad when it is wrong.

[26] *A Defense of Poetry.*

BIOGRAPHICAL NOTES

Dana Gioia is a businessman in New York. He is the author of *Daily Horoscope*, a collection of poems. He is the editor of *The Ceremony and Other Stories* by Weldon Kees and co-editor (with William Jay Smith) of *Poems From Italy: A Comprehensive Bilingual Anthology of Italian Verse*. He has recently edited *Formal Introductions*, an anthology of New Formalist Poems. In 1984 *Esquire* chose Mr. Gioia for their first Register as "One of the Best of the New Generation: Men and Women Under 40 Who Are Changing America."

Frederick Feirstein is a psychoanalyst in New York City. He has published four books of poetry. His first, *Survivors*, was selected as an Outstanding Book of 1975 by the American Library Association. His fifth, *City Life*, a collection of narrative and dramatic poems will be published by *Story Line Press*. He has been the recipient of a Guggenheim Fellowship in poetry, a CAPS Fellowship, the John Masefield Prize from the Poetry Society of America, and a *Quarterly Review of Literature* Colladay Award for his book-length poem *Family History*.

Richard Moore is a graduate of Yale, has been a pilot in the Air Force, a Fulbright Scholar, and a Fannie Hurst Professor at Brandeis. Four collections of his poetry have been published: *A Question of Survival, Word from the Hills, Empires*, and *The Education of a Mouse*. His poems and essays regularly appear in such journals as *The Atlantic Monthly, Harper's, The Hudson Review, The New Yorker, Poetry, Salmagundi*.

Christopher Clausen is a Professor of English at The Pennsylvania State University. He is the author of *The Place of Poetry* (University Press of Kentucky, 1981) and *The Moral Imagination* (University of Iowa, 1986), as well as many essays, poems and reviews.

Dick Allen is the author of four books of poetry including *Flight and Pursuit* and *Overnight In The Guest House of the Mystic*, a National Book Critics Circle Award nominee. He has received many national awards including a National Endowment For The Arts Fellowship and an Ingram-Merrill Fellowship in poetry. His poetry appears regularly in such magazines as *The New Yorker*, *Poetry*, *The New Criterion*, and *The Hudson Review* for which he is a regular reviewer. In 1989 he guest-edited the special edition of *Crosscurrents* on Expansive Poetry.

Mark Jarman's fourth book of poetry, *The Black Riviera*, will be published by Wesleyan University Press. In 1985 he guest-edited a special issue of *The New England Review and Bread Loaf Quarterly*, which examined the New Narrative. He has received numerous awards in poetry, including two National Endowment for the Arts fellowships, the Joseph Henry Jackson Award, a Sotheby's International Award, and a Pushcart Prize. He teaches at Vanderbilt University and is the co-editor of *The Reaper*.

Robert McDowell's first book of poetry, *Quiet Money*, was published by Henry Holt And Company, Inc. in 1987. He is the co-editor of *The Reaper* and the Publisher of Story Line Press.

Paul Lake's first book of poems, *Another Kind of Travel* was published by the University of Chicago Press in 1988. He held a Mirrielees Creative Writing Fellowship in poetry at Stanford. He has had poems in *The New Republic*, *American Scholar*, *Partisan Review*, and *Yale Review*.

Timothy Steele has received a Guggenheim Fellowship in poetry and a Lavan Younger Poets Award from the Academy of American Poets. His latest book is *Sapphics Against Anger And Other Poems*, published by Random House.

Wyatt Prunty's books of poems are *Domestics of the Outer Bank*, *The Times Between*, *What Women Know*, *What Men Believe*, and *Balance As Belief*. In 1989 Oxford University Press will publish a critical study of figure and form in contemporary poetry, entitled *Fallen From The Symboled World: Precedents For The New Formalism*.

Robert McPhillips writes frequently on contemporary literature for such publications as *The Sewanee Review*, *The Nation*, *Prairie Schooner*, *Crosscurrents*, and *American Literature*. He is a graduate of Colgate University where he was elected to Phi Beta Kappa and recently received his Ph.D. in English from the University of Minnesota. He currently teaches English at Iona College.

Frederick Turner is an English-born American poet and scholar. He is Founders Professor of Arts and Humanities at the University of Texas at Dallas. He is the author of two epic poems, *The New World* (Princeton University Press) and *Genesis* (Saybrook Publishers). He is a regular contributor to *Harper's*, appears from time to time in the Smithsonian World Public Television series, and has published dozens of articles, books, and poems in America and several foreign countries.

Ernst Pöppel is the head of the auditory research division of the
Institute for Medical Psychology at the University of Munich
and an internationally distinguished psychophysicist. One of
his books, *Mindworks,* has been translated into English and
received enthusiastic reviews in America.

THE EDITOR

Frederick Feirstein has published four books of poetry. His most recent, *Family History* (1986), won a *Quarterly Review of Literature* Colladay Prize. His first book, *Survivors*, was selected as an Outstanding Book of 1975–76 by *Choice*.

He has won a Guggenheim fellowship in poetry, a CAPS fellowship, the Poetry Society of America's John Masefield Award, and England's Arvon Foundation Special Commendation. He has also received a Rockefeller Foundation OADR Award in playwriting.

His poems are in many anthologies such as Avon's *New York: Poems*, Faber & Faber's *Arvon Poems*, Harper & Row's *Strong Measures*, and Princeton University Press's *Contemporary Poetry*.

He is a psycholanalyst in private practice in New York City.

BOOKS BY FREDERICK FEIRSTEIN

Survivors. David Lewis, 1974.
Manhattan Carnival. Countryman, 1981.
Fathering. Apple-Wood, 1982.
Family History. Quarterly Review of Literature
  (Poetry Series VII) Vol. XXVI, 1986.